Digital Video

FOR

DUMMIES®

4TH EDITION

by Keith Underdahl

WILEY

Wiley Publishing, Inc.

Digital Video For Dummies, 4th Edition

Published by
Wiley Publishing, Inc.
111 River Street
Hoboken, NJ 07030-5774
www.wiley.com

Copyright © 2006 by Wiley Publishing, Inc., Indianapolis, Indiana

Published by Wiley Publishing, Inc., Indianapolis, Indiana

Published simultaneously in Canada

For general information on our other products and services, please contact our Customer Care Department within the U.S. at 800-762-2974, outside the U.S. at 317-572-3993, or fax 317-572-4002.

For technical support, please visit www.wiley.com/techsupport.

Wiley also publishes its books in a variety of electronic formats. Some content that appears in print may not be available in electronic books.

Library of Congress Control Number: 2005936653

ISBN-13: 978-0-471-78278-0

ISBN-10: 0-471-78278-5

Manufactured in the United States of America

10 9 8 7 6 5 4 3 2 1

4O/TR/QR/QW/IN

WILEY

About the Author

Keith Underdahl lives in Albany, Oregon. Professionally, Keith is an electronic-publishing specialist for AGES Software, where he serves as program manager, interface designer, video-media producer, multimedia specialist, graphic artist, and when the day is over, he even sweeps out the place. Keith has written numerous books, including *Microsoft Windows Movie Maker For Dummies*, *Macworld Final Cut Pro 2 Bible* (coauthor), *Adobe Premiere Elements For Dummies*, and *Adobe Premiere Pro For Dummies*.

Digital Video

FOR

DUMMIES®

4TH EDITION

Author's Acknowledgments

When people find out that I have written several books, they usually react with awe and amazement because writing an entire book seems like a monumental task. To be completely honest, it doesn't feel like a monumental task, mainly because I have so many great people helping me. First and foremost is my wife Christa, who has served as my support staff, cheerleader, business manager, and inspiration throughout my writing career. Without Christa's initial encouragement and tireless ongoing support, I would not be writing.

Once again I must also thank my favorite movie subjects, Soren and Cole Underdahl. Not only do they take direction well, but they are also incredibly intelligent and look great on camera! Soren and Cole are featured in screen shots throughout this book. Best of all, because they're my own boys, the Wiley Publishing legal department doesn't make me fill out all kinds of model releases and other daunting forms. If someone writes *Boilerplate For Dummies,* I'll buy the first copy.

Of course, I was working on this book before I even knew I was working on this book, making videos and developing my skills. I've received a lot of help from people in and out of the video and software business, including Jon D'Angelica, Patrick BeauLieu, John Bowne, Ingrid de la Fuente, havoc23, Linda Herd, Pete Langlois, Andy Marken, Rick Muldoon, Paulien Ruijssenaars, Carol Schaubach, and probably a lot of other people I can't remember right at the moment.

Last but certainly not least, I wish to give my unwavering gratitude to the wonderful Composition Services team at Wiley Publishing. After I finished scribbling this book on a stack of cocktail napkins, it was up to the folks at Wiley to turn it all into a coherent book. I wish to thank Steve Hayes, Linda Morris, Luke Hale, and everyone else at Wiley. Keep up the great work, folks!

Publisher's Acknowledgments

We're proud of this book; please send us your comments through our online registration form located at www.dummies.com/register/.

Some of the people who helped bring this book to market include the following:

Acquisitions, Editorial, and Media Development

Project Editor: Linda Morris

Senior Acquisitions Editor: Steve Hayes

Copy Editor: Linda Morris

Technical Editor: Luke Hale

Editorial Manager: Jodi Jensen

Media Development Manager:
Laura VanWinkle

Editorial Assistant: Amanda Foxworth

Cartoons: Rich Tennant
(www.the5thwave.com)

Composition Services

Project Coordinator: Kristie Rees

Layout and Graphics: Carl Byers, Andrea Dahl, Barbara Moore, Lynsey Osborn

Proofreaders: Leeann Harney, TECHBOOKS Production Services

Indexer: TECHBOOKS Production Services

Publishing and Editorial for Technology Dummies

Richard Swadley, Vice President and Executive Group Publisher

Andy Cummings, Vice President and Publisher

Mary Bednarek, Executive Acquisitions Director

Mary C. Corder, Editorial Director

Publishing for Consumer Dummies

Diane Graves Steele, Vice President and Publisher

Joyce Pepple, Acquisitions Director

Composition Services

Gerry Fahey, Vice President of Production Services

Debbie Stailey, Director of Composition Services

Contents at a Glance

Table of Contents

Introduction

*W*alk into any consumer electronics store today and everything has "digital" splashed all over it. You see digital cameras, digital music players, digital cable tuners . . . even the laundry machines now have digital controls! If you're reading this, I'm guessing you're interested in digital video, which is the high-quality video you shoot with digital camcorders, and then edit into great digital movies using your computer.

Of course, the ability to record your own movies isn't new. Affordable film movie cameras have been available since the 1950s, and video cameras that record directly onto videotape have been with us for almost three decades. But after you recorded some video or film with one of those old cameras, you couldn't do much else with it. You could show your movies to friends and family in raw, unedited form, but no one would ever confuse your home movies with professional Hollywood productions.

Digital camcorders provide a slight quality improvement over older camcorders, but the real advantage of digital video is that you can now easily edit your video on a computer. I don't have to tell you how far computer technology has progressed over the last few years, and you know that modern Macs and PCs can now do some pretty amazing things. In a matter of seconds, you can import video from your digital camcorder into your computer, cut out the scenes you don't want, add some special effects, and then instantly send your movies to friends over the Internet — or burn them to a DVD. The capability to easily edit your own movies adds a whole new level of creativity that was — just a few years ago — the exclusive realm of broadcast and movie professionals.

In a culture so accustomed to and influenced by video images, it's actually kind of surprising that personal moviemaking hasn't burgeoned sooner. Video is the high art of our time, and now — at last — you have the power to use this art for your own expression. What will you draw on your digital-video canvas?

Why This Book?

Digital video is a big, highly technical subject, so you need a guide to help you understand and use this technology. But you don't need a big book that is so highly technical that it just gathers dust on your bookshelf. You need easy-to-follow step-by-step instructions for the most important tasks, and you need tips and tricks to make your movies more successful. You need *Digital Video For Dummies,* 4th Edition.

Needless to say, you're no "dummy." If you were, you wouldn't be reading this book and trying to figure out how to use digital video. Thanks to digital video, high-quality moviemaking has never been easier or more affordable. I have included instructions on performing the most important video-editing tasks, including lots of graphics so you can better visualize what I'm talking about. You can also find tips and other ideas in this book that you wouldn't find in the documentation that comes with your editing software.

Digital Video For Dummies doesn't just help you use software or understand a new technology. It's about the art of moviemaking, and how you can apply this exciting new technology to make movies of your very own. I have designed this book to serve as a primer to moviemaking in general. Sections of this book help you choose a good camcorder, shoot better video, publish movies online, and speak the industry technobabble like a Hollywood pro.

Foolish Assumptions

I've made a few basic assumptions about you as I have written this book. First, I assume that you have an intermediate knowledge of how to use a computer. Movie editing is one of the more technically advanced things you can do with a computer, so I assume that if you're ready to edit video, you already know how to locate and move files around on hard drives, open and close programs, and perform other such tasks. I assume that you are using either a Macintosh running OS X or a PC running Windows XP or better. In writing this book, I used both Mac and Windows software, so this book is use to you no matter which platform you use.

I assume that you already own a digital camcorder, or you are ready to buy one. A digital camcorder is the first thing you need before you can take advantage of digital video. If you haven't bought a digital camcorder yet, Chapter 3 provides some tips and recommendations on things to look for when choosing a new camera. And don't worry, if you want to work with some older footage that you shot with an analog camcorder, I show you how to do that too in Chapter 6.

Another basic assumption I made is that you are not an experienced, professional moviemaker or video editor. I explain the fundamentals of videography and editing in ways that help you immediately get to work on your movie projects. Most of this book is based on the assumption that you are producing movies for fun or as a hobby. I also assume that you're not yet ready to spend many hundreds of dollars on highly advanced editing programs. In this book, I show you how to make amazing movies using software that is already installed on your computer (or that you can purchase for a modest sum). I have elected to show how to perform editing tasks primarily using Apple iMovie and Windows Movie Maker. iMovie is free for all Mac users, and Movie Maker is free for all Windows users. I also show how to do a few more advanced techniques using Adobe Premiere Elements, which at $99 (MSRP) is an excellent choice when you think you're ready to step up to slightly more advanced software.

Even if you are working in a professional environment and have just been tasked with creating your first company training or kiosk video, this book helps you grasp the fundamentals of digital video. Not only does this help you get to work quickly and efficiently, but I also include information to help you make an educated decision when your company gives you a budget to buy fancier editing software.

Conventions Used in This Book

Digital Video For Dummies helps you get started with moviemaking quickly and efficiently. Much of this book shows you how to perform tasks on your computer, which means you will find that this book is a bit different from other kinds of texts you have read. The following are some unusual conventions that you will encounter in this book:

- ✔ Filenames or lines of computer code will look like THIS or this. This style of print usually indicates something you should type in exactly as you see it in the book.

- ✔ Internet addresses will look something like this: www.dummies.com. Notice that we've left the http:// part off the address because you never actually need to type it in your Web browser anymore.

- ✔ You will often be instructed to access commands from the menu bar of your video-editing program. The *menu bar* is that strip that lives along the top of the program window and usually includes menus like File,

Edit, Window, and Help. When I tell you to access the Save command in the File menu, it looks like this: File⇨Save.

✔ You'll be using your mouse a lot. Sometimes you'll be told to click something to select it. This means that you should click *once* on whatever it is you are supposed to click, using the *left* mouse button if you use Microsoft Windows. Other times you will be told to *double-click* something; again, you double-click with the *left* mouse button if you are using Windows.

How This Book Is Organized

I put all of the chapters of *Digital Video For Dummies* in a bucket, stirred them up using a large stick, and, amazingly, they came out perfectly organized into the six parts described in the following sections.

Part 1: Getting Ready for Digital Video

You may be wondering, "Just what is this whole digital video thing, anyway?" Part I introduces you to digital video. I show you what digital video is and what you can do with it. I also show you how to get your computer ready to work with digital video, and I help you choose a camcorder and other important moviemaking gear.

Part 11: Gathering Footage

Editing video on your computer is just one part of the digital video experience. Before you can do any editing, you need something to actually edit. Part II shows you how to shoot better video, and then I show you how to get that video into your computer — even if you don't yet have a digital camcorder, or you just have some footage on old VHS tapes that you want to use. I also help you record and import better audio because good audio is just as important as video when you're making movies.

Part 111: Editing Your Movie

Until just a few years ago, video editing was something that required professional-grade equipment, which cost in the hundreds of thousands of dollars.

But with digital video and a semi-modern computer, editing video is now easy and very affordable. In Part III of this book, I introduce you to the basics of editing. You'll find out how to arrange scenes in the order you like and trim out the unwanted parts. I show you how to add cool transitions between video clips, use titles (text that appears onscreen), and top off your creation with sound effects, musical soundtracks, still graphics, and special effects.

Part IV: Sharing Your Video

When you've poured your heart into a movie project, you definitely want to share it with others. This part helps you share your movies on the Internet or on videotape. You even find out how to make your own DVDs in this part.

Part V: The Part of Tens

I wouldn't be able to call this a *For Dummies* book without a "Part of Tens" (really, it's in my contract). Actually, the Part of Tens always serves an important purpose. In this book, it gives me a chance to show you ten advanced movie-making tricks and techniques, as well as ten tools to improve your movies and make your work easier. Because there are a lot of video-editing programs out there to choose from, I also provide a chapter that compares ten of them, feature by feature.

Part VI: Appendixes

The appendixes provide quick, handy references on several important subjects. First I provide a glossary to help you decrypt the alphabet soup of video-editing terms and acronyms. Additional appendixes help you install and update the editing programs shown throughout this book.

Icons Used in This Book

Occasionally you'll find some icons in the margins of this book. The text next to these icons includes information and tips that deserve special attention, and some warn you of potential hazards and pitfalls you may encounter.

Although every word of *Digital Video For Dummies* is important (of course!), I sometimes feel the need to emphasize certain points or remind you of something that was mentioned elsewhere in the book. I use the Remember icon to provide this occasional emphasis.

Tips are usually brief instructions or ideas that, although not always documented, can greatly improve your movies and make your life easier. Tips are among the most valuable tidbits in this book.

Heed warnings carefully. Some warn of things that will merely inconvenience you, whereas others tell you when a wrong move could cause expensive and painful damage to your equipment and/or person.

Computer books are often stuffed with yards of technobabble, and if it's sprinkled everywhere, it can make the whole book a drag and just plain difficult to read. As much as possible, I have tried to pull some of the deeply technical stuff out into these icons. This way, the information is easy to find if you need it, and just as easy to skip if you already have a headache.

Where to Go From Here

You are about to enter the mad, mad world of moviemaking. Exciting, isn't it? If you're not sure whether your computer is ready for digital video, head on over to Chapter 2. If you still need to buy some gear or set up your movie studio, I suggest you visit Chapter 3. For tips on shooting better video with your new camcorder, spend some time in Chapter 4. Otherwise, you should jump right in and familiarize yourself with digital video, beginning with Chapter 1.

Part I
Getting Ready for Digital Video

In this part . . .

Until recently, home movies consisted mainly of crude video tapes or 8mm films full of raw, unedited footage. But now, thanks to digital video, you can shoot near broadcast-quality video with affordable digital camcorders. Then you can copy that digital video onto your computer, where you can pick out the best scenes and add some special effects.

This first part of *Digital Video For Dummies* introduces you to digital video. You start out right away with the basics in Chapter 1, and I guide you through the process of making a simple movie. Subsequent chapters show you how to prepare your computer for working with digital video, and I review some of the other gear you need for moviemaking.

Chapter 1

Introducing Digital Video

*I*t is often said that we live in the Digital Age. We call each other on digital cell phones, we take snap shots with digital cameras, we download digital music from online digital stores to our digital audio players, and when we make home movies, we make them using digital video.

Digital video first appeared over a decade ago. Sony and Panasonic released the first consumer-oriented digital video camcorders in 1995. Also in 1995, Apple introduced the high-speed FireWire interface. In theory, FireWire would allow camcorders to easily connect to computers, making it easy to store video on your computer and edit that video into professional-style movies. In practice, few computers back then could handle digital video.

If you buy a new camcorder today, chances are it's a digital camcorder. Likewise, so long as your computer isn't more than about four or five years old, you can probably use it to copy digital video from a camcorder, pick and choose scenes, add some special effects, and turn it into a real movie. This chapter introduces you to digital video and shows you how easy it is to edit and share your movies with others.

What Is Digital Video?

Human beings experience the world as an analog environment. When we take in the serene beauty of a rose garden, the mournful song of a cello, or the graceful motion of an eagle in flight, we are receiving a steady stream of infinitely variable data through our various senses. Of course, we don't think of all these things as "data" but rather as light, sound, smell, and touch.

Computers are pretty dumb compared to the human brain. They can't comprehend the analog data of the world; all computers understand are *yes* (one) and *no* (zero). In spite of this limitation, we force our computers to show pictures, play music, and display moving video; infinitely variable sounds, colors, and shapes must be converted into the language of computers — ones and zeros. This conversion process is called *digitizing*. Digital video — often abbreviated as *DV* — is video that has been digitized.

To fully understand the difference between analog data and digital data, suppose you want to draw the profile of a hill. An analog representation of the profile (shown in Figure 1-1) would follow the contour of the hill perfectly because analog values are infinitely variable. However, a digital contour of that same hill would not be able to follow every single detail of the hill because, as shown in Figure 1-2, digital values are made up of specifically defined, individual bits of data.

Figure 1-1:
Analog data
is infinitely
variable.

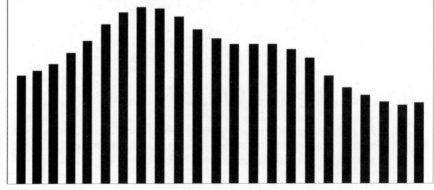

Figure 1-2:
Digital data
contains
specific
values.

Comparing analog and digital video

We're often led to believe that digital is better, but believe it or not, digital recordings are *theoretically* inferior to analog recordings. This is because analog recordings can *theoretically* contain more information. But the truth is, major advances in digital technology mean that this really doesn't matter. Yes, a digital recording must be made up of specific individual values, but modern recordings have so many discrete values packed so closely together that human eyes and ears can barely tell the difference. Casual observation often reveals that digital recordings actually seem to be of a higher quality than analog recordings. Why?

A major problem with analog recordings is that they are highly susceptible to deterioration. Every time analog data is copied, some of the original, infinitely variable data is lost. This phenomenon, called *generational loss,* can be observed in that dark, grainy copy of a copy of a copy of a wedding video that was first shot more than 10 years ago. However, digital data doesn't have this problem. A one is always a one, no matter how many times it is copied, and a zero is always a zero. Likewise, analog recordings are more susceptible to deterioration after every playback, which explains why your 1964-vintage *Meet the Beatles* LP pops, hisses, and has lost many of its highs and lows over the years. Digital recordings are based on instructions that tell the computer how to create the data; as long as the computer can read the instructions, it creates the data the same way every time.

Whether you are editing analog or digital material, always work from a copy of the master and keep the master safe. When adding analog material to your project, the fewer generations your recording is from the original, the better.

When you consider the implications of generational loss on video editing, you begin to see what a blessing digital video really is. You're constantly copying, editing, and recopying content as you edit your movie projects — and with digital video, you can edit to your heart's content, confident that the quality won't diminish with each new copy you make.

Warming up to FireWire

FireWire is one of the technologies that makes digital video so fun and easy to work with. FireWire — also sometimes called IEEE 1394 or i.LINK — was originally developed by Apple Computer and is actually an interface format for computer peripherals. Various peripherals including scanners, CD burners, external hard drives, and of course digital video cameras use FireWire technology. Key features of FireWire include

- ✔ **Speed:** FireWire is really fast, way faster than USB or serial ports. FireWire is capable of transfer rates up to 400Mbps (megabits per second). Digital video contains a lot of data that must be transferred quickly, making FireWire an ideal format.

- ✔ **Mac and PC compatibility:** (What a concept.) Although FireWire was developed by Apple, it is widely implemented in the PC world as well. This has helped make FireWire an industry standard.

- ✔ **Plug-and-play connectivity:** When you connect your digital camcorder to a FireWire port on your computer (whether Mac or PC), the camera is automatically detected. You won't have to spend hours installing software drivers or messing with obscure computer settings just to get everything working.

- ✔ **Device control:** OK, this one isn't actually a feature *of* FireWire, it's just one of the things that makes using FireWire really neat. If your digital camcorder is connected to your computer's FireWire port, most video-editing programs can control the camcorder's playback features. This means you don't have to juggle your fingers and try to press Play on the camcorder and Record in the software at exactly the same time. Just click Capture in a program like Apple iMovie or Windows Movie Maker, and the software automatically starts and stops your camcorder as needed.

- ✔ **Hot-swap capability:** You can connect or disconnect FireWire components whenever you want. You don't need to shut down the computer, unplug power cables, or confer with your local public utility district before connecting or disconnecting a FireWire component.

All new Macintosh computers come with FireWire ports. Some — but not all — Windows PCs have FireWire ports as well. If your PC does not have a FireWire port, you can usually add one using an expansion card. (I cover all kinds of optional upgrades and adjustments to your system in Chapter 2.) If you're buying a new PC and you plan to do a lot of video editing, consider a FireWire port a must-have feature.

Virtually all digital camcorders offer FireWire ports as well, although the port isn't always called FireWire. Sometimes FireWire ports are instead called "i.LINK" or simply "DV" by camcorder manufacturers that don't want to use Apple's trademarked FireWire name. FireWire truly makes video editing easy, and if you are buying a new camcorder, I strongly recommend that you buy a camcorder that includes a FireWire port. Chapter 3 provides more detail on choosing a great digital camcorder.

Some camcorders can transfer video using a USB (Universal Serial Bus) 2.0 port instead of FireWire. In fact, a few digital camcorders on the market offer only USB 2.0 connectivity, and not FireWire. The reason for this is that USB 2.0 ports are more common on modern Windows PCs than FireWire ports. Video transfer via USB 2.0 might work for you, but if possible I recommend FireWire instead. When it comes to working with digital video, FireWire is less likely to offer unexpected technical surprises than USB 2.0.

Editing Video

Until a few years ago, the only practical way for the average person to edit video was to connect two VCRs and use the Record and Pause buttons to cut out unwanted parts. This was a tedious and inefficient process. The up-to-date (and vastly improved) way to edit video is to use a computer — and the following sections introduce you to the video-editing techniques you're most likely to use. In this chapter, I show how to edit video using Apple iMovie and Windows Movie Maker, the free video-editing programs that come with the Macintosh OS or Microsoft Windows, respectively.

Editing a short video project

Editing video is really cool and easy to do if you have a reasonably modern computer. But why talk about editing when you can jump right into it? Here's the drill:

1. **Open Windows Movie Maker (Windows) or Apple iMovie (Macintosh).**

Comparing editing methods

Video (and audio, for that matter) is considered a linear medium because it comes at you in a linear stream through time. A still picture, on the other hand, just sits there — you take it in all at once — and a Web site lets you jump randomly from page to page. Because neither photos nor Web pages are perceived as linear streams, they're both examples of nonlinear media.

You tweak a linear medium (such as video) by using one of two basic methods — *linear* or *nonlinear* editing. If your approach to editing is linear, you must do all the editing work in chronological order, from the start of the movie to the finish. Here's an old-fashioned example: If you "edit" video by dubbing certain parts from a camcorder tape onto a VHS tape in your VCR, you have to do all your edits in one session, in chronological order. As you probably guessed, linear editing is terribly inefficient. If you dub a program and then decide to perform an additional edit, subsequent video usually has to be redubbed. (Oh, the pain, the tedium!)

What is the alternative? Thinking outside the line: *nonlinear editing!* You can do nonlinear edits in any order; you don't have to start at the beginning and slog on through to the end every time. The magical gizmo that makes nonlinear editing possible is a combination of the personal computer and programs designed for nonlinear editing (NLE). Using such a program (for example, Apple iMovie or Windows Movie Maker), you can navigate to any scene in the movie, insert scenes, move them around, cut them out of the timeline altogether, and slice, dice, tweak and fine-tune to your heart's content.

2. **Connect your digital camcorder to your computer's FireWire port, and turn the camcorder on to Player or VTR mode.**

   If you're not sure how to connect the camcorder, see Chapter 5, where I discuss video capture in greater detail.

3. **Choose File⇨Capture Video in Windows Movie Maker, or slide the Mode button to Camera in iMovie as shown in Figure 1-3.**

   In Windows Movie Maker, you are asked to provide a name for your captured video. The name should be descriptive so that you'll be able to identify the file later. Movie Maker also asks you to choose a video quality setting. For now, just choose Digital Device Format (DV-AVI).

4. **Use the Play, Fast Forward, and Rewind buttons in the capture window to locate video you want to capture.**

5. **When you are ready to start capturing, click Import (iMovie) or Start Capture (Movie Maker).**

Figure 1-3: Use the playback buttons to find some video you want to capture.

Mode button   Storyboard   Clip browser

6. **Click Import (iMovie) again or Stop Capture (Movie Maker) to stop capturing video.**

7. **In Windows Movie Maker, click Finish to close the Video Capture Wizard. In Apple iMovie, slide the Mode button over to Edit.**

   You should now see a selection of video clips in the clip browser.

8. **Click and drag a clip from the clip browser and drop it on the storyboard.**

9. **Click and drag a second clip from the clip browser and drop it on the storyboard just after the first clip.**

Congratulations! You've just made your first movie edit. You should now have two clips on the storyboard, looking similar to Figure 1-4.

If your Windows Movie Maker window doesn't look quite like this, click the Show Storyboard button (if you see it onscreen).

Figure 1-4: Two clips have been placed in the storyboard.

Storyboard   Clip browser

After you've added a couple of scenes to your movie, you may decide that you want to insert a scene between them. With a nonlinear editing program like iMovie or Windows Movie Maker, this edit is easy. Just click and drag a clip and drop it right between two clips that are already in the storyboard. The software automatically shifts clips over to make room for the inserted clip, as shown in Figure 1-5. Almost as easy as shuffling cards, edits like these are the essence of nonlinear video editing.

Figure 1-5:
A clip
has been
inserted in
the middle
of the
storyboard.

Inserted clip

Performing Hollywood magic at the click of a mouse

The previous section shows the basics of making a movie by assembling clips in a specific order — and frankly, most of your editing work will probably consist of simple tasks like that. But when you want to go beyond ordinary, you can really spice up your movies by adding special effects or transitions between clips. (Special effects are covered in Chapter 11, and I show you just about everything you'll ever need to know about transitions in Chapter 9.)

Of course, there's no need to wait until later. Modern video-editing programs make it really easy to add special creative touches to your movies.

Creating a transition

You can add a transition to the simple movie you put together in the previous section by following these steps:

1. **Create a movie project with a couple of clips in the storyboard, as described in the previous section.**

   You can follow these steps using any movie project that includes two or more clips.

2. **Open the list of video transitions in your editing program.**

   In Apple iMovie, click the Trans button just below the browser window. In Windows Movie Maker, click View Video Transitions in the Movie Tasks list on the left side of the screen, or choose Tools➪Transitions.

3. **Click and drag one of the Circle transitions to a spot between two clips on the storyboard.**

   A transition indicator appears between the two clips, as shown in Figure 1-6.

4. **Click Play in the preview window to preview the transition.**

   If you are using iMovie, the transition may not appear immediately. If you see a tiny red progress bar under the transition, wait a few seconds for it to finish. When the progress bar is complete, you should be able to preview the transition.

OLD FAITHFUL
GEYSER

Figure 1-6:
Transitions
add a
special
touch to
your movies.

Drop transition here.

Pretty cool, huh? But wait, that's not all!

Creating special effects

Adding special effects to your video is pretty easy too. Here's one that makes a video clip look like it came from a really old reel of film:

1. **Click a clip in the storyboard to select it.**

2. **Open the list of video effects in your video-editing program.**

   In iMovie, click the Effects button under the browser window. In Windows Movie Maker, click View Video Effects in the Movie Tasks list, or choose Tools⇨Video Effects.

3. **Click an Aged Film effect to select it.**

   In iMovie, there is only one Aged Film effect. In Windows Movie Maker, scroll down in the list of effects and choose one of the Film Age effects. It doesn't matter if you choose Old, Older, or Oldest.

4. Apply the effect to the clip.

In iMovie, click Apply at the top of the effects window. In Windows Movie Maker, click and drag the effect onto the clip on the storyboard.

5. Click Play in the preview window to preview the effect as shown in Figure 1-7.

Again, if you're using iMovie, you will probably have to wait for the tiny red progress bar on the clip to finish before you can preview the effect.

These are just a couple of the cool things you can do with digital video. Part III of this book helps you explore the wonders of video editing in greater detail. So break out your director's chair and get ready to make some movie magic!

Click to apply effect.

Figure 1-7: Making video look like aged film is just one of many special video effects you can use.

Choose an effect.

Click to browse effects.

Sharing Video

One of the best things about digital video is that it enables you to get really creative with your own movie projects. To make your work worthwhile, you may want to share your video work with others. Thankfully, sharing digital video is pretty easy too. Part IV of this book shows you all the details of sharing video on tape, DVD, or the Internet, but the following sections provide a handy, brief glimpse of what you can do.

Exporting a movie

Modern video-editing programs are designed to make it as easy as possible to share your movie projects — often with no more than a couple of mouse clicks. For now, I show you how to export a movie that is suitable for viewing over the Internet. The steps for exporting your movie are a little different depending on whether you are using Apple iMovie or Windows Movie Maker, so I'll address each program separately.

Exporting from Apple iMovie

Apple iMovie exports movies in QuickTime format, or you can export directly to your camcorder's videotape or Apple iDVD. To export your project in iMovie, follow these steps:

1. **Open the project you want to export.**

2. **Choose File⇨Export.**

   The iMovie Export dialog box appears.

3. **Choose how you want to export your movie from the Export menu.**

   For now, I recommend that you choose To QuickTime (as shown in Figure 1-8).

4. **Choose a Format, such as Web.**

5. **Click Export.**

6. **Give a name for your movie file in the Save As box.**

   Make a note of the folder in which you are saving the movie. Choose a different folder if you wish.

   If you remove the .mov filename extension, Windows users (you probably know a few) will have a hard time viewing your movie.

7. **Click Save.**

Figure 1-8:
Choose
export
settings
in this
dialog box.

iMovie exports your movie. The export process may take a few minutes, depending on how long your movie is.

Exporting from Windows Movie Maker

Like iMovie, Windows Movie Maker also enables you to export video for a variety of applications. Windows Movie Maker is especially well suited to exporting movies for Internet playback. To export a movie for online viewing, follow these steps:

1. **Open the project that you want to export.**

2. **Choose File⇨Save Movie File.**

   The Save Movie Wizard appears.

3. **Choose an export format for your movie and then click Next.**

   For now, I recommend choosing My Computer.

4. **Enter a filename for your movie and choose a location in which to save the file.**

5. **Click Next again.**

   The Save Movie Wizard shows details about the file, including the file size (see Figure 1-9).

6. **Click Next again.**

   The export process begins.

7. **When export is done, click Finish.**

Your movie will probably begin playing in Windows Media Player. Enjoy!

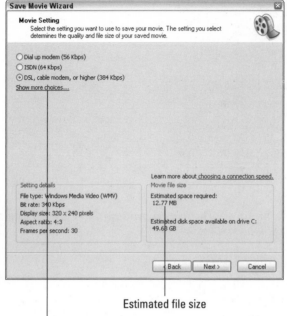

Figure 1-9:
Review
movie
details here.

Estimated file size

Click for more quality options.

Playing your movie

After your movie has been exported, playing it is pretty easy. Simply locate
the file on your hard drive and double-click its name. The movie should automatically open and start to play, as shown in Figure 1-10.

If you exported your movie from Windows Movie Maker, the movie file will be
in Windows Media (WMV) format. Despite the name, you don't have to be a
Windows user to view Windows Media video. You do need Windows Media
Player to view Windows Media files, but Microsoft does offer a version of
Windows Media Player for Macintosh. Figure 1-10 shows a Windows Media
version of the Chapter 1 movie, playing contentedly on my Mac.

Movies created on a Mac are also cross-platform–friendly. iMovie outputs
videos in Apple QuickTime format, and Windows versions of QuickTime
(shown in Figure 1-11) have been available for years. Chapter 14 tells you
more about available video-player programs.

Figure 1-10:
Windows
Media
movies can
be played
on a Mac . . .

Figure 1-11:
. . . and
QuickTime
files can be
played in
Windows.

After you have previewed your movie, you can either share it with others or
edit it some more. I usually go through the preview and re-edit process dozens
of times before I decide that a movie project is ready for release, but thanks to
digital video, re-editing is no problem at all. Chapter 13 offers some tips for
previewing your movies more effectively.

Chapter 2

Getting Your Computer Ready for Digital Video

In This Chapter

▶ Deciding between a Mac or a PC

▶ Computer upgrading tips

▶ Using a Mac for video work

▶ Using a Windows PC with digital video

▶ Choosing video capture hardware

*I*f you like to spend money, you've come to the right hobby — a lot of cool digital video gadgets are out there, just ready for you to buy. A digital camcorder is the most obvious gadget, and I talk about those in Chapter 3. Almost as important as a camcorder is a good computer capable of editing video and recording DVDs.

This chapter helps you decide if your current computer is a good digital video gadget, and, if it isn't, I show you how to upgrade your computer or buy a new one. I also give some important tips on choosing video-editing software, as well as hardware to help you capture video into your computer. But first, I start with something simple — trying to resolve the age-old debate of whether a Mac or Windows PC is better.

Resolving the Mac-versus-PC Debate Once and for All

Yeah. Right.

Wanna start a ruckus? Wear an "I ♥ Bill Gates" t-shirt to a *Macworld* convention. Go ahead, I dare you.

> *Legal disclaimer: Wiley Publishing, Inc., is not responsible for physical or emotional harm that may result from compliance with the preceding foolish suggestion.*

Like the debate over whether cats or dogs make better pets, the question of whether to use a Mac or a PC has been disputed tirelessly between the true believers. It has been a largely unproductive dispute: For the most part, Mac people are still Mac people, and PC people are still PC people.

But who is right? If you want the best computer for working with digital video, should you choose a PC or a Mac? Well, look at the important factors:

- ✔ **Ease of use:** Macintosh users often boast that their computers are exceedingly easy to use, and they are right. But if you're a long-time Windows user, you might not think so. Some things *are* easier to do on a Mac, but other things are easier to do in Windows. Neither system offers a clear advantage, so if you're a creature of habit, you'll probably be happiest if you stick with what you know.

- ✔ **Reliability:** The Windows Blue Screen of Death (you know, the dreaded screen that often appears when a Windows PC crashes) is world-famous and the butt of countless jokes. But the dirty little secret of the Macintosh world is that until recently, most Macs crashed nearly as often as Windows PCs. Apple's modern operating system — Mac OS X — is exceedingly stable and refined, but Windows XP is pretty dependable as well. Reliability is important to you because video pushes your computer's performance to its limits. Use a Mac with OS X or a PC with Windows XP, and you should be just fine.

- ✔ **Digital video support:** I can't be wishy-washy any longer; if you want a great computer ready to edit digital video right out of the box, a new Macintosh is often the safer bet. All new Macs come with built-in FireWire ports, making it easy to hook up your digital camcorder. Some new Windows PCs also come with built-in FireWire, but many don't. If your PC doesn't have FireWire, you'll have to buy some extra video capture hardware (see "Choosing Video Capture Hardware" later in this chapter).

So there you have it: Macs and PCs are both pretty good. Sure, Macs all come with FireWire, but if you shop around, you should be able to find a Windows

PC with FireWire for about the same price as a new Mac. Both platforms can make excellent video-editing machines, so if you're already dedicated to one or the other, you should be fine.

Upgrading Your Computer

Picture this: Our hero carefully unscrews an access panel on the blinking device, revealing a rat's nest of wires and circuits. A drop of sweat runs down his face as the precious seconds tick away, and he knows that fate hangs by a slender thread. The hero's brow creases as he tries to remember the procedure: "Do I cut the blue wire or the red wire?"

If the thought of opening up your computer and performing upgrades fills you with a similar level of anxiety, you're not alone. The insides of modern computers can seem pretty mysterious, and you might be understandably nervous about tearing apart your expensive PC or Mac to perform hardware upgrades. Indeed, all the chips, circuit boards, and other electronic flotsam inside the computer case are sensitive and easily damaged. You can even hurt yourself if you're not careful, so if you don't have any experience with hardware upgrades, you are probably better off consulting a professional before making any changes or repairs to your PC.

But if you have done hardware upgrades before, digital video may well inspire you to make more upgrades now or in the near future. If you do decide to upgrade your computer, some basic rules include

- ✔ **Review your warranty.** Hardware upgrades might invalidate your computer's warranty if it still has one.

- ✔ **RTM.** This is geek-speak for, "Read The Manual." The owner's manual that came with your computer almost certainly contains important information about what can be upgraded and what can't. The manual may even have detailed instructions for performing common upgrades.

- ✔ **Back up your data.** Back up your important files on recordable CDs or another storage device available to you. You don't want to lose work, pictures, or other data that are difficult or impossible to replace.

- ✔ **Gather license numbers and ISP (Internet Service Provider) information.** If you have any important things like software licenses stored in saved e-mails, print them out so that you have hard copies. Also, make sure that you have all the access information for your ISP (account name, password, dial-up numbers, server addresses, and so on) handy in case you need to re-install your Internet service.

- ✔ **Gather all your software CDs.** Locate all your original installation discs for your various programs, including your operating system (Mac OS or Windows), so that you can reinstall them later if necessary.

✔ **Turn off the power.** The computer's power should be turned off to avoid damage to components and electrocution to yourself.

✔ **Avoid static electricity build-up.** Even if you didn't just walk across a shag carpet and pet your cat, your body probably has some static electricity stored inside. A tiny shock can instantly destroy the tiny circuits in expensive computer components. Before touching any components, touch your finger to a bare metal spot on your computer's case to ground yourself. I also recommend wearing a grounding strap, which can be purchased at most electronics stores for $2–3. Now *that's* what I call cheap insurance!

✔ **Handle with care.** Avoid touching chips and circuitry on the various computer components. Try to handle parts by touching only the edges or other less-delicate parts.

✔ **Protect those old parts.** If you are taking out an old component (such as a 128MB memory module) and replacing it with something better (like a 512MB memory module), the old part may still be worth something to somebody. And if your newly purchased part is defective, at least you can put the old part back in to get your computer running again. If the new part works fine, you may be able to salvage a few bucks by auctioning the old part on the Internet!

Again, when in doubt, you should consult with a computer hardware professional. In fact, many computer parts retailers offer free or low-cost installation on memory, FireWire cards, and other upgrades.

Using a Macintosh

Apple likes to tout the great multimedia capabilities of modern Macintosh computers. And it has a lot to tout: Apple has been at the forefront of many important developments in digital video. Any new Macintosh works quite well with digital video, and almost any Mac sold in the last couple of years is also ready for video or can be easily upgraded. The following sections show you what to consider when choosing a new Mac, how to decide if your current Mac can handle digital video, and what video-editing software is available for your Mac.

Buying a new Mac

To work with digital video, your computer needs a powerful processor, lots of memory, a big hard drive, and a FireWire port. Any new Macintosh meets these requirements. That said, not all new Macs are created equal. Generally speaking, the more money you spend, the better the Mac will be, and a new iMac or better is the best choice. That said, even the most affordable eMacs and MacMinis are adequate for basic video editing. If you're serious about video, I recommend that your new Mac meet the following requirements:

- **512MB of RAM:** Video-editing software needs a lot of RAM (Random Access Memory) to work with, so the more the better. Virtually all modern Macs come with at least 512MB of RAM, but check the specs carefully before you buy. Fortunately, the RAM in most Macs can be easily upgraded through a handy little access panel that enables you to upgrade RAM in mere seconds.

- **80GB hard drive:** I just know I'm going to get e-mails from the video pros who don't think that even 80GB is enough! Video files take up lots and lots and lots of drive space. At one time, 80GB (gigabytes) was considered insanely massive for a hard drive, but when you are working with digital video, you'll eat up that space in a hurry. Less than five minutes of video eats up an entire gigabyte on your hard drive, which also has to hold software files, system files, e-mails from video pros, and other important information. Lots of people will tell you that you need at least 200GB of drive space, and they're right: 200GB or more would be really nice. But you should be able to get away with an 80GB hard drive if your budget is tight. If you can afford a bigger drive, it's worth the expense.

- **SuperDrive:** Most — but not all — modern Macs come with a SuperDrive, which is a drive that can record DVDs. If you're buying a new Mac with the intention of working with video, you'll definitely want a SuperDrive because DVD is a great way to share your video.

- **OS X:** Any new Mac includes the latest version of Apple's operating system software. But if you are buying a previously enjoyed Mac, I strongly recommend that you buy one that already has OS version 10.1.5 or higher.

Another important specification is the processor. Faster processors are better for video work, but all modern Macs come with a processor that I would consider adequate for video work. If you're buying a preowned Mac, try to get one that has at *least* a 500MHz G3 processor, or a G4 processor, if your budget allows.

The video display adapter is also an important feature for video work, but as with processors, all modern Macs have pretty good display adapters with dedicated video memory. Dedicated video memory is a huge plus when you are working with video.

If you're considering a portable iBook or PowerBook computer, pay special attention to the specifications before you buy. Portable computers usually have considerably less RAM and hard drive space than similarly priced eMacs, MacMins, iMacs, and PowerMacs.

Upgrading ye olde Mac

If you already have a Mac that is a year or two old, you should still be able to use it with digital video if it meets the basic requirements described in the previous section. If it doesn't meet those requirements, you might be able to upgrade it. As a general rule, however, if your Mac doesn't already have a G3 or higher processor, upgrading is probably going to be more expensive or challenging than simply buying a new Mac. And in the end, a very old upgraded Mac probably will not perform that well anyway.

One of the biggest obstacles you'll face involves FireWire. If your Mac does not already have a FireWire port, you may have difficulty adding one. PowerMacs can usually be upgraded with a FireWire card, but most other Macs cannot. If your Mac is so old that it doesn't already have FireWire, you should seriously consider a newer model.

Before you think you can get away without FireWire, keep in mind that if your Mac is too old for FireWire, its USB port won't be fast enough to capture full-quality digital video either.

Some parts of your Mac may be more easily upgradeable, as described in the following sections. For more details on upgrade information and installation instructions, check out *The iMac For Dummies* by David Pogue, or *Mac OS X All-in-One Desk Reference For Dummies* by Mark Chambers (both published by Wiley Publishing, Inc.). Macworld (www.macworld.com) also provides online articles and tutorials to help you upgrade your Mac. And of course, follow all the safe computer upgrade guidelines I provided earlier in this chapter.

Improving your Mac's memory

Digital video editing uses a lot of computer memory, so you should see significant performance improvements if you upgrade your RAM. Memory is usually pretty easy to upgrade in most desktop Macs. In fact, most Macs incorporate a handy access panel that enables you to add memory in mere seconds. Memory comes on little cards called *DIMMs* (dual inline memory modules), and they easily snap into place in special memory slots on the computer's motherboard. Figure 2-1 illustrates what a DIMM looks like. Read the documentation from Apple that came with your Mac for specific instructions on installing more memory.

Make sure you obtain memory that is specifically designed for your Mac — specify the model as well as its processor type and speed (for example: 1.42 GHz G4). Memory modules come in various sizes, so even if all memory slots in your Mac appear full, you might be able to upgrade by replacing your current DIMMs with bigger ones.

Figure 2-1:
Memory
modules
(DIMMs)
look
something
like this.

Portable Macs can also receive memory upgrades, but the task is more technically challenging. It usually requires that you remove the keyboard and some other parts of your iBook or PowerBook. I recommend that you leave such upgrades to a professional unless you really know exactly what you are doing.

Upgrading Mac hard drives

The hard drive in virtually any Mac can be replaced with a bigger unit. Most modern Macs have EIDE (Enhanced Integrated Drive Electronics) hard drives, a standardized hard drive format that's ubiquitous in the PC world. Standardization keeps the initial cost of new Macs affordable, and it tends to make replacement parts cheaper and easier to find. But resist the urge to run off and buy (for example) that gargantuan 300GB EIDE drive advertised in a Sunday flyer to replace the 4GB drive in your six-year-old Bondi blue iMac. Hold your horses until you consider two potential problems:

- **The new hard drive may be too big.** Older Macs may not support some of the massive newer hard drives available today.

- **The new hard drive may be too hot.** Literally. One of the greatest challenges facing computer hardware engineers today involves heat management. Modern processors and hard drives put off a lot of heat, and if too much heat is allowed to build up inside the computer's case, the life of your Mac is greatly shortened. Many older iMacs were not designed to manage the heat generated by the newest, fastest hard drives.

You should only buy a hard drive recommended for your specific Macintosh model. This means you're best off buying a new hard drive from a knowledgeable Macintosh retailer. As with memory, make sure you specify your Mac's model and processor when purchasing a hard drive.

Choosing Mac video-editing software

Apple offers a pretty good selection of video-editing software for the Macintosh — good thing it does, too, because not many other software vendors offer Mac-compatible editing programs. Chapter 19 provides a comprehensive comparison of various editing programs; if you're a Mac user, your choices are pretty much limited to these:

- ✔ **Apple iMovie:** It comes free with all new Macintosh computers, and you can download the latest version of iMovie for free from www.apple.com. The new iMovie HD supports new High-Definition (HD) camcorders.

- ✔ **Apple Final Cut Pro:** If you *can* afford pro-level prices and you want one of the most cutting-edge video-editing programs available, consider Final Cut Pro (about $1,000). Final Cut Pro is used by many professional video editors.

- ✔ **Apple Final Cut Express:** This program offers many of the features of Final Cut Pro for a fraction of the price (about $300). Final Cut Express is a good choice if you want pro-style editing features but can't afford pro-level prices.

- ✔ **Avid Xpress DV:** Avid has been making professional video-editing workstations and gear for years, so it's no surprise that it also offers one of the most advanced video-editing programs as well. Avid Xpress DV retails for about $500, or you can step up to the even more advanced "Pro" version for about $1,700.

As you can see, if you're a professional video editor, you can choose between several programs for your Mac. If you're not a pro, however, your choices are a little more limited. Fortunately, iMovie is a reasonably capable program. You can even expand the capabilities of iMovie with plug-ins from Apple (and some third parties). Visit www.apple.com/imovie/ and check out the iMovie Downloads section for more information.

Using a Windows PC for Digital Video

Graphic and video professionals have long favored Macs, but you can do advanced video editing on a Windows PCs, too. In fact, one advantage of a PC is that there is now a much greater variety of editing software available for Windows. The next few sections show you what to consider when choosing and configuring a Windows PC for digital video.

Buying a new PC

Countless PC vendors offer computers running Windows for just about any budget these days. For about the same amount of money as you would have spent just to buy a printer 10 years ago, you can now buy a new PC — including monitor — and if you shop around, you might even find someone to throw in the printer for free.

You may find, however, that a bargain-basement PC is not quite good enough for digital video. The hard drive may be too slow and small, the processor may not be fast enough, the computer might not have enough memory, or some other features may not be ideal. Look for these features when you're shopping for a new PC:

✔ **Windows XP or better:** Any new PC you buy should have Windows XP or better. Older versions of Windows such as Windows 98 and Windows ME may have serious performance problems that make video editing difficult or impossible.

✔ **512MB RAM:** Video editing requires a lot of random-access memory (RAM) — the more the better. Most new PCs have DDR RAM, which operates much more quickly and efficiently than older SDRAM.

✔ **32MB video RAM:** The video image on your monitor is generated by a component in your computer called the *video card* or *display adapter*. The video card has its own memory — I recommend at least 32MB. Some video cards share system RAM (the computer's spec sheet might say something like "integrated" or "shared" in reference to video RAM), which tends to slow down the performance of your computer. Avoid shared video RAM if at all possible.

✔ **1GHz (gigahertz) processor:** I recommend a processor speed of at least 1GHz (equal to 1000MHz) or faster. This shouldn't be a problem because there aren't too many PCs still being sold with processors slower than 1GHz. The best processors for working with video are Intel Pentium IVs and AMD Athlon XPs. The faster the better, naturally.

✔ **FireWire:** Unlike Macs, not all PCs come with FireWire (also called IEEE-1394) ports. You can upgrade most PCs with a FireWire card, but buying a computer that already has FireWire is a lot easier.

✔ **80GB hard drive:** When it comes to hard drives, bigger is better. If you plan to do a lot of video-editing work, 80GB is an absolute minimum. Sure, it *sounds* like a lot, but you'll use it up in a hurry as you work with digital video.

Another option, of course, is to build your own computer. For some, the act of building a PC from scratch remains a vaunted geek tradition (you know who you are). If you choose to build your own, make sure that your system meets — preferably *exceeds* — the guidelines given here. But know what you're doing before you start down this path; it's definitely not the path of least resistance. Heed the wisdom of this ancient computer-geek proverb: *Building your own PC is cheap only if your time is worthless!*

If you're a Linux devotee, good for you! However, if you plan to do much with digital video, you're going to have to bite the proverbial bullet and use either a Mac or the dreaded Windoze. Currently the mainstream offers no video-editing programs designed for Linux. Although some tools allow you to run some Windows or Mac programs, system performance often deteriorates, meaning you probably won't be able to capture and edit video efficiently.

Upgrading your PC for digital video

If you already have a PC, you can probably do some things to make it better-suited for video work. These tweaks may or may not be simple, however. The diversity of the PC market means your computer can probably be upgraded, but performing hardware upgrades requires experience and expertise (whether your own or somebody else's).

When considering any upgrade, your first step is to check your PC's documentation for information about what upgrades can be performed. The manufacturer may offer upgrade kits designed specifically for your computer. The following sections address some specific upgrades you may be considering. Of course, make sure you follow the computer-upgrade guidelines I provide earlier in this chapter, in the section "Upgrading Your Computer." I also recommend buying a book that specifically covers PC upgrades, such as *Upgrading and Fixing PCs For Dummies,* by Andy Rathbone, published by Wiley Publishing, Inc.

Choosing a new hard drive

About 10 years ago I bought a 1.6GB hard drive for *just* $200. At the time, I couldn't imagine using up all that space, and the price seemed like an almost unbelievably good deal. But drive sizes have grown, and prices have dropped — fast enough to make a lot of heads spin. Nowadays that $200 buys you a 300GB hard drive or more.

Big, cheap hard drives are a popular PC upgrade these days. They have become so ubiquitous that even one of my local grocery stores sells hard drives. Digital video consumes hard drive space almost as fast as my kids gobble chips and salsa at the local Tex-Mex restaurant, so there's a good chance that you may be considering a hard drive upgrade of your own. If so, here are some important considerations before you nab that hard drive along with the broccoli at your local supermarket:

✔ **Interface format:** Your hard drive connects to the rest of the computer through a special disk interface. Until recently, most modern PCs used the EIDE (Enhanced Integrated Drive Electronics) interface, also known as the ATA (Advanced Technology Attachment) interface. Some newer computers use a new format called Serial ATA, or SATA. SATA drives are faster than ATA drives and cost a little more. They also have different connectors, so only buy a serial ATA drive if you know that your computer's motherboard has a SATA interface.

✔ **Drive speed:** Common hard drive speeds are 4200 rpm, 5400 rpm, or 7200 rpm. This speed is always clearly marked on the drive's packaging. For digital video work, a 7200-rpm drive is virtually mandatory. Laptops usually have slower hard drives, making them less than ideal for video editing.

✔ **Windows installation:** If you're replacing your old hard drive with a newer, bigger drive, you have to (you guessed it) reinstall Windows. Do you have a Windows installation CD? You should have received an installation disc with your PC. If not, figure on spending at least $199 for a new Windows CD (you need to buy the Full Version, not a cheaper Upgrade Version).

✔ **Support for big hard drives:** Maybe your computer won't support the biggest hard drives sold today (admittedly, a remote possibility). Check the BIOS section of your PC's documentation to see whether your computer has any drive-size limitations.

If you do decide to upgrade to a bigger hard drive, you can either replace your current hard drive, or (in many cases) simply add a second hard drive to your computer. If you look inside your computer case, you probably see a gray ribbon cable running from the motherboard to the hard drive. In some systems, that cable has two connectors — one connecting to the hard drive and the other to the CD-ROM drive. This arrangement is called *daisy-chaining,* and sometimes you can get away with daisy-chaining two hard drives together. If you can, it's really cool — you just keep your applications where they are and add a second great big hard drive to use exclusively as a scratch pad for all your video work. Again, consult your PC's documentation (and a book like *Upgrading and Fixing PCs For Dummies*) to see whether daisy-chaining is an option.

Upgrading Windows

Earlier I recommended that you run Windows XP or better if you plan to work with digital video. Windows XP is vastly more stable than previous versions of Windows (especially Windows 95, 98, and Me) — and it does a much better job of managing system memory, which is crucial when you work with video.

If you don't already have Windows XP or better, you need to upgrade. If you already have a version of Windows on your computer, you can purchase upgrades for as little as $99, or full versions starting at $199. Any edition of a modern version of Windows (such as Home, Professional, or Media Center) is adequate for video editing.

You may have heard horror stories from friends who tried to upgrade their old computers to Windows XP. To be honest, I have a horror story of my own (but I'll spare you the gruesome details). For now, I can offer this advice:

✔ **Avoid installing Windows XP on any computer that is more than three or four years old.** XP is a snob about modernity, and may not support some of your older components and hardware. A quick way to check the hardware in your computer is to use Microsoft's online Upgrade Advisor. Visit www.microsoft.com/windowsxp/pro/upgrading/advisor. asp for instructions on how to download and use the Upgrade Advisor, which inspects your system and advises whether your computer is ready for Windows XP.

✔ **Perform a "clean" installation.** Although the installation CD provides an option to upgrade your current version of Windows, there is a really, really, *really* good chance that this approach will cause you troubles in the near future. So back up all your important data *before you begin installing,* and let the installer program reformat and repartition your hard drive using the NTFS (NT File System) when you are presented with these options. The rest of the installation process is pretty simple. (Oh, yeah, you'll have to restore all the data from your backup onto that reformatted hard drive. You could be at it for a while.)

✔ **Check for online updates immediately after installation.** Microsoft is constantly developing updates and fixes for Windows XP, and you can quickly download and install those updates by choosing Start⇨All Programs⇨Windows Update. You have to connect to the Internet to do so, so make sure you have all the necessary information handy to rein-stall your Internet service.

Installing a FireWire card

If you have a PC and want to work with digital video, perhaps the one upgrade you are most likely to perform is to install a FireWire (IEEE-1394) card. A FireWire card is crucial if you want to capture video from a digital camcorder into your computer.

To install a FireWire card, you must have an empty PCI slot inside your computer. PCI slots are white and look like the empty slot in Figure 2-2.

If you have an empty PCI slot, you should be able to install a FireWire card. Numerous cards are available for less than $100. Most FireWire cards also come packaged with video-editing software, so consider the value of that software when you make your buying decision.

When you purchase a FireWire card, read the box to make sure your computer meets the system requirements. Follow the installation instructions that come with the card to install and configure your FireWire card for use. After the card is installed, Windows automatically detects your digital camcorder when you connect it to a FireWire port and turn on the camcorder's power. You can then use Windows Movie Maker or other video software to capture video.

PCI slot

Figure 2-2:
Make sure
you have an
empty PCI
slot to
accom-
modate a
new
FireWire
card.

Choosing Windows video-editing software

A nice thing about using a Windows PC is that no matter what you want to do, lots of software is available to help you. Countless video-editing programs are available, and in Chapter 19, I provide a feature-specific cross-reference of several popular choices. Video-editing software for Windows breaks down into three basic categories:

- ✓ **Basic:** At the low end of the price-and-feature scale are free programs (such as Windows Movie Maker) or programs that come free with cheaper FireWire cards (such as Ulead VideoStudio or Roxio VideoWave). These programs are usually pretty limited in terms of what you can do with them; I recommend moving up to the next level as soon as your budget allows.

- ✓ **Intermediate:** A growing number of video-editing programs now offer more advanced editing features at a price that is not out of the average consumer's reach. Adobe Premiere Elements — featured throughout this book — is an excellent example. Premiere Elements retails for $99 and offers a diverse package of advanced editing features at an incredible

> price. Another good choice is Pinnacle Studio, which has a suggested retail price of $99 but usually sells for much less.
>
> ✔ **Advanced:** If you're willing to spend $400 or more, you can get some of the same programs that the video pros use. Advanced video-editing programs include Adobe Premiere Pro, Avid Xpress DV, Pinnacle Edition, and Sonic Foundry Vegas.

The software you choose depends greatly upon your budget and your needs. Again, check out Chapter 19 for a complete feature-and-price comparison of some top video-editing programs currently available for your PC.

Optimizing Windows for video work

Even if you have a brand new computer with a wicked-fast processor and lots of RAM, you may experience problems when you work with digital video. The most common problem is dropped frames during capture or export. A *dropped frame* occurs when your computer can't keep up with the capture or export process and loses one or more video frames. You editing software should report dropped frames if they occur. If you encounter dropped frames (or you just want to help your computer run more efficiently for video work), try the tips in the following sections to improve performance.

Updating video drivers

Windows operates the various components in your computer by using software tools called *drivers.* Outdated drivers can cause your computer to run slowly — or even crash. This is especially true of video display drivers in Windows XP. The *display adapter* (another name for the video card) is the component that generates the video image for your computer's monitor. Hardware vendors frequently provide updates, so check the manufacturers' Web sites regularly for downloadable updates. If you aren't sure who made your display adapter, follow these steps:

1. **Choose Start⇨Control Panel.**

2. **In the Windows Control Panel, click Performance and Maintenance if you see that option, and then double-click the System icon.**

   If you do not see a Performance and Maintenance listing, simply double-click the System icon.

   The System Properties dialog box appears.

3. **Click the Hardware tab to bring it to the front, and then click Device Manager.**

   The Windows Device Manager opens.

4. Click the plus sign next to Display Adapter.

More information about Display Adapter appears in the list, including the manufacturer and model of your display adapter.

5. Click the Close (X) button when you are done to close the Device Manager.

As you can see in Figure 2-3, my display adapter is made by NVIDIA. To check for updated drivers, I can do a Web search for the manufacturer's name, and then visit its Web site to see if updates are available. The Web site should contain installation instructions for the driver updates. Make sure that any driver updates you download are designed specifically for Windows XP (or specifically for the version of Windows you're using).

Figure 2-3:
Use the
Windows
Device
Manager to
review
information
about the
hardware
components
on your
computer.

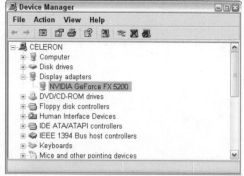

Adjusting power settings and screen savers

Your computer is probably set to power down after a period of inactivity. Normally this is a good thing because it conserves energy, but it can cause problems during video capture, DVD burning, and other video-editing actions. To temporarily disable power-saving options, follow these steps:

1. Choose Start➪Control Panel.

2. In the Windows Control Panel, click Performance and Maintenance if you see that option, and then double-click the Power Options icon.

If you do not see a Performance and Maintenance listing, simply double-click the Power Options icon.

The Power Options Properties dialog box appears.

3. **On the Power Schemes tab, set all pull-down menus (near the bottom of the dialog box) to Never, as shown in Figure 2-4.**

   You may see three or four pull-down menus, depending on your system configuration.

4. **Click Save As, name the power scheme** Video **in the Save Scheme dialog box that appears, and then click OK.**

5. **Click OK again to apply the changes and close the Power Options Properties dialog box.**

If you want to conserve power in the future, you can turn on the power-saving features by simply choosing a different power scheme.

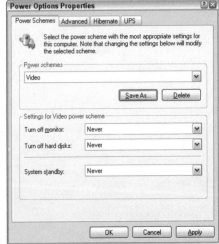

Figure 2-4:
Turn off power-saving features for video work.

I also recommend that you disable screen savers when you are getting ready to work with video. To do so, right-click an empty area of the Windows desktop and choose Properties. In the Display Properties dialog box, click the Screen Saver tab and choose (None) in the Screen saver menu. Click OK to close the Display Properties dialog box.

Choosing Video Capture Hardware

If you want to capture video from a digital camcorder, the best way to do so is with a FireWire port. But if you want to capture analog video — whether from a VCR, Hi8 camcorder, or other analog source — you need some specialized hardware. You can install a video-capture card in your computer, or (possibly) use an external *analog video converter* that connects the analog device to your computer's FireWire or USB port.

Choosing external hard drives

By far, the easiest way to add storage space to a Mac or PC is to use an external hard drive. External drives that connect to a FireWire or USB port are widely available, and although they tend to be more expensive than internal drives, their ease of installation and use makes them attractive.

Unfortunately, external drives are less than ideal for working with digital video. Even a FireWire or USB 2.0 external drive is slower than an internal drive — and drive speed is crucial when you are capturing or exporting video. External hard drives are fine if you need a big place to store music or other files, but consider them only as a last resort for video storage.

Read the packaging carefully before you buy any video-capture hardware and make sure that it is designed to capture analog hardware. Some FireWire cards are marketed simply as video-capture cards, even though they can only capture *digital* video.

When choosing an analog video-capture device, check the packaging to make sure your computer meets the system requirements. The device should also be capable of capturing the following:

- ✔ NTSC or PAL video, whichever matches your local standard (see Chapter 3 for more on broadcast video standards)
- ✔ 30 frames per second (fps) for NTSC video or 25 fps for PAL video
- ✔ 720 x 480 (NTSC) or 720 x 576 (PAL) video frames
- ✔ Stereo audio

If your analog capture device has an S-Video connector (it looks like Figure 2-5), use that for capturing video instead of the standard yellow RCA-style composite video jack. S-Video provides higher image quality.

Figure 2-5:
Use the S-Video connector to capture analog video, if one is available.

Selecting capture cards

Earlier in this chapter, I provide an overview of how to install a FireWire card in a Windows PC. Analog video-capture cards are usually installed inside your computer in much the same way. That means you'll have to have some expertise in upgrading computer hardware, and you should follow the computer-upgrade guidelines I detail in "Upgrading Your Computer," earlier in this chapter.

OK, it may seem obvious, but I'll say it anyway: Make sure your computer has an open PCI expansion slot in which you can install the card.

Many capture cards have neat little accessories called *breakout boxes*. The space available on the back of an expansion card is pretty small, and may not provide enough room for all the needed audio and video ports. Instead, the ports reside in a breakout box — which can sit conveniently on your desk. The breakout box connects to the capture card using a special (included) cable.

Selecting external video converters

If you don't feel like ripping into the innards of your computer, you may want to consider an external analog video converter, such as the Dazzle Digital Video Creator or Pinnacle Studio Moviebox USB. These devices usually connect to your computer's USB (Universal Serial Bus) port. You connect your VCR or analog camcorder to the converter, connect the converter to your computer, and the analog video is converted into digital video as it is captured into your computer. Chapter 18 gives more information on a couple of popular video converters.

If you buy a USB converter, make sure that both the device and your computer use USB 2.0 (a newer, faster version of USB). The original version of USB could only transfer data at 12Mbps (megabits per second), which is not quite enough for full-quality video capture. USB 2.0, however, can transfer at a much faster rate of 480Mbps.

Chapter 3

Gearing Up for Digital Video

Having successfully resolved the Mac versus PC debate once and for all in Chapter 2, I decided to tackle the subject of world peace here in Chapter 3. Although I would like to address that subject, the editors remind me that my approved *Digital Video For Dummies* outline calls for a discussion of camcorders and other video gear instead. (By the way, if your name is Jimmy Carter and you're interested in writing *World Peace For Dummies*, please contact the publisher.)

So, camcorders it is then. Fortunately, camcorders are actually a pretty fascinating topic, and there are now many great, high-tech choices on the market at affordable prices only dreamed of a few years ago. In this chapter, I help you understand the different kinds of camcorders sold today to ensure you pick the best one for your needs. I also help you pick out audio gear, lighting, tripods, and other gear that can help you make better movies.

Selecting a Camcorder

Digital camcorders — also called *DV* (digital video) camcorders — are among *the* hot consumer electronics products today. This is good news for you because it means there is a great selection of makes and models, with cameras to fit virtually any budget. But cost isn't the only important factor when choosing a camera. You need to read and understand the spec sheet for each camera and determine if it will fit your needs. The next few sections help you understand the basic mechanics of how a camera works, as well as compare the different types of cameras available.

I won't make specific camera model recommendations — the market is constantly changing — but I can list some up-to-date resources to help you compare the latest and greatest digital camcorders. My favorites are

- ✔ **CNET.com (www.cnet.com):** This is a great online resource for information on various computer and electronics products. The editorial reviews are helpful, and you can read comments from actual owners of the products being reviewed. The Web site also provides links to various online retailers. If you order a camcorder online, consider more than just the price. Find out how much shipping costs, and pay close attention to the retailer's customer satisfaction rating. Retailers earn high ratings by being honest and fulfilling orders when promised.

- ✔ **The local magazine rack:** Visit Barnes & Noble, Borders, Waldenbooks, or any other bookstore that has a good magazine selection. There you should find magazines and buyer's guides tailored to you, the digital video enthusiast. *Computer Videomaker* is one of my favorites, although many of its articles are aimed at professional and semi-pro videographers.

Mastering Video Fundamentals

Before you go looking for a camcorder, it's worth reviewing the fundamentals of video and how camcorders work. In modern camcorders, an image is captured by a *charged coupled device* (CCD) — a sort of electronic eye. The image is converted into digital data and then that data is recorded on tape, DVD, flash memory, or in some cases internal hard drives.

The mechanics of video recording

It is the springtime of love as John and Marsha bound toward each other across the green meadow. The lovers' adoring eyes meet as they race to each other, arms raised in anticipation of a passionate embrace. Suddenly, John is distracted by a ringing cell phone, and he stumbles, sliding face-first into the grass and flowers at Marsha's feet. A cloud of pollen flutters up on the gentle breeze, irritating Marsha's allergies, which erupt in a massive sneezing attack.

As this scene unfolds, light photons bounce off John, Marsha, the blossoming meadow, the flying dust from John's mishap, and everything else in the shot. Some of those photons pass through the lens of your camcorder. The lens focuses the photons on transistors in the CCD. The transistors are excited, and the CCD converts this excitement into data, which is then recorded for later playback and editing. This process, illustrated in Figure 3-1, is repeated approximately 30 times per second. Most camcorders record to tape, but other recording formats are sometimes used as well. I talk about those formats later in this chapter.

Most mass-market DV camcorders have a single CCD, but higher-quality cameras have three CCDs. In such cameras, individual CCDs capture red, green, and blue light, respectively. Multi-CCD cameras are expensive (typically over $1,000), but the image produced is near-broadcast quality.

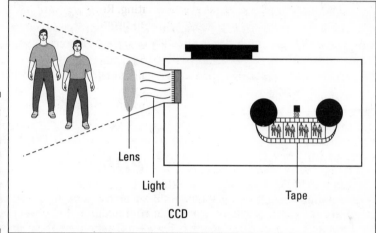

Figure 3-1:
The CCD
converts
light into
the video
image
recorded
on tape.

Lens

Light

CCD

Tape

Broadcast video formats

A lot of new terms have entered the videophile's lexicon in recent years: NTSC, PAL, SECAM. These terms identify broadcast television standards, which are vitally important to you if you plan to edit video — because your cameras, TVs, tape decks, and DVD players probably conform to only one broadcast standard. Which standard is for you? That depends mainly on where you live:

- ✔ **NTSC (National Television Standards Committee):** Used primarily in North America, Japan, and the Philippines.

- ✔ **PAL (Phase Alternating Line):** Used primarily in Western Europe, Australia, Southeast Asia, and South America.

- ✔ **SECAM (Sequential Couleur Avec Memoire):** This category covers several similar standards used primarily in France, Russia, Eastern Europe, and Central Asia.

What you need to know about video standards

The most important thing to know about the three broadcast standards is that they are *not* compatible with each other. If you try to play an NTSC-format videotape in a PAL video deck (for example), the tape won't work, even if both decks use VHS tapes. This is because VHS is merely a physical *tape* format, and not a *video* format.

On a more practical note, make sure you buy the right kind of equipment. Usually this isn't a problem. If you live in the United States or Canada, your local electronics stores only sells NTSC equipment. But if you are shopping online and find a store in the United Kingdom that seems to offer a really great deal on a camcorder, beware: That UK store probably only sells PAL equipment. A PAL camcorder is virtually useless if all your TVs are NTSC.

Some nice-to-know stuff about video standards

Video standards differ in two primary ways. First, they have different frame rates. The *frame rate* of video is the number of individual images that appear per second, thus providing the illusion that onscreen subjects are moving. Frame rate is usually abbreviated *fps* (frames per second). Second, the standards use different resolutions. Table 3-1 details the differences.

You're probably familiar with resolution measurements for computer monitors. Computer resolution is measured in pixels. If your monitor's resolution is set to 1024 x 768, the display image is 1024 pixels wide by 768 pixels high. TV resolution, on the other hand, is usually measured by the number of horizontal lines in the image. An NTSC video image, for example, has 525 lines of resolution. This means that the video image is drawn in 525 separate horizontal lines across the screen.

Table 3-1	Video Standards	
Standard	*Frame Rate*	*Resolution*
NTSC	29.97 fps	525 lines
PAL, SECAM	25 fps	625 lines

Interlacing versus progressive scan

A video picture is usually drawn as a series of horizontal lines. An electron gun at the back of the picture tube draws lines of the video picture back and forth, much like the printer head on your printer moves back and forth as it prints words on a page. All three broadcast video standards — NTSC, PAL, and SECAM — are *interlaced;* the horizontal lines are drawn in two passes rather than one. Every other line is drawn on each consecutive pass, and each of these passes is called a *field*. So on a PAL display, which shows 25 fps, there are actually 50 fields per second.

Noninterlaced displays are becoming more common. Modern computer monitors, for example, are all *noninterlaced* — all the lines are drawn in a single pass. Some HDTV (high-definition television) formats are noninterlaced; others are interlaced.

Most camcorders record interlaced video, but some high-end camcorders also offer a progressive-scan mode. *Progressive scan* — a fancy way of saying noninterlaced — is a worthwhile feature if you can afford it, especially if you shoot a lot of video of fast-moving subjects. With an interlaced camera, a problem I call *interlacing jaggies* can show up on video with fast movement. Figure 3-2, for example, shows video of a fast-moving subject that was shot using an interlaced camera. The stick seems to have some horizontal slices taken out of it, an unfortunate illusion created because the subject was moving so fast that the stick was in different places when each field of the video frame was captured. If the entire frame had been captured in one pass (as would have happened with a progressive-scan camcorder), the horizontal anomalies would not appear.

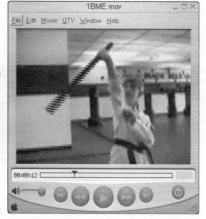

Figure 3-2: Interlaced cameras can cause interlacing jaggies on fast-moving subjects.

The many aspects of aspect ratios

Different moving picture displays have different shapes. The screens in movie theaters, for example, look like long rectangles; TV screens and computer monitors are usually more square. The shape of a video display is called the *aspect ratio*. The following two sections look at how aspect ratios affect your video work.

Image aspect ratios

The aspect ratio of a typical TV screen or computer monitor is 4:3 (four to three) — for any given size, the display is four units wide and three units high. To put this in real numbers, measure the width and height of a TV or computer monitor that you have nearby. If the display is 32 cm wide, for example, you should notice that it's also about 24 cm high. If a picture completely fills this display, the picture has a 4:3 aspect ratio.

Different numbers are sometimes used to describe the same aspect ratio. Basically, some people who make the packaging for movies and videos get carried away with their calculators, so rather than call an aspect ratio 4:3, they divide each number by three and call it 1.33:1 instead. Likewise, sometimes the aspect ratio 16:9 is divided by nine to give the more cryptic-looking number 1.78:1. Mathematically, these are just different numbers that mean the same thing.

A lot of movies are distributed on tape and DVD in *widescreen* format. The aspect ratio of a widescreen picture is often (but not always) 16:9. If you watch a widescreen movie on a 4:3 TV screen, you will see black bars (also called letterboxes) at the top and bottom of the screen. This format is popular because it more closely matches the aspect ratio of the movie-theater screens for which films are usually shot. Figure 3-3 illustrates the difference between the 4:3 and 16:9 aspect ratios.

Figure 3-3:
The two most common image aspect ratios.

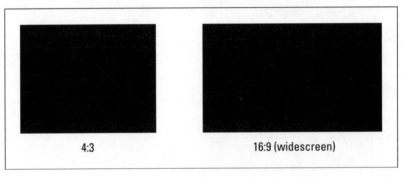

4:3   16:9 (widescreen)

A common misconception is that 16:9 is the aspect ratio of all big-screen movies. In fact, various aspect ratios for film have been used over the years. Many movies have an aspect ratio of over 2:1, meaning that the image is more than twice as wide as it is high! But for many films, 16:9 is considered close enough. More to the point, it's just right for you — because if your camcorder has a widescreen mode, its aspect ratio is probably 16:9.

Pixel aspect ratios

You may already be familiar with image aspect ratios, but did you know that pixels can have various aspect ratios too? If you have ever worked with a drawing or graphics program on a computer, you're probably familiar with pixels. A *pixel* is the smallest piece of a digital image. Thousands — or even millions — of uniquely colored pixels combine in a grid to form an image on a television or computer screen. On computer displays, pixels are square. But in standard video, pixels are rectangular. In NTSC video, pixels are taller than they are wide, and in PAL or SECAM, pixels are wider than they are tall.

Pixel aspect ratios become an issue when you start using still images created as computer graphics — for example, a JPEG photo you took with a digital camera and imported into your computer — in projects that also contain standard video. If you don't prepare the still graphic carefully, it could appear distorted when viewed on a TV. See Chapter 12 for more on using still graphics in your movie projects.

Color

Remember back in the old days when many personal computers used regular televisions for monitors? In the early 1980s, I had a Commodore 64 hooked up to a TV — it made sense at the time — but these days it's hard to believe, especially when you consider how dissimilar TVs and computer monitors have become. Differences include interlacing versus progressive scan, horizontal resolution lines, and unique pixel aspect ratios. On top of all that, TVs and computer monitors use different kinds of color.

Computer monitors utilize what is called the *RGB color space.* RGB stands for *red-green-blue,* meaning that all the colors you see on a computer monitor are combined by blending those three colors. TVs, on the other hand, use the *YUV color space.* YUV stands for *luminance-chrominance.* This tells us two things:

- ✔ Whoever's in charge of making up video acronyms can't spell.

- ✔ Brightness in video is treated as a separate component from color. *Luminance* is basically just a fancy word for *brightness,* and *chrominance* means *color* in non-techie speak.

I could go on for pages describing the technicalities of the YUV color space, but there are really only two important things you need to know about color:

- ✔ **Some RGB colors won't show up properly on a TV.** This is an issue mainly when you try to use JPEGs or other computer-generated graphics in a video project, or when you adjust the colors of a video image using effects and color settings in your video-editing program. RGB colors that won't appear properly in the YUV color space are often said to be *illegal* or *out of gamut.* You won't get arrested for trying to use them, but they will stubbornly refuse to look right. Generally speaking, illegal colors are ones with RGB values below 20 or above 230. Graphics programs can usually tell you RGB values for the colors in your images. Some graphics programs (like Adobe Photoshop) even have special filters that help you filter out broadcast "illegal" colors from your images.

✔ **Video colors won't look exactly right when you view them on a computer monitor.** Because you probably do most of your video editing while looking at a computer monitor, you don't necessarily see the same colors that appear when the video is viewed on a TV. That's one reason professional video editors connect broadcast-style video monitors to their computer workstations. An external video monitor allows an editor to preview colors as they actually appear on a TV. (See Chapter 13 for more on using a video monitor with your computer.)

Choosing a Camera Format

Virtually all camcorders sold today are digital, and there are models available to fit almost any budget. Most digital camcorders record video on MiniDV tapes, but some other formats exist as well. I describe the most common digital video formats in the following sections.

With any recording format, the first two things you should consider are price and availability of recording media. How many stores sell blank media? How much does it cost? Will the media still be available five years from now?

MiniDV camcorders

MiniDV is the most common format for digital camcorders, and if you want to be able to edit video on your computer and produce pro-quality movies, MiniDV is the best choice. MiniDV tapes are small — more compact even than audio cassette tapes. Small is good because smaller tape-drive mechanisms mean smaller, lighter camcorders. Tapes come in a variety of lengths, the most common length being 60 minutes.

All MiniDV cameras use the IEEE-1394 FireWire interface to connect to computers and transfer video, and the DV codec serves to compress and capture video. (A *codec* — short for *compressor/decompressor* — is a compression scheme. Chapter 13 tells you more about codecs.) The DV codec is supported by virtually all FireWire hardware and video-editing software. Some new MiniDV camcorders can also transfer video via USB 2.0. This may come in handy if your computer has USB 2.0 but not FireWire.

Although video can be captured reliably using USB 2.0 ports — also called "High-Speed USB" — older USB 1.1 (sometimes called "Full-Speed USB") ports aren't fast enough to capture video. Check your computer's documentation as well as Chapter 2 if you're not sure whether or not your USB port is fast enough for digital video.

DVD-based camcorders

Many new camcorders record video directly to recordable DVD discs rather than tape. This is a tempting feature because you can just pop a recorded disc into a DVD player and start watching your video in seconds. However, if you plan to edit your raw video footage into great movies, DVD camcorders have several important drawbacks:

✓ **DVD video is difficult, and sometimes impossible, to capture.** Most video-editing programs cannot capture video directly from DVD camcorders. A few programs – such as Adobe Premiere Elements 2.0 and higher – can import DVD video, but many other programs – like Apple iMovie and Windows Movie Maker – cannot.

✓ **Video quality is slightly inferior.** Most DVD camcorders offer video quality that is slightly inferior to MiniDV camcorders.

✓ **Poor Mac compatibility.** Most DVD-based camcorders offer limited or no compatibility with Macintosh computers.

✓ **DVD camcorders are often bulky.** Camcorders that use full-size recordable DVDs tend to be bulky because they must accommodate the large discs. Some cameras use smaller mini-DVDs, but mini-DVDs offer less storage capacity and are harder to find at electronics retailers.

If you have already purchased a DVD camcorder, don't despair. You should still be able to edit video from it on your Windows PC, keeping in mind that you may have to spend a little more on editing software that supports DVDs. But if you're still shopping for a new camcorder, I recommend a MiniDV-based camcorder instead.

Flash memory camcorders

A new genre of digital camcorders record video onto flash-style memory such as MemorySticks or internal flash memory. This type of recording media promises several advantages, including compact camcorder size and longer battery life. Unfortunately, there are a few potential disadvantages as well. These include difficult video capture, much like DVD-based camcorders, and inconsistent video quality. Be sure to check out online reviews before choosing a flash-based camcorder.

Digital8 camcorders

When MiniDV tapes were first introduced in the late 1990s, they were expensive and hard to find. Sony found a more affordable way to introduce digital video to the masses by creating the Digital8 format, which records high-quality digital video onto cheap Hi-8 tapes. Digital8 camcorders use the DV codec and have FireWire ports, meaning that it's just as easy to capture video from a Digital8 camcorder as from a MiniDV camcorder.

For many years Digital8 camcorders enjoyed a significant price advantage over MiniDV, but because of major price drops in recent years for both MiniDV camcorders and tapes, the price advantage of Digital8 no longer exists. If you're shopping for a new camcorder today, you are better off to choose a low-price, more compact MiniDV camera.

Analog cameras

A handful of analog camcorders remain on the market, but they are so rare and cheaply priced that one is left with the impression that stores are simply trying to clear out old stock. With MiniDV camcorders starting at well under $300, there is no good reason to buy a new analog camcorder today. If you still have an analog camcorder, see Chapter 6 for information on how to capture video from it into your computer.

Choosing a Camera with the Right Features

When you go shopping for a new digital camcorder, you may find the myriad of specifications and features overwhelming. Your challenge is to sort through all the hoopla and figure out whether the camera will meet your specific needs. When reviewing the spec sheet for any new camcorder, pay special attention to these items:

 ✔ **CCDs:** As mentioned earlier, 3-CCD (also called *3-chip*) camcorders provide much better image quality, but they are also a lot more expensive. A 3-CCD camera is by no means mandatory, but it is nice to have. Several 3-chip camcorders now retail for well under $1,000.

 ✔ **Progressive scan:** This is another feature that is nice but not absolutely mandatory. (To get a line on whether it's indispensable to your project, you may want to review the section on interlaced video earlier in this chapter.)

✔ **Resolution:** Some spec sheets list horizontal lines of resolution (for example: 525 lines); others list the number of pixels (for example: 690,000 pixels). Either way, more is better when it comes to resolution.

✔ **Optical zoom:** Spec sheets usually list optical and digital zoom separately. *Digital zoom* numbers are usually huge (200x, for example). Ignore the big digital zoom number and focus (get it?) on the *optical zoom factor* — it describes how well the camera lens actually sees — and it should be in the 12x-25x range. Digital zoom just crops the picture captured by the CCD and then makes each remaining pixel bigger to fill the screen, resulting in greatly reduced image quality. Optical zoom allows you to zoom in while maintaining maximum video quality.

✔ **Recording format:** MiniDV is the most common format, but (as mentioned earlier) other formats might make more sense for your needs.

✔ **Batteries:** How long does the included battery supposedly last, and how much do extra batteries cost? I recommend you buy a camcorder that uses Lithium Ion or NiMH (nickel-metal-hydride) batteries. Ni-Cad (nickel-cadmium) batteries don't last as long and are harder to maintain.

✔ **Microphone connector:** For the sake of sound quality, the camcorder should have some provisions for connecting an external microphone. (You don't want your audience to think, "Gee, it'd be a great movie if it didn't have all that whirring and sneezing.") Most camcorders have a standard mini-jack connector for an external mic, and some high-end camcorders have a three-pin XLR connector. XLR connectors — also sometimes called *balanced* audio connectors — are used by many high-quality microphones and PA (public address) systems.

✔ **Manual controls:** Virtually all modern camcorders offer automatic focus and exposure control, but sometimes (see Chapter 4) manual control is preferable. Control rings around the lens are easier to use than tiny knobs or slider switches on the side of the camera — and they'll be familiar if you already know how to use 35mm film cameras.

The spec sheet may try to draw your attention to various other camcorder features as well, but not all these features are as useful as the salesman might claim. Features that are generally less important include

✔ **Night vision:** Some camcorders have an infrared mode that enables you to record video even in total darkness. Sony's NightShot is an example of this feature. If you want to shoot nocturnal nature videos this feature may appeal to you, but for day-to-day videography, it's less useful than you might think.

✔ **Still photos:** Many new digital camcorders can also take still photos. Some even have an extra still-camera lens built into the housing. This is handy if you want to shoot both video and stills but don't want to lug along two cameras — but keep in mind that photo quality usually isn't the best. A 3-megapixel digital camera costing as little as $70 will take far better still pictures than almost any camcorder.

✔ **Built-in light:** If a camcorder's built-in light works as a flash for still photos, it at least serves a semi-useful purpose. But on-camera lights often have unfavorable lighting effects on your subjects; I recommend that you rely on other light sources instead when you shoot video.

And then there are some features that are essentially useless. Don't pay extra for these:

✔ **In-camera special effects:** Most digital camcorders boast some built-in effects. But why? Special effects can be added much more *effectively* (so to speak) in your computer, using your editing software.

✔ **Bluetooth:** This is a new wireless networking technology that allows various types of electronic components — including camcorders and computers — to connect to each other using radio waves instead of cables. Bluetooth is a handy technology for wireless cell phone headsets, GPS antennas, and PDAs, but Bluetooth connections are far too slow to be used for video capture.

✔ **Digital zoom:** Digital zoom makes the image appear blocky and pixelated — again, why do it? I tend to ignore the big digital-zoom claims that camcorder manufacturers like to advertise. When you test the zoom feature on a camcorder, make sure you can *disable* digital zoom. Some cameras automatically switch to digital zoom when you reach the limit of optical zoom, meaning that you could inadvertently zoom in too much and reduce your video quality.

What about HD camcorders?

In the not too-distant future, we are told, all televisions will be High Definition (HD) TVs. HDTVs display non-interlaced video images at much higher resolution than regular TVs. A few HD camcorders are now offered on the marketplace, allowing you to shoot high-definition video that takes full advantage of the capabilities of HDTV. HD camcorders are cutting edge and expensive (about $2,000 or more). Unfortunately, footage that you shoot with an HD camcorder can't be viewed on regular TVs, and you must use special HD-capable editing software to edit it. Unless you are a die-hard HD video enthusiast, you should wait a couple more years before embracing this emerging technology.

Accessorizing Your Camcorder

Few pieces of digital video gear are as underappreciated as camcorder accessories. Beyond the obvious things like a camcorder bag and spare tapes, a couple of extras are critical whenever you shoot video. These include

✔ **Extra batteries:** Your new camcorder should come with at least one battery, and I recommend buying at least one extra. Lithium Ion or NiMH batteries are preferable to Ni-Cad because Lithium and NiMH batteries last longer, and you don't have to worry about completely discharging them before recharging. (Ni-Cad batteries have always been a pain because you were supposed to *completely* discharge them before recharging, and then you had to recharge them as fully as possible because Ni-Cad batteries had a "memory" that would often prevent them from accepting a full charge.) A Lithium Ion or NiMH battery, on the other hand, is more like the gas tank in your car: You can top it off whenever you want!

✔ **Lens cleaner:** Your camcorder's lens inevitably needs to be cleaned. Purchase a cleaning kit specifically recommended by your camcorder's manufacturer. This is important because the lens on your camcorder might have a special coating that can be damaged by the wrong kind of cleaner. Avoid touching the camcorder lens with *anything* (as much as humanly possible). I like to use canned air (available at computer stores, right next to the dehydrated water) to blow dust or sand off the lens.

✔ **Lens hood:** Some high-end camcorders have hoods that extend out in front of the lens. A hood shades the lens surface to prevent light flares or other problems that occur when the sun or some other bright light source reflects directly on the lens. If your camcorder didn't come with a hood and your manufacturer doesn't offer one as an accessory, you can make a hood using black photographic paper tape (available at photographic supply stores). Make sure you check the camcorder's viewfinder, however, to ensure that your homemade hood doesn't show up in the picture!

✔ **Lens filters:** Filters fit onto the front of your lens and serve a variety of purposes. Some filters correct or modify the light that comes into the lens. *Polarizing filters* reduce reflections on glass or water that appear in a video shot. A *neutral density filter* improves color in bright sunlight. A *clear* or *UV (ultraviolet) filter* is often used simply to protect the camera's lens from getting dirty or scratched. Filters usually screw into a threaded fitting just in front of the lens, and you can purchase them from consumer electronics or photographic supply stores. If your camcorder doesn't accept a standard filter size (such as 37mm or 58mm), you will probably have to order filters specially designed for your camcorder by its manufacturer.

Some high-end cameras (like the Canon GL2 or Sony DCR-VX2100) have built-in neutral density filters that you can turn on and off or adjust. This is a handy feature, but I still recommend that you always install at least a UV filter in front of your camcorder's lens to protect it from damage. A $15 UV filter is a lot easier and cheaper to replace than the glass lens in your camcorder. Tiffen (www.tiffen.com) sells a variety of camcorder filters; its Web site includes some excellent photographs that illustrate the effects of various lens filters on your video image.

Sounding Out Audio Equipment

All digital camcorders have built-in microphones, and most of them record audio adequately. You will probably notice, however, that the quality of the audio recorded with your camcorder's mic never *exceeds* "adequate." Most professional videographers emphasize the importance of good audio. They note that while audiences tolerate some flaws in the video presentation, poor audio quality has an immediate negative effect on your viewers. To record better audio, you have two options:

- ✔ Use a high-quality accessory microphone.
- ✔ Record audio using a separate recorder.

Choosing a microphone

If you want to connect a better microphone to your camcorder, the best place to start is with your camcorder's manufacturer — you'll need a *really* long cable. (Just kidding.) Accessory microphones are usually available from the

---

What's wrong with my camcorder's mic?

After spending hundreds if not thousands of dollars for a high-tech digital camcorder, you may be frustrated by the so-so quality of the audio recorded by the built-in microphone. The problem is that the camcorder's mic is prone to pick up a lot of noise you don't want, while not recording enough of the audio you actually want. Unwanted noise includes wind roar, people chatting next to or behind the camera, and even the camcorder's own tape drive. A separate microphone can be positioned to better record your intended subject. Chapter 4 provides specific tips on recording better audio.

manufacturer. These accessory units make use of connections, accessory shoes, and other features on your camcorder.

One type of special microphone you may want to use is a *lavalier* microphone — a tiny unit that usually clips to a subject's clothing to pick up his or her voice. You often see lavalier mics clipped to the lapels of TV newscasters. Some lavalier units are designed to fit inside clothing or costumes, although some practice and special shielding may be required to eliminate rubbing noises.

You might also consider a hand-held mic. These can be either held by or close to your subject, mounted to a boom (make your own out of a broom handle and duct tape!), or suspended over your subject. Suspending a microphone overhead prevents unwanted noise caused by breathing, rustling clothes, or simply bumping the microphone stand. Just make sure that whoever holds the microphone boom doesn't bump anyone in the head!

Microphones are generally defined by the directional pattern in which they pick up sound. The three basic categories are *cardioid* (which has a heart-shaped pattern), *omnidirectional* (which picks up sound from all directions), and *bidirectional* (which picks up sound from the sides). Figure 3-4 illustrates these patterns.

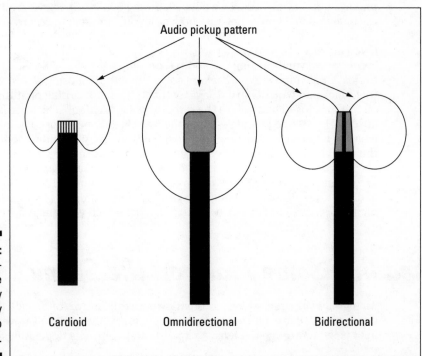

Figure 3-4: Micro-phones are defined by how they pick up sound.

A good place to look for high-quality microphones is at a musician's supply store. Just make sure that the connectors and frequency range are compatible with your camcorder or other recording device (check the camcorder's documentation). Finally, the Internet is always a good resource as well. One good resource is www.shure.com, the Web site of Shure Incorporated. Shure sells microphones and other audio products, and the Web site is an excellent resource for general information about choosing and using microphones.

Selecting an audio recorder

Separate sound recorders give you more flexibility, especially if you just want to record audio in a certain location but not video. Many professionals use DAT (digital audio tape) recorders to record audio, but DAT recorders usually cost hundreds or (more likely) thousands of dollars. For a good balance of quality and affordability, the two best options are

- ✔ MiniDisc recorder
- ✔ MP3 player with external recording capability

Many MP3 players can record audio, but make sure that you can connect a good external microphone to the player. Some MP3 players have built-in microphones, but they provide very poor recording quality. Check your MP3 player's documentation if you're not sure how or if you can use it to record audio.

If you do record audio with a separate recorder, one problem you'll have later is precisely synchronizing the audio recording with your video image. Professional video and filmmakers solve this problem using *slates*. A *slate* is that black-and-white board thingie with all the chalk writing on it that someone snaps closed just before the director yells, "Action!" The slate isn't just a kitschy Hollywood gimmick. When the slate is snapped closed in front of the camera, it makes a loud snapping noise picked up by all audio recorders on the set. That sound and the video image of the slate can be used later to precisely synchronize the separate audio and video recordings. If you plan to record audio with a separate audio recorder, I recommend that you construct and use a simple slate of your own. You can make it using two boards and a hinge purchased at any hardware store. (Just watch your fingers, okay?)

Shedding Some Light on the Scene

All digital camcorders have automatic aperture control (often called *exposure*). The *aperture* is the part of the camera that controls how much light is let in through the lens. It expands and contracts depending on light conditions, much like the iris in the human eye. But all the automatic controls in the world won't make up for a poorly lit scene. In Chapter 4, I provide some tips for properly lighting your scenes, and, in Chapter 18, I recommend a couple of specific lighting products you may want to buy. But basically, you are going to need these key bits of gear to better light your scene:

- **Lights:** Right about now, you're probably thinking, "No kidding." You can buy professional lights if you wish, but you don't need to spend hundreds of dollars to get good lights. Fluorescent shop lights are affordable and provide good-quality light, as do halogen work lights available at many hardware stores.

- **Backdrop material:** For some shots, you may want a backdrop behind your subject. You can make a backdrop frame out of pipe or cheap 1 x 3 pine boards (also known as *furring strips*) from your local lumber yard, and then tie, clamp, or staple the backdrop material to the frame. In Chapter 11, I show you how a backdrop of blue vinyl tablecloth material can be used to create a "bluescreen" special effect.

- **Clamps:** While you're at the hardware store buying lights and backdrop stuff, pick up some cheap spring clamps. Clamps can be used for holding backdrops together, holding lights in position, or playfully pinching unsuspecting crew members as they walk past.

- **Extension cords:** You'll need to plug in all your fancy lights somehow.

- **Duct tape:** If you can't do it with duct tape, it probably can't be done! I like to use duct tape to secure extension cords to the ground so that they aren't a trip hazard.

- **Translucent plastic sheets and cheesecloth:** Get these at your local art supply store to help diffuse and soften intense lights.

- **Reflective surfaces:** Use poster board, aluminum foil, or even black plastic garbage bags to bounce light onto your subjects. Crumple foil to provide a more diffuse reflection, and tape the foil or plastic bags to boards so they're easier to handle.

Lights get hot, so use care when handling them after they've been in use for a while. Also, if you use plastic, cheesecloth, or other materials to diffuse light, position those materials so they aren't too close to hot lights.

Stabilizing Your Video Image

Although modern camcorders are small and easy to carry around, you'll probably find that most of your shots benefit from a tripod or other method of stabilization. Even the cheap $20 tripod that you got for free with your camcorder purchase is better than nothing for stationary shots. If you're looking for a higher-quality tripod, here are some features that can make it worth the extra cash:

- ✓ **Strong legs and bracing:** Dual-stanchion legs and strong bracing greatly improve the stability of the camera.

- ✓ **Lightweight:** The best tripod in the world doesn't do you any good if it's so heavy that you never take it with you. Better tripods use high-tech materials like aircraft aluminum, titanium, and carbon fiber to provide lightness without sacrificing strength.

- ✓ **Bubble levels:** Some tripods have bubble levels (like those carpenters use) to help ensure that the camera is level. Few things are more disorienting in a video shot than an image that is slightly skewed from level.

- ✓ **Counterweights:** Adjustable counterweights help you keep the tripod head and camera balanced even if you're using a heavy telephoto lens or other camcorder accessory.

- ✓ **Fluid heads:** This is probably the most important feature of a high-quality tripod. A fluid head enables you to pan the camera smoothly, eliminating the jerky panning motion associated with cheaper tripods.

Chapter 18 discusses some other stabilization devices that you may want to consider, especially if you shoot a lot of high-action video.

Part II
Gathering Footage

The 5th Wave   By Rich Tennant

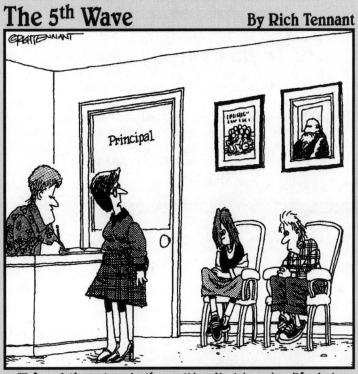

"I found these two in the multimedia lab, using iMovie to morph faculty members into farm animals."

In this part . . .

Digital video isn't all about editing. After all, you can't do any video editing if you don't have anything to edit! That means you're going to have to choose some video, record some audio, take some pictures, and obtain other source material. This part shows you how to shoot great video, record better audio, and import that audio and video into your computer.

Chapter 4

Shooting Better Video

Not so long ago, the only way to enjoy your home video was to watch tapes of raw footage, warts and all. But thanks to digital video, it's now easy for you to edit your raw footage, using only the best parts to make a great home movie.

Of course, you can improve your footage using editing software only so much. It is still important to shoot the best footage possible, so that you have a good selection of material to work with later. This chapter helps you shoot and record better audio and video. I show you how to plan a video project, and how to shoot video and record audio effectively.

Planning a Video Production

Modern camcorders are easy to use, encouraging seat-of-the-pants videography. Just grabbing your camcorder and hastily shooting may be fine if you're shooting the UFO that happens to be flying overhead, but for most other situations, some careful planning will vastly improve the quality of your movie.

The first thing you're probably going to do in any movie project is shoot some video. Even if you are shooting a simple school play or family gathering, you can and should plan many aspects of the shoot:

✔ **Make a checklist of shots that you need for your project.** While you're at it, make an equipment checklist too.

✔ **Survey the shooting location.** Make sure passersby won't trip over your cables or bump the camera. (It makes you unpopular, and can ruin your footage to boot.)

Enlisting a crew

If you're like me, most of your video shoots will actually be pretty informal, so assigning a director, sound engineer, and key grip probably seems a little silly. Besides, people who are formally assigned to such jobs will want special t-shirts and name tags and catered lunches and all kinds of other stuff that isn't allowed by your shoestring budget.

Still, you're probably going to need some help — with setting up equipment, holding lighting props and microphones, standing guard to prevent passersby from walking in front of the camera, and (of course) hauling gear. I've found that my kids are extremely helpful when it comes to videography because they *know* that moviemaking is cool. (Why are children always smarter than everybody else?) You'll want to take a few minutes to indoctrinate whomever you enlist for your video crew on the finer points

of moviemaking and provide some do's and don'ts to follow while they're on the set. Helpers should be trained on any equipment they're going to use, and they should know where they can (and cannot) stand to avoid showing up in the picture. Anyone holding a microphone must be told that little hand movements may cause loud thumps and other noise; anyone holding a light reflector should be reminded to sit still lest strange shadows pan wildly back and forth on the scene.

Perhaps most importantly, remind all helpers that silence is golden. A camera lens may be limited to a specific field of vision, but a microphone isn't. When little Johnny comes over to you behind the camera and whispers, "Daddy, I have to go to the bathroom," his revelation will be recorded loud and clear on the tape.

✔ **Talk to property owners or other responsible parties.** Identify potential disruptions, and make sure you have permission to shoot. For example, your kids' school probably doesn't mind if you shoot video of Suzie's band concert, but commercial concerts or sporting events usually have rules against recording performances.

✔ **Plan the time of the shoot.** Timing is especially important if you are shooting outside. What direction will sunlight be coming from? Do you want to take advantage of the special light available at sunrise or sunset?

✔ **Bring more blank tapes and charged batteries than you think you'll need.** You never know what may go wrong, and preparing for the worst is always a good idea. When it comes to blank tapes and spare (charged) batteries, too many is better than almost enough.

If you want to shoot high-quality video, you'll be happy to learn that staging an elaborate video production with dozens of staff members, acres of expensive equipment, and professional catering is not necessary. But you can do some simple things to improve any shooting situation — whether you are casually recording a family gathering or producing your own low-budget sci-fi movie. The following sections help you shoot better video in any situation.

Composing a Shot

Like a photograph, a great video image must be thoughtfully composed. Start by evaluating the type of shot you plan to take. Does the shot include people, landscapes, or some other subject? Consider what kind of tone or feel you want to achieve. Figure 4-1 illustrates how different compositions of the same shot can affect its overall tone. In the first shot, the camera looks down on the subject. Children are shot like this much too often: This approach makes them look smaller and inferior. The second shot is level with the subject and portrays him more favorably. The third shot looks up at the subject and makes him seem important, dominant, almost larger than life.

Figure 4-1: Composition can greatly affect how your subject is perceived.

Dressing your cast for video success

My guess is that most of your video "shoots" will actually be pretty informal affairs, where you basically record an event that was scheduled to happen whether you brought your camcorder or not. Thus, you may have a hard time convincing everyone who is attending that they should dress appropriately for video. But there definitely are some types of clothes that work better in video than others — and if you have any control at all over what the people in your movies wear, try making these suggestions:

✔ **Avoid clothes with lots of thin parallel lines or stripes.** Thin parallel lines (like those you'd find on coarse corduroy or pinstripe suits) don't get along well with TV screens; they create a crawling or wavy visual effect called a *moiré pattern*.

✔ **Limit the use of very bright shades of red and blue.** Red is especially problematic because it tends to bleed into neighboring portions of the video image. This doesn't mean everyone in your movie should wear dark, drab colors, however. In the best of all possible shoots, your subjects' clothing is bright enough to lend some interest, but contrasts with the background somewhat so they don't get lost in the video image.

Evaluating Lighting

For the purposes of shooting video, light can be subdivided into two categories: good light and bad light. Good light allows you to see your subject, and it flatters your subject by exposing details you want shown. Good light doesn't completely eliminate shadows, but the shadows don't dominate large portions of the subject either. Bad light, on the other hand, washes out color and creates *lens flares* (the reflections and bright spots that show up when the sun shines across the lens) and other undesired effects. Consider Figure 4-2: The right side of the subject's face is a featureless white glow because it's washed out by intense sunlight. Meanwhile, the left side of the face is obscured in shadow. Not good.

Figure 4-2:
This is what happens when you don't pay attention to light.

How do you light your shots effectively? Remain ever aware of both the good light and the bad. If you don't have control over lighting in a location, try to compose the shot to best take advantage of the lighting that is available. The following sections provide more specific lighting tips.

Choosing lights

Professional photographers and videographers typically use several different lights of varying type and intensity. Multiple light sources provide more control over shadows and image detail, and different kinds of lights have different effects. Lights that you'll use break down into three basic types:

- ✔ **Incandescent:** These are your good old-fashioned light bulbs like the ones Thomas Edison invented. Most of the light bulbs around your house are probably incandescent. Incandescent lights are usually cheap, but the light temperature is lower than with other types of lighting (meaning they are not as bright) and they can provide inconsistent performance.

- ✔ **Halogen:** Okay, *technically* halogen lights are also incandescent, but they usually burn at a much higher temperature (and provide more consistent light over their lifetimes) than do regular bulbs. Many professional video-lighting systems are tungsten-halogen lights, which means they have a tungsten filament passing through a sealed tube of halogen gas. Good, cheap halogen work lights (available at the local hardware store) also work well for video lighting, but their intensity should often be diffused or reflected as described in the next section.

- ✔ **Fluorescent:** Fluorescents also tend to give off a high-temperature light, although the temperature can vary greatly depending on the condition and age of the bulb. Fluorescent light is usually both very white and soft, making it ideal for video lighting. Fluorescent fixtures and bulbs can be purchased for less than $20 and can be easily suspended above your subject.

If you use fluorescent bulbs, let them warm up for a few minutes before shooting your video. This should prevent flicker. If the bulbs still flicker after they've warmed for a bit, try using new or different bulbs. Also, pay attention to how fluorescent lights affect your audio recordings. Fluorescent bulbs tend to produce a hum in audio recordings, so some practice and testing may be necessary. If fluorescent humming in your audio recording is a problem, record audio separately or use a different kind of light.

Bouncing light

Shining a light directly on a subject is not necessarily the best way to illuminate it. You can often get a more diffuse, flattering effect by bouncing light off a reflective surface, as shown in Figure 4-3. You can make reflectors out of a variety of materials, depending on your desired lighting effect:

- ✔ **Poster board:** White poster board is a good, cheap material you can find just about anywhere. Thicker poster board is easier to work with because it's rigid (meaning it won't flop all over the place and make noise while a helper holds it). With some spray paint, paint one side of a poster board gold and the other silver. Experiment using each side to gain just the right light quality.

- ✔ **Aluminum foil:** Crumple a large sheet of foil, and then spread it out again and tape it to a backing board. Crumpling the foil provides a more diffuse reflection than you can get from flat foil, but its reflection is still highly effective.

✔ **Black plastic garbage bag:** Yep, black plastic bags are pretty good reflectors even though they have a dark color. As with foil, you can tape or staple the bag to a backing board to make it easier to work with.

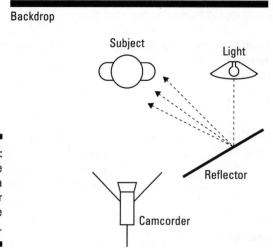

Figure 4-3:
Bounce
light off a
reflector
for a more
diffuse light.

Reflectors can also be used to "fill" the lighting of your subject. Consider Figure 4-4: A light is directed at the subject to light up his face. This light is often called the *key light*. A reflector is positioned so some of the light that goes past the subject is bounced back onto the other side to fill in facial or other details.

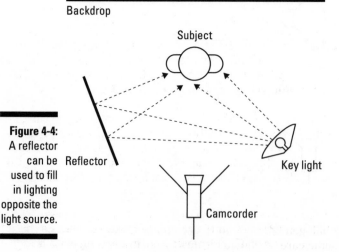

Figure 4-4:
A reflector
can be
used to fill
in lighting
opposite the
light source.

Diffusing light

Sometimes you may find that a light you're using to illuminate a subject is too intense. This is especially common with key lights such as the one shown in Figure 4-4. If you get a glaring white spot on your subject's face, you can diffuse the light by putting something between it and your subject:

✔ **Cheesecloth:** Available at art and cooking supply stores (and some grocery stores), cheesecloth has a coarse mesh and is useful both for diffusing light and straining beans or yogurt in the kitchen.

✔ **Translucent plastic:** Sheets of translucent plastic are also available at arts and craft stores. Professional videographers call these *gels*.

Colored gels are often placed in front of lights that illuminate a backdrop for special lighting effects. If you do this, make sure you place a barrier between your key light and the backdrop (as shown in Figure 4-5) so the colored light from the gel isn't washed out by the white key light. A barrier may be a piece of cardboard that is held up by a stand or helper.

If you diffuse your light, you may have to move your lights closer to the subject. Experiment for the best results.

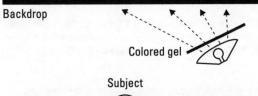

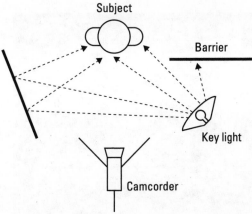

Figure 4-5: If using colored gels, be sure to place a barrier between the backdrop and key light.

Lights (especially halogen lights) tend to get very hot. To avoid fire hazards, you must use extreme care when placing gels or cheesecloth in front of lights. *Never* attach diffusers directly to lights. Position your diffusers some distance away from the lights so that they don't melt or catch on fire, and check the condition of your lights and diffusers regularly. Read and heed all safety warnings on your lights before using them. Also, if you use extension cords, make sure they are rated to handle the amperage used by your lights. Don't leave plugged-in cords coiled: Unplug cords when not in use, and regularly check their temperature. If a cord feels warm, unplug it immediately.

Dealing with backlighting

Among the most common lighting problems you'll encounter when you shoot video are backlit situations. Backlit images occur when a relatively dark subject is shot against a relatively light background, as shown in Figure 4-6. The automatic exposure control in the camera adjusts exposure based primarily on that bright background, making the subject a dark, indistinguishable blob. To deal with a backlit situation

- ✔ **Avoid it:** When possible, try to shoot subjects so that they are not in front of a bright background, such as the sky.

- ✔ **Fight light with light:** Try to put more light on the subject. You may look silly toting a bright light around a sunny beach in the middle of the afternoon, but that is exactly what the pros do. If possible, try to shoot with the sun behind the camera.

- ✔ **Use camera settings:** Many camcorders have settings that automatically compensate for backlighting by increasing exposure. The results aren't always favorable, however, as you can see in Figure 4-7.

Figure 4-6:
Who is that shadowy figure in this severely backlit situation?

Figure 4-7:
Ah, there
he is. But
now the
background
is terribly
overexposed
by the
camcorder's
backlight
compen-
sator.

Your camera probably has settings to accommodate many special lighting situations. Always read the camcorder's documentation to see what features may be available to you — and practice using those features to see which ones work well and which ones don't.

Using lens filters

Your camcorder can probably accept some lens filters that screw on in front of the lens (see Chapter 3 for more on filters). Filters can be used to improve various lighting situations. For example, if you are shooting outdoors in a brightly sunlit location, you may find that colors look kind of washed out in the light. A *neutral-density filter* can compensate for the light and improve the way colors look.

Other lens filters can provide special lighting effects. For example, a *star filter* causes star patterns to shoot out from light points that appear in the image. This can give the scene a magical look. For more on how lens filters can change and improve the way your video images look, check out the Tiffen Web site at www.tiffen.com.

Controlling Focus and Exposure

Virtually all modern camcorders control exposure and focus automatically. Automation is really handy most of the time, but it's not perfect. If you always rely on auto focus, you will inevitably see the lens "hunting" for the right setting during some shots. This will happen a lot if you shoot moving subjects. Likewise, if you are shooting a school play over a crowd, the camera might focus on the crowd instead of the stage. If your camera has a manual focus mode, you can avoid focus hunting by turning off auto focus.

Manual focus is pretty difficult to control if you're using a small dial or slider switch on the side of a camcorder. As I mention in Chapter 3, try to get a camera with a focus ring around the lens. This makes manual focus a lot easier to control.

I also urge you to learn how to use the manual exposure control (also called the *iris*). Exposure determines how much light is allowed to pass through the lens. It dilates and contracts much like the iris in a human eye. Manual exposure control allows you to fine-tune exposure if the automatic control or camcorder presets aren't providing the desired light levels. Some high-end digital camcorders have a helpful feature called a *zebra* pattern. As you adjust exposure, a striped zebra pattern appears in overexposed portions of the image. Overexposed areas appear as washed-out, colorless white blobs in your video image. A zebra pattern makes controlling exposure a lot easier: I have found that overexposing a video shot when you are manually adjusting exposure is very easy. Figure 4-7 is a good example of an overexposed image.

Although every camera is different, most camcorders have an infinite setting (∞) on the manual focus control. In most cases, anything that is more than about 10 feet away is in focus when the lens is set to infinite. Ten feet isn't a long distance, so you may be able to resolve many focus problems by simply using the infinite setting.

Setting Up Your Camcorder

Perhaps the most important tip for shooting better video is this: Know your camera. Even today's least expensive digital camcorders are packed with features that were wildly advanced (and expensive) just a few years ago. Most digital camcorders include image stabilization, in-camera effects, and the ability to record 16-bit stereo audio. But these advanced features only help you if they're turned on and configured properly. Spend a few hours reviewing the manual that came with your camcorder, and practice using every feature and setting. In particular, check the following:

- ✔ **Audio:** New camcorders are sometimes set to record 12-bit audio, also sometimes called the 32-KHz (kilohertz) setting. Fire up your camcorder right now and make sure that it is set to 16-bit (48KHz) audio instead, and never change it back. 16-bit audio is higher quality, and it won't cause any problems later on when you capture video into your computer. For more on working with audio and understanding the bit and kilohertz settings, see Chapter 7. Audio recording is also described later in this chapter.

✔ **Focus and exposure:** In the previous section, I mention those times when you want to control focus and exposure manually. If you use manual focus or exposure control, switch them back to automatic before you turn off the camcorder. That way, the camcorder is ready for quick use later on when Bigfoot momentarily stumbles into your camp.

✔ **Special effects and exposure modes:** A lot of the built-in special effects in camcorders are too gimmicky, but you should find out how to use the effects in case any of them turn out to be useful. The same thing goes for special exposure modes.

✔ **Stow the lens cap securely:** It seems obvious, I know, but if there is a clip or something that allows you to securely stow the camcorder's lens cap, use it. If you let the cap hang loose on its string, it will probably bang into the microphone and other parts periodically, making a lot of noise you don't want to record.

✔ **Use a new tape:** Even though digital video doesn't suffer from the same generational loss problems as analog video (where each play of the tape degrades the recording quality), various problems can still occur if you reuse digital tapes. Potential problems include timecode breaks (described later in this chapter) and tapes that just get old and physically wear out.

Keep the camcorder manual in your gear bag when you hit the road. It may provide you with an invaluable reference when you're shooting. Also, review the manual from time to time: Your camcorder may have some cool features that you forgot about. If you've lost your manual, check the manufacturer's Web site. You might be able to download a replacement manual.

Shooting Video

After your camcorder is configured and set up the way you want it, it's time to start shooting some video. Yay! One of the most important things you'll want to work on as you shoot video is to keep the image as stable as possible. Your camcorder probably has an image stabilization feature built in, but this automatic feature can do only so much. I recommend using a tripod for all static shots, and a monopod or sling for moving shots. (See Chapter 18 for more on monopods and slings.)

Pay special attention to the camera's perspective. As I mentioned earlier (and demonstrated in Figure 4-1), the angle of the camera greatly affects the look and feel of the video you shoot. I often find that lowering the level of the camera greatly improves the image. Some high-end camcorders have handles on top that make shooting from a lower level easier. Virtually all digital camcorders have LCD panels that can be swiveled up so you can easily see what you're recording, even if you're holding the camera down low.

Be especially careful to avoid letting the camera roll to one side or the other. This skews the video image as shown in Figure 4-8, which is extremely disorienting to the viewer. Try to keep the camera level with the horizon at all times. The following sections give additional recommendations for shooting better video.

Figure 4-8:
Don't let the video image get skewed like this — it's very disorienting.

If you're shooting a person in a studio-like situation, complete with a backdrop and fancy lighting, provide a stool for your subject to sit on. A stool will help your subject remain still and relaxed during a long shoot, and (unlike a chair) a stool also helps the subject maintain an erect posture.

Panning effectively

Moving the camera across a scene is called *panning*. You'll often see home videos that are shot while the person holding the camcorder pans the camera back-and-forth and up-and-down, either to follow a moving subject or to show a lot of things that don't fit in a single shot. This technique (if you can call it that) is called *firehosing* — usually not a good idea. Practice these rules when panning:

✔ **Pan only once per shot.**

✔ **Start panning slowly, gradually speed up, and slow down again before stopping.**

✔ **Slow down!** Panning too quickly — say, over a landscape — is a common mistake.

✔ **If you have a cheap tripod, you may find it difficult to pan smoothly.** Try lubricating the tripod's swivel head with WD-40 or silicon spray lubricant. If that doesn't work, limit tripod use to stationary shots. Ideally you should use a higher-quality tripod with a fluid head for smooth panning (see Chapter 18 for more on choosing a tripod).

✔ **If you're shooting a moving subject, try moving the camera with the subject, rather than panning across a scene.** Doing so reduces out-of-focus issues with the camera lens, and helps keep the subject in-frame.

Using (not abusing) the zoom lens

Most camcorders have a handy zoom feature. A zoom lens is basically a lens with an adjustable focal length. A longer lens — also called a *telephoto* lens — makes far-away subjects appear closer. A shorter lens — also called a *wide angle* lens — allows more of a scene to fit in the shot. Zoom lenses allow you to adjust between wide-angle and telephoto.

Because the zoom feature is easy to use and fun to play with, amateur videographers tend to zoom in and out a lot. I recommend that you avoid zooming during a shot as much as possible. Overuse of the zoom lens disorients the viewer, and it creates focal and light problems for the camcorder. Some zoom lens tips include

✔ **Avoid zooming whenever possible.** I know how tempting it is to zoom in on something cool or interesting in a video shot, but you should exercise restraint whenever possible.

✔ **Try to zoom while not recording.** I like to record a wide shot, stop recording, and then zoom in for a close up before recording again.

✔ **If you must zoom while recording, zoom slowly.** You may need to practice a bit to get a feel for your camera's zoom control.

✔ **Consider repositioning the camera instead of using the zoom lens to compose the shot.** Wide-angle lenses (remember, when you zoom out you make the camcorder's lens more of a wide-angle lens) have greater *depth of field*. This means more of the shot is in focus if you're zoomed out. If you shoot subjects by zooming in on them from across a room, they may move in and out of focus. But if you move the camera in and zoom the lens out, focus is less of a problem.

Avoiding timecode breaks

As I describe in Chapter 8, each frame of video is identified using a number called a *timecode*. When you edit video on your computer, timecode identifies the exact places where you make edits. On your camcorder, a timecode indicator tells you how much video has been recorded on the tape. This indicator usually shows up in the camcorder's viewfinder or the LCD panel. A typical timecode looks something like this:

```
00:07:18:07
```

This number stands for zero hours, seven minutes, eighteen seconds, and seven frames. If you have a 60-minute tape, timecode on that tape probably starts at 00:00:00:00 and ends at 00:59:59:29. In some cases, however, the timecode on a tape can become inconsistent. For example, suppose you record one minute of video, rewind the tape 20 seconds, and then start recording again. Depending on your camcorder, the timecode might count up to 00:00:40:00 and then start over at zero again. An inconsistency like this is called a *timecode break*. A timecode break is more likely to occur if you fast-forward a tape past a blank, unrecorded section and then start recording again.

When you capture video from a digital camcorder into your computer, the capture software reads the timecode from the tape in your camcorder. If the

Blacking and coding your tapes

Years ago, computer geeks used lots of floppy disks for storing and moving files. Before they could be used, brand new disks had to be *formatted,* a simple process that allowed the computer to read and access the disk. Video pros also have a formatting process for new videotapes called *blacking and coding.* As the name suggests, blacking and coding is the process of recording black video and timecode onto new tapes. This helps ensure consistent timecode throughout the entire tape, thus avoiding potential timecode breaks.

You don't need special equipment to black and code new camcorder tapes. All you need is a lens cap. Place the lens cap on the camcorder and start recording from the start of the tape all the way to the end. You should do this in a quiet, darkened room in case the lens cap leaks a little light. As the black video is recorded onto the tape, consistent timecode is also recorded on the entire tape from start to finish. If consistent timecode is recorded on the entire tape, timecode breaks are not likely to occur when you use the tape to record real video later on.

Blacking and coding tapes is not absolutely mandatory with modern MiniDV camcorders: As long as you follow the basic recording guidelines mentioned earlier, you should be able to avoid timecode breaks. But if you do find that timecode breaks are a problem with your particular camera, blacking and coding all new tapes before you use them is a good idea.

software encounters a timecode break, it will probably stop capture and be unable to capture any video past the break.

The best way to avoid timecode breaks is to make sure you don't *shuttle* the tape (fast-forward or rewind it) between recording segments. An alternative approach is to pre-timecode your tapes before shooting (as described in the sidebar "Blacking and coding your tapes" in this chapter). If you do have to rewind the tape — say, someone wants to see a playback of what you just recorded — make sure you cue the tape back to the end of the recorded video *before* you start recording again. Many camcorders have an *end-search* feature that automatically shuttles the tape to the end of the current timecode. Check your camcorder's documentation to see whether it has such a feature.

Recording Sound

Recording great-quality audio is no simple matter. Professional recording studios spend thousands (sometimes even millions) of dollars to set up acoustically superior sound rooms. I'm guessing you don't have that kind of budgetary firepower handy, but if you're recording your own sound, you can get pro-sounding results if you follow these basic tips:

- ✔ **Use an external microphone whenever possible.** The microphones built into modern camcorders have improved greatly in recent years, but they still present problems. They often record undesired ambient sound near the camcorder (such as audience members at a play) or mechanical sound from the camcorder's tape drive. If possible, connect an external microphone to the camcorder's mic input.

  Don't let power cords cross your microphone cable. This can cause a hum in the audio you record.

- ✔ **Eliminate unwanted noise sources.** If you *must* use the camcorder's built-in mic, be aware of your movements and other things that can cause loud, distracting noises on tape. Common problems include loose lens caps, fingers rubbing against the mic, wind blowing across the mic, and the *swish-swish* of those nylon workout pants you wore this morning. I discuss ambient noise in greater detail in the following section.

- ✔ **Obtain and use a high-quality microphone.** If you're recording narration or other sounds in your "studio" (also known as your office) use the best microphone you can afford. A good mic isn't cheap, but it can make a huge difference in recording quality. The cheap little microphone that came with your computer probably gives poor results.

- ✔ **Position the microphone for best quality.** If possible, suspend the mic above the subject. A suspended microphone is less likely to pick up noises made by the subject's clothes or bumping the microphone stand.

- ✔ **Watch for trip hazards!** In your haste to record great sound, don't forget that your microphone cables can be a hazard on-scene. Not only is this a safety hazard to anyone walking by, but if someone snags a cable, your equipment could be damaged as well. If necessary, bring along some duct tape to temporarily cover cables that run across the floor.

Earlier I mentioned that you should plan which video scenes you want to record. Planning the *audio* scenes that you want to record is also important. For example, suppose I want to make a video about a visit to the beach. In such a project I would like to have a consistent recording of waves crashing on the shore to use in the background. But if I record short, 5-to-10–second video clips, I'll never get a single, consistent *audio* clip. So, in addition to my various video clips, I'll also record a long, unbroken clip of the ocean.

Managing ambient noise

Ambient noise is the general noise that we don't usually think much about because it surrounds us constantly. Ambient noise might come from chirping birds, an airplane flying overhead, chattering bystanders, passing cars, a blowing furnace, the little fans spinning inside your computer, and even the tiny motor turning the tape reels in your camcorder or tape recorder. Although it's easy to tune out these noises when you're immersed in them, they'll turn up loud and ugly in your audio recordings later on.

If you're recording outdoors or in a public gathering place, you probably can't do much to eliminate the actual sources of ambient noise. But wherever you are recording, you can take some basic steps to manage ambient noise:

- ✔ **Use a microphone.** I know, this is about the millionth time I've said it, but a microphone placed close to your subject will go a long way toward ensuring that the sound you actually *want* to record is not totally over-whelmed by ambient noise.

- ✔ **Wear headphones.** Camcorders and tape recorders almost always have headphone jacks. If you plug headphones into the headphone jack, you can listen to the audio that is actually being recorded, and possibly detect potential problems.

- ✔ **Shield the camcorder's mic from wind.** A gentle breeze may seem almost silent to your ear, but the camcorder's microphone may pick it up as a loud roar that overwhelms all other sound. If nothing else, you can position your hand to block wind from blowing directly across the screen on the front of your camcorder's mic.

✔ **Try to minimize sound reflection.** Audio waves reflect off any hard surface, which can cause echoing in a recording. Hanging blankets on walls and other hard surfaces significantly reduces reflection.

✔ **Turn off fans, heaters, and air conditioners.** Air rushing through vents creates a surprising amount of unwanted ambient noise. If possible, temporarily turn off your furnace, air conditioner, or fans while you record your audio.

✔ **Turn off cell phones and pagers.** You know how annoying it is when someone's cell phone rings while you're trying to *watch* a movie; just imagine how bothersome it is when you're *making* a movie! Make sure that you and everyone else on the set turns those things off. Even the sound of a vibrating pager might be picked up by your microphones.

✔ **Shut down your computer.** Obviously this is impossible if you are recording using a microphone that is connected to your computer, but computers do tend to make a lot of noise, so shut them down if you can.

✔ **Warn everyone else to be quiet.** If anyone else is in the building or general area, ask him to be quiet while you are recording audio. Noises from the next room may be muffled, but they still contribute to ambient noise. Likewise, you may want to wait until your neighbor is done mowing his lawn before recording your audio.

✔ **Record and preview some audio.** Record a little bit of audio, and then play it back. This might help you identify ambient noise or other audio problems.

Creating your own sound effects

As you watch a TV show or movie, it's easy to forget that many of the subtle little sounds you hear are actually sound effects that were added in during editing, rather than "real" sounds that were recorded with the video image. This is often because the microphone was focused on the voice of a speaking subject as opposed to other actions in the scene. Subtle sounds like footsteps, a knock on the door, or splashing water are often recorded separately and added to the movie later. These sound effects are often called *Foley* sounds by movie pros, and someone who makes Foley sounds is called a *Foley artist.* Foley sound effects are named after audio pioneer Jack Foley, who invented the technique in the 1950s.

Recording your own sound effects is pretty easy. Many sounds actually sound better in a video project if they're simulated, as opposed to recording the real thing. For example:

- **Breaking bone:** Snap carrots or celery in half. Fruit and vegetables can be used to produce many disgusting sounds, and they don't complain about being broken in half nearly as much as human actors.

- **Buzzing insect:** Wrap wax paper tightly around a comb, place your lips so that they are just barely touching the paper, and hum so that the wax paper makes a buzzing sound.

- **Fire:** Crumple cellophane or wax paper to simulate the sound of a crackling fire.

- **Footsteps:** Hold two shoes and tap the heels together followed by the toes. Experiment with different shoe types for different sounds. This may take some practice to get the timing of each footstep just right.

- **Gravel or snow:** Walk on cat litter to simulate the sound of walking through snow or gravel.

- **Horse hooves:** This is one of *the* classic sound effects. The clop-clop-clopping of horse hooves is often made by clapping two halves of a coconut shell together.

- **Kiss:** Pucker up and give your forearm a nice big smooch to make the sound of a kiss.

- **Punch:** Punch a raw piece of steak or a raw chicken.

- **Thunder:** Shake a large piece of sheet metal to simulate a thunderstorm.

- **Town bell:** To replicate the sound of a large bell ringing, hold the handle of a metal stew pot lid, and tap the edge with a spoon or other metal object. Experiment with various strikers and lids for just the right effect.

Some sound effects might be included with your editing software or are available for download. For Windows, Pinnacle Studio comes with a library of sound effects. Apple iMovie also includes some built-in sound effects, which you can view by clicking the Audio button in iMovie. To view a list of sound effects, make sure you have iMovie Sound Effects listed in the menu at the top of the audio browser (as shown in Figure 4-9). You may also be able to download additional sound effects periodically from www.apple.com/ilife/imovie/soundeffects.html.

Figure 4-9:
Many video programs include sound effects you can use in your movies.

Chapter 5

Capturing Digital Video

*O*nce upon a time, a computer's operating system allowed you to turn the computer on and get it up and running, but not much more. If you wanted to actually do anything with your computer, you had to install programs created by other programmers and software companies. But over the years, Apple and Microsoft have been adding value to their operating systems in the form of handy little utilities and programs. These include text editors, Web browsers, e-mail clients, and drawing programs.

Add to that list video-editing programs. Apple was the first to offer built-in video editing with its excellent program iMovie, and Microsoft quickly followed up with Windows Movie Maker. If your computer has a FireWire port and runs a modern version of Windows or Mac OS X, you have all you need to start capturing and editing your digital video. This chapter shows you how to capture video into your computer from a digital camcorder using iMovie and Windows Movie Maker, as well as with a more advanced editing program such as Adobe Premiere Elements.

Preparing to Capture Digital Video

The process of transferring video into your computer is called *capturing*. Capturing digital video is really easy, but you should take some steps beforehand to make sure everything goes smoothly:

> ✔ **Install your hardware.** Your computer needs the right components to capture video — which means (among other things) having a FireWire or other capture card installed. (See Chapter 2 for more details on prepping your computer.)

✔ **Turn off unnecessary programs.** If you are like most people, you probably have several different programs running on your computer right now. Video capture requires a lot of memory and processor power, and every running program on your computer uses some of those resources. E-mail, Web browser, and MP3 jukebox? Close 'em down. Cute desktop schemes and screen savers? Disable those too. You may even want to temporarily disable your antivirus software during video capture, especially if you encounter capture problems (see the section titled "Troubleshooting Capture Problems," later in this chapter).

If you're using Windows, take a look at the System Tray. (That's the area in the lower right corner of your screen, next to the clock.) Most of the little icons you see down there represent a running program. Right-click each icon and close or disable as many of them as possible. Eventually (well, okay, ideally) your System Tray and Windows Taskbar looks something like Figure 5-1. You don't have to get rid of every single item, but do try to close or disable as many as possible. After all, it's a temporary arrangement. You should also disable your Internet connection if possible during video capture as well. You can reactivate System Tray items later — including your antivirus software — by simply restarting your computer.

If you have Windows XP Service Pack 2 (SP2) or later installed and you disable your anti-virus program, your System Tray displays a red security warning icon as shown in Figure 5-1. This icon (as well as the speaker icon) won't use enough memory to affect video capture, but it is a handy warning to re-activate your anti-virus program when you're done capturing.

Figure 5-1:
The Windows Taskbar ideally looks like this when you're ready to capture video.

System Tray

If you're using a Macintosh, look at the OS X Dock to make sure your programs are closed. (Any active program has a little arrow under it, as shown in Figure 5-2.) To quit a program, click its icon in the Dock and press ⌘+Q. The only icon you won't be able to quit is the Finder, of course.

Figure 5-2:
Use the OS X
Dock to
make sure
all open
programs
are closed.

The Finder icon   An active program

✔ **Defragment your hard drive.** When your computer's operating system puts files on your hard drive, those files may wind up spread all over the place. This means that even if you have 100GB of free space, that 100GB might be broken up into little chunks here and there. This can cause trouble during video capture, especially with Windows machines, and *most* especially with versions of Windows before Windows XP (such as Windows Me). Even if you have a Mac, defragging is still a good regular computer maintenance practice, and if you experience dropped frames during video capture, defragmentation can only help.

I recommend you defragment your hard drive monthly, or right before video capture if the drive hasn't been defragmented recently. Defragmentation organizes the files on your hard drive so that the empty space is in larger, more usable chunks. Some computer experts will probably tell you that defragmentation isn't as important with modern operating systems like OS X and Windows XP, but that advice does not really apply when you're working with video. Video is one of the few remaining tasks that still benefits from a defragmented hard drive.

To defragment a hard drive in Windows, choose Start⇨All Programs⇨ Accessories⇨System Tools⇨Disk Defragmenter. Choose the hard drive you want to defragment, and click Defragment (Windows XP) or OK (Windows Me and earlier).

The Macintosh OS doesn't come with a built-in defragmenter, but you can use an aftermarket defragmentation utility such as Norton DiskDoctor or Apple Disk First Aid.

✔ **Make sure you have enough hard-drive space.** I address this more in the next section, "Making room for video files."

Why is the process of transferring video to the hard drive called *capturing* instead of just *copying?* Even though the video is stored as digital data on your camcorder tape, that data must be turned into a computer file in order to be stored on your hard drive. *Capturing* is the process of turning video data into a computer file.

Making room for video files

Video files consume a lot of space. Digital video normally uses 3.6MB (megabytes) of hard drive space for every second of video, which (if you do the math) means that 1GB (gigabyte) holds about five minutes of video. You'll also need working space on the hard drive — so figure out approximately how much video you want to capture and multiply that number by four. For example, if you want to capture 15 minutes of video, you'll need at least 3GB of disk space to store it. Multiply that by four, and you should have at least 12GB of free space on your hard drive to get the job done.

When I say you need at least 12GB of space for 15 minutes of video, I do mean *at least.* Even though hard-drive space may appear empty, your operating system — as well as your video-editing program — has to use that empty space periodically while working in the background. When it comes to hard-drive space, more truly is better when you're working with video.

The first thing you need to do is figure out how much free space is available on your hard drive. In Windows, open My Computer (Start⇨My Computer). Right-click the icon representing your hard drive; choose Properties from the menu that appears. A Properties dialog box appears, similar to the one shown in Figure 5-3. It tells you (among other things) how much free space is available. Click OK to close the box.

Figure 5-3:
This hard drive has plenty of free space to capture some video.

On a Macintosh, click the icon for your hard drive just once; then press ⌘+I. An Info dialog box (similar to Figure 5-4) appears, showing you how much free space is available. Click the Close button or press ⌘+W to close the Info dialog box.

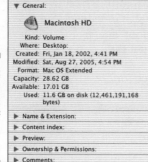

Figure 5-4:
This hard drive has 17.01GB of free space available.

What if you need more space? Your options may be limited, but here are some things to consider:

- ✔ **Take out the garbage.** Empty the Recycle Bin (Windows) or Trash (Mac).

- ✔ **Clean up unneeded Internet files.** The cache for your Web browser could be taking up a lot of hard-drive space. The Windows Disk Cleanup utility (pictured in Figure 5-3) can help you get rid of these and other unnecessary files. On a Mac, you can empty the cache or control how much disk space is devoted to cache using the Preferences window for your Web browser.

- ✔ **Add a hard drive to your computer.** Adding a second hard drive to your computer can be a little complicated, but it's a good way to gain more storage space. (See Chapter 2 for more on how to do this.)

Connecting a digital camcorder to your computer

Before you can edit video on your computer, you need to get the video *into* the computer somehow. Sorry, a shoehorn won't work — usually you connect a cable between your camcorder and the FireWire or USB port on your computer. Of the two, FireWire (also called IEEE-1394) is usually preferable.

FireWire ports have two basic styles: 6-pin and 4-pin. The FireWire port on your computer probably uses a 6-pin connector, and the port on your camcorder probably uses a 4-pin connector. This means you'll probably have to buy a 6-pin to 4-pin FireWire cable if you don't already have one. Figure 5-5 illustrates the differences between FireWire connectors.

Figure 5-5:
The two styles of FireWire connectors are 6-pin and 4-pin.

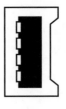

6-pin   4-pin

The FireWire connector on your camcorder may not be labeled "FireWire." It may be called IEEE-1394 (the "official" term for FireWire), DV, or i.Link. Whatever it's called, if the camcorder is digital and it has a port that looks like one of the connectors in Figure 5-5, it's FireWire-compatible.

FireWire is a "hot-swappable" port technology. This means you don't have to turn the power off on your computer when you want to connect a camcorder or other FireWire device to a FireWire port. Just plug the device in, turn it on, and away you go. (Meanwhile, you may want to practice saying buzzwords like "hot-swappable" with a straight face.)

Connect the FireWire cable between the camcorder and your computer, and then turn on the power on your camcorder. Your camcorder probably has two power modes. One is a *camera* mode, which is the mode you use when you shoot video. The second mode is a *player* or *VTR* mode. This second mode is the one you want to use when you capture video.

When you turn on the camcorder, your Windows PC probably chimes and then displays the Digital Video Device window, which asks you what you want to do. This window is one of those handy yet slightly-annoying features that tries to make everything more automatic in Windows. Click Cancel to close that window for now.

One really cool feature of FireWire is a technology called *device control*. In effect, it allows software on your computer to control devices that are connected to your FireWire ports — including digital camcorders. This means that when you want to play, rewind, or pause video playback on the camcorder, you can usually do it using Play, Rewind, Pause, and other control buttons in your Windows Movie Maker or Apple iMovie application.

Some camcorders can use USB 2.0 *(Universal Serial Bus)* ports instead of FireWire ports. The nice thing about USB ports is that — unlike FireWire ports — virtually all PCs made in the last five years have them. The not-so-nice thing is that only USB 2.0 ports are fast enough to capture video. Older USB 1.1 ports are too slow, resulting in very poor video quality when you capture. I recommend that you use FireWire whenever possible.

Capturing Digital Video

Capturing digital video is really easy in a program like iMovie, Windows Movie Maker, or Premiere Elements. In the following sections, I show you how to capture video using Windows Movie Maker or Premiere Elements on a Windows PC, and iMovie on a Mac. Fortunately, the capture process in most programs is pretty similar, so you should be able to follow along no matter what software you are using.

Even if your FireWire card came with a separate capture utility, I recommend that you capture video in the program you plan to use for editing whenever possible. This saves you time later trying to figure out how to transfer video between two different programs.

Capturing video in Windows Movie Maker

Windows Movie Maker is to video-editing programs what Microsoft Paint is to graphics programs. It's simple and rudimentary, but it gets the job done. To launch Windows Movie Maker, choose Start➪All Programs➪Accessories➪ Windows Movie Maker. Windows Movie Maker opens.

I strongly recommend that you use Windows Movie Maker version 2 or better. To check Movie Maker's version number, choose Help➪About Windows Movie Maker. A dialog box appears showing the version number and other information. If you need to upgrade, choose Help➪Windows Movie Maker on the Web and look for a link to download the latest update from Microsoft's Web site.

To capture video, follow these steps:

1. **Click Capture from Video Device in the Tasks list on the left.**

   The Video Capture Wizard appears. If you receive an error message instead, make sure that your camcorder is connected to the port and turned on. You may need to disconnect and reconnect the cable, and restart Windows Movie Maker.

 2. **Enter a name for the video you want to capture, choose a folder for saving the video (or just accept the default location), and click Next.**

 3. **Choose a video setting as shown in Figure 5-6.**

 This is where you choose the quality of the video you want to capture. Notice that for each setting, the window shows an estimate of how much hard-drive space will be consumed. I recommend the middle option — Digital Device Format (DV-AVI) — because it captures video at the highest possible quality. You can always reduce the quality later when you output your movie for Internet viewing. Only choose the other options if your hard-drive space is limited.

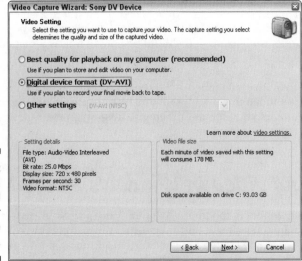

Figure 5-6:
Choose a
quality level
for your
capture
video.

 4. **Click Next again, and then choose whether you want to capture the whole tape or just certain portions.**

 Capturing the whole tape is easier, but choosing to manually capture only certain portions of the tape means you won't waste hard-drive space on unwanted video clips.

 5. **Uncheck the Show Preview During Capture option and click Next.**

 The onscreen preview wastes computer memory and processing power. Instead, use the camcorder's viewfinder or display screen to preview the video.

 If you are automatically capturing the whole tape, you're done! Windows Movie Maker does the rest. But if you are manually capturing just certain portions, continue with the following steps.

6. **Use the DV camera controls to locate portions of video you want to capture, as shown in Figure 5-7.**

   The Play, Pause, Stop, Rewind, and Fast Forward buttons in the Video Capture Wizard control the tape in your camcorder. Use the Previous Frame and Next Frame windows to move — or *shuttle* in video-tech speak — the tape a single frame at a time.

7. **Click Start Capture to start capturing video.**

   While video is being captured, the Capture Wizard shows you how much time has been captured, and how much hard-drive space is being used. In Figure 5-7, you can see that thus far I have captured 13 minutes and 49 seconds of video, consuming 2.79GB of disk space.

   One of the options in the Video Capture Wizard is Create Clips when Wizard Finishes. This is a handy option because it automatically divides your captured video into separate clips at every scene break. This feature comes in handy later when you are editing.

8. **Click Stop to stop capturing a segment of video.**

   Repeat steps 7 and 8 to capture additional segments.

9. **When you are done capturing video, click Finish to close the Video Capture Wizard.**

When you are done capturing video, Windows Movie Maker automatically imports clips into the program window. You are now ready to edit your clips into a movie!

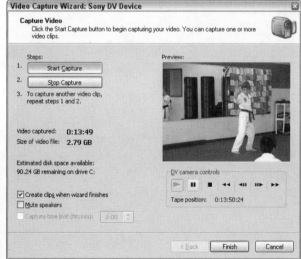

Figure 5-7:
The Video Capture Wizard makes capturing pretty easy.

Capturing video in Apple iMovie

Like Windows Movie Maker, Apple's iMovie makes the capture process as simple as possible. In fact, there are just two video capture options to worry about. To adjust capture preferences, choose iMovie⇨Preferences. The Preferences dialog box appears, as shown in Figure 5-8. The two options relating to video capture are as follows:

- ✔ **New Clips Go To:** This default setting sends incoming clips to the Clips Pane. This is the best place to send new clips unless you want to quickly convert your imported video into a movie without any editing. What's the fun in that?

- ✔ **Automatically Start New Clip at Scene Break:** iMovie automatically recognizes when one scene ends and a new one begins. This useful feature often makes editing easier, so I recommend that you leave this option checked.

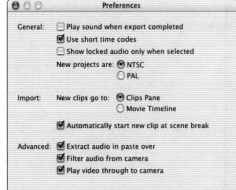

Figure 5-8: Import options also apply to captured video.

The iMovie interface is simple and easy to use. To capture video, follow these steps:

1. **Connect your camcorder to the FireWire port as described earlier in this chapter.**

2. **Switch the camera to VTR mode.**

3. **In iMovie, click the Camera button to switch iMovie to the Camera mode.**

   The Preview pane displays the message `Camera Connected` (as shown in Figure 5-9).

4. **Use the camera controls to identify a portion of video that you want to capture.**

   When you are ready, rewind the tape about ten seconds before the point at which you want to start capturing.

5. **Click the Play button in the camera controls.**

6. **Click the Import button when you want to start importing.**

7. **Click the Import button again when you want to stop importing.**

It's just that simple. Your captured clips automatically appear in the Clips Pane, where you can then use them in your movie projects.

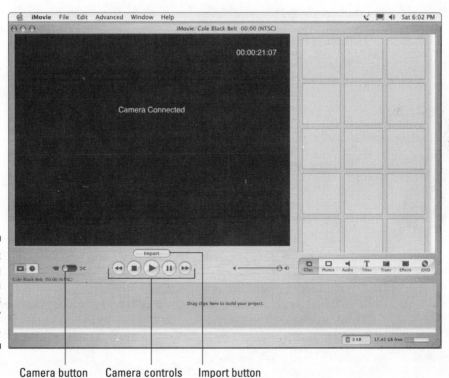

Figure 5-9:
Capturing
video in
iMovie is
pretty
simple.

Camera button   Camera controls   Import button

Capturing Video in Adobe Premiere Elements

World leaders and video editors alike know that more power brings greater responsibility. When you choose a more advanced video-editing program like Adobe Premiere Elements, you have a lot more video-editing power at your command, but you also have a lot more steps to follow and choices to make as you try to get your work done. The task of capturing video is no exception; when you capture video in Premiere, you have to spend a little more time adjusting settings and choosing capture formats.

Although I cover Adobe Premiere Elements here, most advanced video-editing programs look and work pretty much the same. You should be able to follow these same basic steps in Final Cut Express, Vegas Video, and other advanced editors.

To capture video in Premiere Elements, follow these steps:

1. **Open a Premiere Elements project.**

   If you don't yet have a project in which to work, open the Premiere Elements program and click New Project in the welcome screen. Enter a name for the project and click OK. A new project is created, and the Edit workspace appears.

2. **Choose Edit➪Preferences➪Device Control.**

3. **In the Preferences dialog box, click the Options button next to the Devices menu.**

   If you have Premiere Elements version 2 or later, choose USB Video Class 1.0 Device Control in the Devices menu to capture video using a USB 2.0 port instead of FireWire.

4. **In the Options dialog box, choose the brand and device model of your camcorder if they are listed, as shown in Figure 5-10.**

   If your brand or model isn't listed, choose Standard in the Device Type menu and Generic in the Device Brand menu. Make sure that your local video standard (NTSC or PAL; see Chapter 3 for more on video standards) is selected in the Video Standard menu. If you use NTSC video, choose Drop-Frame in the Timecode Format menu. If you use PAL, choose Non Drop-Frame instead.

   After you have told Premiere Elements what kind of camcorder you have, you won't have to repeat this step the next time you capture video, unless, of course, you get a new camcorder.

Figure 5-10:
Tell
Premiere
Elements
what kind of
camcorder
you have.

5. **Click OK to close the Options dialog box.**

6. **In the Preferences dialog box, click Capture in the menu on the left to reveal capture options on the right.**

   Premiere Elements gives three capture options:

   • Abort Capture on Dropped Frames. If the computer runs short on memory or processing power, it may miss some video frames during capture. This is called *dropped frames,* and it creates a serious video quality problem. I recommend that you enable this option.

   • Report Dropped Frames. If some frames get dropped during capture, you'll definitely want to know about it. Keep this option enabled.

   • Use Device Control Timecode. This option makes Premiere Elements use the same timecode recorded on your videotape. This isn't absolutely necessary, but it may help you find a needed section of video later if you need to re-capture anything. Timecode is used to identify video frames, and is explained in detail in Chapter 8.

7. **Click OK to close the Preferences dialog box.**

8. **Click the Capture button on the Premiere Elements toolbar, or choose Window➪Workspace➪Capture.**

   The capture workspace appears as shown in Figure 5-11.

9. **Use the camera controls under the capture preview window to identify segments of video that you want to capture.**

   The Play, Stop, Rewind, and Fast Forward buttons control your camcorder. Use the Step Back or Step Forward to move back or forward a single frame at a time. The Shuttle slider allows you to dynamically shuttle video forward or back, much like the shuttle on professional video equipment.

10. Click Capture to start capturing video.

If there's a specific segment of video that you want to capture, start capturing a few seconds before the desired segment begins. This ensures that you successfully capture the whole segment, and that it's easier to edit later.

11. Click Stop Capture when you are done capturing a segment.

Premiere Elements saves your clip in the Media window, where they can later be used in your movie project.

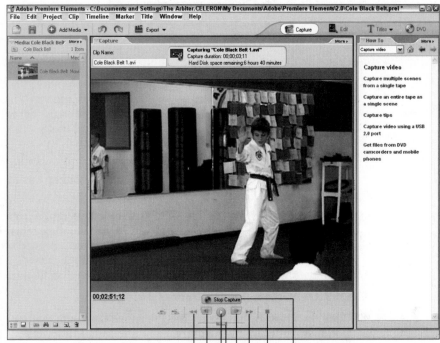

Figure 5-11:
Use the Capture workspace to capture video.

Rewind
Step Back
Play/Pause
Shuttle
Step Forward
Fast Forward
Stop
Capture/Stop Capture

Importing video from phones and digital cameras

Several decades ago, the only way to record moving pictures was with an expensive film movie camera, and the film had to be expensively developed before it could be viewed. A movie camera was a luxury few enjoyed.

Today people record video with almost anything, including camcorders, Web cams, digital still cameras, and even cell phones! Most of these devices record video in the MPG format, which is good because MPG video is supported by Apple iMovie, Adobe Premiere Elements, Windows Movie Maker, and virtually every other video-editing program on the market. To import MPG video files into a movie project,

choose File⇨Import (File⇨Add Media in Adobe Premiere) and browse to the file you want to import. Once imported, the file can be used in your movie projects.

Just keep in mind, however, that video files imported from camera phones, Web cams, and digital still cameras usually have much lower video quality than a digital camcorder. The reduced quality of a camera phone clip may not be a big deal for videos you plan to compress and share online, but if you record the movie to DVD or tape, the low-res video clips will stick out like sore thumbs.

Troubleshooting Capture Problems

Video capture usually works pretty easily and efficiently with modern hardware, but some problems can still occur. Here's a quick tour of some common digital-capture problems — and their potential solutions.

You can't control your camera through your capture software

When you click Play or Rewind on the camera controls in your video-capture software, your digital camcorder *should* respond. If not, check the following items:

- ✔ **Check all the obvious things first:** Are the cables connected properly? Is your camcorder turned on to VTR mode? Does the camera have a dead battery?

- ✔ **Did the camera automatically power down due to inactivity?** If so, check the camera's documentation to see if you can temporarily disable the power saver mode. Also, consider plugging the camera in to a charger or AC power adaptor so that you aren't just running on battery juice.

✔ **Is your FireWire card installed correctly?** Open the System icon in the Performance and Maintenance section of the Windows Control Panel. Click the Hardware tab, and then click the Device Manager button. If you see a yellow exclamation mark under IEEE 1394 Bus host controllers, you have a hardware problem. See Chapter 2 for more on configuring hardware.

✔ **Is your camcorder supported?** Most modern digital camcorders are supported by Apple iMovie, Adobe Premiere, Windows Movie Maker, and other programs. But if the software just doesn't seem to recognize the camera, check the software vendor's Web site (www.apple.com, www.adobe.com, or www.microsoft.com, respectively) for camera compatibility information. If your camera is so new that it wasn't originally supported by your editing software, check the publisher's Web site to see if software updates are available to accommodate newer camcorder models.

Frames drop out during capture

Video usually has about 30 frames per second, but if the capture process doesn't go smoothly, some of those frames could get missed or *dropped,* as video pros call it. *Dropped frames* show up as jerky video and cause all kinds of other editing problems, and usually point an accusing finger at your hardware, for one of four possible reasons:

✔ **Your computer isn't fast enough.** Does your computer meet the system requirements that I recommend in Chapter 2? How fast is the processor? Does it have enough RAM?

✔ **Your computer isn't operating efficiently.** Make sure all unnecessary programs are closed as I described earlier in this chapter. You may also be able to tweak your computer's settings for better video-capture performance. Check out the OS Tweaks in the Tech Support section of www.videoguys.com for tips and tricks for helping your computer make the best possible use of its resources.

✔ **You left programs running.** Make sure that your e-mail program, Internet browser, music jukebox, and other programs are closed. I also recommend that you disable your Internet connection during video capture, even if you have a broadband (cable modem, DSL) connection. When your connection is active, you probably have a few utilities running in the background looking for software updates to your operating system and other programs. A well-meaning message that updates are available for download might appear right in the middle of video capture, causing dropped frames.

✔ **Your hard drive can't handle the data rate.** First off, does your hard drive meet the requirements I outline in Chapter 2? If so, maybe some hard-drive maintenance is in order. The more stuff that is packed onto your hard drive, the slower it will be. This is one reason I recommend (pretty often, in fact) that you *multiply the amount of space you think you'll need by four.*

To keep your hard drive working efficiently and quickly, defragment your hard drive periodically (at least once a month). In Windows, choose Start⇨All Programs⇨Accessories⇨System Tools⇨Disk Defragmenter. On a Mac, you'll need to obtain a third-party disk-maintenance tool such as Norton Disk Doctor.

Capture stops unexpectedly

If the capture process stops before you want it to, your culprit could be mechanical. Check the following:

✔ **Did you forget to rewind the camcorder tape?** This is a classic "oops" that happens to nearly everybody sooner or later.

✔ **Is your hard drive full?** This is bad juju, by the way. Try to avoid filling up your hard drive at all costs.

✔ **Is there a timecode break on the tape?** Inconsistent timecode on a digital videotape can create all sorts of havoc when software tries to capture video. (See Chapter 4 for tips on avoiding timecode breaks.)

✔ **Did Fluffy or Junior step on the Esc key?** It happens. My cat has fouled more than one capture process. (Hey, biomechanical still counts as "mechanical," right?)

Chapter 6

Capturing Analog Video

· ·

· ·

*W*ith a high-tech book called *Digital Video For Dummies,* it would be easy to ignore old technologies like analog video. Analog video is on its way out, a true thing of the past. But resigning analog video to history doesn't change the fact that many of your cherished old home movies are still in analog format.

Fortunately, your old movies saved on videotapes aren't necessarily doomed to oblivion. With special hardware and software, you can still capture analog video into your computer, where you can then edit it and share it online or burn it to DVD. The video-editing programs featured throughout this book — Adobe Premiere Elements, Apple iMovie, and Windows Movie Maker — cannot capture video directly from an analog camcorder, so, in this chapter, I show you how to use Pinnacle Studio, which *can* capture analog video if you have the right hardware. But first, I'm going to show you how to capture analog video using a simple shortcut that may be available to you.

Digitizing Analog Video before Capture

Before you go out and buy a special program and analog-capture hardware, there's a shortcut that you may be able to take advantage of. Premiere Elements, iMovie, and Windows Movie Maker can all capture analog video if you use a video converter. A *video converter* is a device that connects to your computer's FireWire or USB 2.0 port. It has analog connectors, so you can connect your old analog camcorder or VCR to the converter. Like the name implies, the converter "converts" your analog video to digital video, which can then be captured by virtually any video-editing program.

Many video converters are available for less than $100. I talk about some of them in Chapter 18. But you may already own a video converter *and not even know it!* Your digital camcorder might work as a video converter. To work as a converter, your digital camcorder must have

- ✔ **Analog audio/video connectors:** Many — but not all — digital camcorders have analog connectors. These may include an S-Video connector, as well as yellow/red/white RCA-style connectors.

- ✔ **Ability to accept analog input:** OK, so your digital camcorder has analog connectors. But can it actually accept video *input* on those connectors? Some digital camcorders can only send video *out* through the analog connectors, not read it in. Your camcorder's owners' manual should tell you whether it can accept analog input.

- ✔ **Ability to send analog input along through the FireWire/USB 2.0 port:** This is the final piece of the puzzle. When you play video into the camcorder's analog inputs, does that video show up in the capture preview window of your video-editing program? If so, you are ready to capture!

If your camcorder accepts analog input, but cannot simultaneously send out digitized video through the FireWire or USB 2.0 port, you can still use your digital camcorder as a converter. Simply record the analog video onto tape in your digital camcorder, and then later capture the digital video as described in Chapter 5.

When you capture analog video using a video converter or your digital camcorder, you follow the same steps described in Chapter 5 for digital video capture. The only difference is that you won't be able to control the analog device using the playback buttons in the capture window. You'll have to manually press the Play, Stop, and Rewind buttons on the analog camcorder or VCR to control playback.

Preparing to Capture Analog Video

In Chapter 5, I showed you how easy it is to capture video from a digital camcorder and your computer's FireWire or USB 2.0 port. Analog video can also be easy to capture *if you have the right hardware*. Because computers only understand digital data, analog video must be converted to digital when you capture it. This conversion process is sometimes called *digitizing*. The next few sections help you prepare your computer for capturing analog video.

If you have a Mac, your best bet is to use an external video converter as described earlier in this chapter. Some high-end analog-capture cards are available for PowerMacs, but these cards usually cost hundreds — if not thousands — of dollars. In Chapter 18, I show which video converters are Macintosh-compatible.

Preparing your computer for analog video

Getting your computer ready to capture analog video is a lot like getting ready to capture digital video. Before you can capture analog video, you have to

- ✔ **Set up your capture hardware.** I show you what hardware you need and how to set it up in the following section, "Setting up capture hardware."

- ✔ **Turn off unnecessary programs.** Whether you're working with analog or digital video, your computer works more efficiently if you close all non-essential programs, including Web browsers, e-mail clients, and media players. See Chapter 5 for more on making sure all unnecessary programs are closed on your Macintosh or Windows PC.

- ✔ **Make sure there's enough free space on your hard drive.** Five minutes of digital video uses about 1GB (gigabyte) of hard-drive space. Unfortunately, there is no single, simple formula for figuring out how much space your analog video requires.

Digital video recorded with a MiniDV camcorder uses the DV codec, which uses a steady 200MB (megabytes) per minute of video. A *codec* — short for compressor/decompressor — is the software scheme used to compress video so it fits reasonably on your computer. (Codecs are described in greater detail in Chapter 13.) Some analog-capture devices let you choose from a list of different codecs to use during video capture; many codecs have settings you can adjust. Which codec you use (and the settings you select) can greatly affect the quality and file size of captured video. I show you how to adjust capture settings later in this chapter in the section, "Adjusting video-capture settings."

Most analog video-capture programs make it easy to determine whether you have enough hard-drive space. The Pinnacle Studio capture window, for example (shown in Figure 6-1), shows you exactly how much free space is available on your hard drive, and it gives you an estimate of how much video you can capture using the current settings.

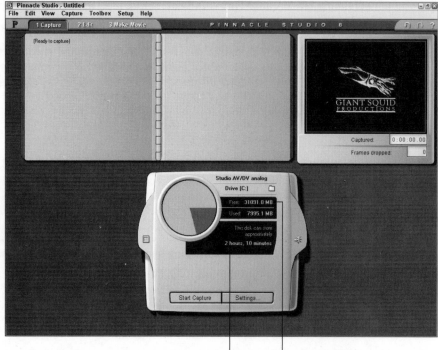

Figure 6-1:
Most
capture
programs
provide an
estimate of
how much
video you
can capture.

You can capture this much video.   Free hard disk space

In Figure 6-1, you can see that the Pinnacle software is telling me that I can squeeze about two hours and ten minutes of video onto my hard drive. But (as I mention in Chapter 5) you need to leave some free space on your hard drive to ensure that your video-editing software and operating system can still work efficiently.

Setting up capture hardware

Before you can capture analog video, you need to have some way to connect your VCR or analog camcorder to your computer. To do so, you have two basic options. You can either use an external video converter as described earlier in this chapter, or you can use an analog-capture card such as the card that comes with Pinnacle Studio AV/DV. The capture card must be physically installed inside your computer. I describe how to install capture cards in Chapter 2.

If you use an analog-capture card, you must use a video-capture program specifically designed to interact with analog-capture cards. Pinnacle Studio is a great choice because Pinnacle's software works seamlessly with its capture card, and at less than $100, it's affordable. As a bonus, the Pinnacle AV/DV card also has a FireWire port, which can be used by Premiere Elements or Windows Movie Maker to capture digital video.

When you buy an analog-capture card, double-check that it can actually capture analog video. Many FireWire cards are marketed as digital-video-capture cards, but if you don't read the packaging carefully, you might be confused about the card's capabilities. If a FireWire card doesn't *specifically* say that it can *also* capture analog video, assume that it can't.

After you have a capture card installed in your computer, all you need to do is connect your VCR or analog camcorder to the appropriate ports. These ports may be located on the back of the card, or on an external break-out box that sits conveniently on your desktop. You will probably have to choose from among several different kinds of connectors:

- **Composite:** Composite connectors — the most common type — are often used to connect video components in a home entertainment system. Composite connectors are also sometimes called *RCA jacks* and use only one connector for the video signal. A composite video connector is usually color-coded yellow. Red and white composite connectors are for audio. Make sure you connect all three.

- **S-Video:** S-video connectors are found on many higher-quality analog camcorders as well as S-VHS VCRs. S-Video provides a higher-quality picture, so use it if it's available as an option. The S-Video connector only carries video, so you'll still need to use the red and white audio connectors for sound.

- **Component:** Component video connectors often look like composite connectors, but the video image is broken up over three separate connectors color-coded red, green, and blue. The red cable is sometimes also labeled R-Y and carries the red portion of the video image, minus brightness information. The green cable — sometimes labeled Y — carries brightness information. Video geeks like to say *luminance* instead of brightness, but it means the same thing. The blue wire — sometimes labeled B-Y — carried the blue portion of the image, minus brightness. Component video provides a higher quality video image, but it's usually only found on the most expensive, professional-grade video-capture cards. Like S-Video, component connectors don't carry audio, so you still need to hook up the red and white audio cables.

When you're done hooking everything up, you'll probably have quite a rat's nest of cables going everywhere. Your capture software won't be able to control your VCR or camcorder through the analog cables, so you'll have to manually press Play on the device before you can start capturing in the software.

Capturing Analog Video

After you have your capture hardware set up and connected properly, you're ready to start capturing video. If you're using an external video converter connected to your computer's FireWire or USB 2.0 port, follow the instructions in Chapter 5 for digital capture. The only difference is you'll have to manually press Play on the analog VCR or camcorder before you can start capturing.

The exact procedure for capturing analog video varies; it depends on the software you're using. In this chapter I show Pinnacle Studio, but most other programs should have similar controls and settings. Begin by opening Studio, and then choose View⇨Capture. Studio's capture window appears, as shown in Figure 6-1. The next section shows you how to adjust Studio settings to get ready for analog capture.

Adjusting video-capture settings

To make sure Studio is ready to capture analog video instead of digital video, click the Settings button at the bottom of the capture window. The Pinnacle Studio Setup Options dialog box appears, as shown in Figure 6-2. Click the Capture Source tab to bring it to the front. On that tab, review the following settings:

- **Video:** Choose your analog-capture source in this menu. The choices in the menu vary depending upon what hardware you have installed.

- **Audio:** This menu should match the Video menu.

- **Use Overlay and Capture Preview:** I recommend that you leave both these options disabled. Leaving these options on may cause dropped frames (that is, some video frames are missed during the capture) on some computers.

- **Scene Detection during Video Capture:** This setting determines when a new scene is created. For most purposes, I recommend choosing Automatic Based on Video Content for analog capture.

- **Data Rate:** This section tells you how fast your hard drive can read or write. Click the Test Data Rate button to get a current speed estimate. Ideally, both numbers should be higher than 10,000 kilobytes per second for analog capture. If your system can't reach that speed, see Chapter 5 for information on what you can do to speed up your hard drive.

If you have trouble with dropped frames when you capture analog video, try disabling automatic scene detection by choosing the No Automatic Scene Detection option. Scene detection uses some computer resources, and it can cause some dropped frames if your computer isn't quite fast enough.

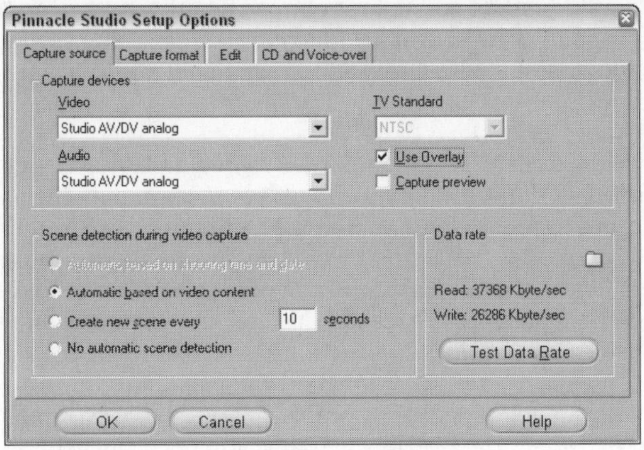

Figure 6-2:
Choose your
analog-
capture
source here.

When you're done reviewing settings on the Capture Source tab, click OK to
close the Setup Options dialog box. You are almost ready to begin capturing
analog video. Like many analog video-capture programs, Studio lets you fine-
tune the audio and video that are captured. Click the buttons on either side
of the capture controller to open the Video Input and Audio Capture control
panels as shown in Figure 6-3. These control panels allow you to adjust color,
brightness, and audio levels of the incoming video.

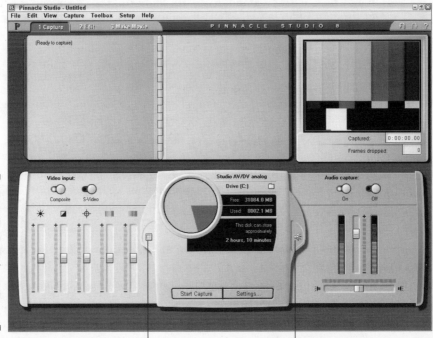

Figure 6-3:
Use these
control
panels to
fine-tune
your
incoming
video and
audio.

Open Video Input control panel   Open Audio Capture control panel

On the Video Input control panel, first choose whether you're going to capture video from the Composite or S-Video connectors using the radio buttons under Video Input. The Audio Capture control panel allows you to turn audio capture on or off.

Now press Play on your VCR or camcorder to begin playing the video you plan to capture, but don't start capturing it yet. As you play the analog video, watch the picture in the preview screen in the upper-right corner of the Studio program window. If you don't like the picture quality, you can use the brightness, contrast, sharpness, hue, and color saturation sliders on the Video Input control panel to adjust the picture. Experiment a bit with the settings to achieve the best result.

As you play your analog tape, you'll probably notice that although you can see the video picture in the preview window, you can't hear the sound through your computer's speakers. That's okay. Keep an eye on the audio meters on the Audio Capture control panel. They should move up and down as the movie plays. Ideally, most audio will be in the high green or low yellow portion of the audio meters. Adjust the audio-level slider between the meters if the levels seem too high or too low. If the audio seems biased too much to the left or right, adjust the balance slider at the bottom of the control panel.

If you're lucky, the tape you're going to capture from has color bars and a tone at the beginning or end (as shown in Figure 6-3). In that case, use the bars and tone to calibrate your video picture and sound. The tone is really handy because it's a standard 1KHz (kilohertz) tone designed specifically for calibrating audio levels. Adjust the audio-level slider so both meters read just at the bottom of the yellow, as shown in Figure 6-3.

When you're done playing with the settings in the Video and Audio control panels, stop the tape in your VCR or camcorder and rewind it back to where you want to begin capturing.

Capturing video in Pinnacle Studio

When all your settings are, uh, *set,* you're ready to start capturing. (Finally!) I recommend that you rewind the tape in your VCR or camcorder to at least 15 seconds *before* the point at which you want to begin capturing. Then follow these steps:

1. **Click the Start Capture button at the bottom of the Studio capture window.**

   The Capture Video dialog box appears, as shown in Figure 6-4.

2. **Enter a descriptive name for the capture.**

3. **If you want to automatically stop capturing after a certain period of time, enter the maximum number of minutes and seconds for the capture.**

   In Figure 6-4, you can see that I want to capture only six minutes of video.

4. **Press Play on the VCR or camcorder.**

5. **Click Start Capture within the Capture Video dialog box.**

   The capture process begins, and you'll notice that the green Start Capture button changes to the red Stop Capture button. As Studio captures your video, keep an eye on the Frames Dropped field under the preview window. If any frames are dropped, try to determine the cause and then recapture the video. (Chapter 5 suggests some things you can do to prevent dropped frames.) Common causes of dropped frames include programs running in the background, power saver modes, or a hard drive that hasn't been defragmented recently.

6. **Click Stop Capture when you're done capturing.**

   Studio reviews the video that has been captured and improves scene detection if possible. When the process is done, the captured clips appear in Studio's clip album.

Figure 6-4:
Choose your analog-capture source here.

Exporting video from Pinnacle Studio

After you have captured video using Pinnacle Studio, you have two options: You can either edit the video into a movie using Pinnacle Studio's editing features, or you can export it for editing in another program. Studio actually has a few more editing features than Windows Movie Maker, but if you have a more advanced program like Adobe Premiere Elements, exporting your video makes a lot of sense. To export your captured video from Studio:

1. **When you are done capturing your analog video, choose View➪Edit.**

   A list of captured video clips appears in the edit window.

2. **Click and drag all of the clips to the video track in the timeline as shown in Figure 6-5.**

3. **Choose View➪Make Movie.**

4. **Click AVI on the left side of the Make Movie window that appears.**

   AVI is the best format to choose if you plan to edit the video in Premiere Elements or another Windows-based program. If you plan to edit the video on a Mac, choose MPEG instead.

5. **Click Create AVI File to create your movie.**

6. **In the dialog box that appears, choose a folder in which to save your movie, and give it a filename.**

7. **Click OK.**

   The export process will probably take a few seconds or even minutes, depending on the length of your movie and the number of effects.

After the file is exported, choose File➪Add Media in Premiere Elements, and browse to the file to import it.

Drag clips from here.

Figure 6-5:
Drag all of your clips to the video track in Studio's timeline.

Drop them here.

Chapter 7

Importing Audio

. . . .

. . . .

*W*hen moviemakers first started adding sound to their moving pictures in the 1920s, the addition was so revolutionary that a new term was coined: *Talkies.* Today, of course, we pretty much take it for granted that movies always include the sounds of people talking, lasers blasting, dinosaurs roaring, and music playing.

Beware of taking audio too much for granted, however. Most moviemaking experts agree that audiences tolerate poor video quality better than poor audio quality. Excellent sound is absolutely crucial to any great movie, which is why I've devoted not one but *two* chapters in this book to audio. This chapter helps you understand the fundamentals of audio, and it helps you obtain and record better quality audio. After you have some audio source material to work with, check out Chapter 10 for more on working with audio in the movie-editing software on your computer.

Understanding Audio

Sound has a tremendous effect on how we perceive a scene in a movie. A creaking door hinge adds fear of the unknown to a scary scene; calling seagulls tell us we're near the ocean; grinding heavy metal music sets a high-energy tone in an extreme-sports movie.

What is audio? According to my notes from high-school science class, audio is produced by sound waves moving through the air, like ripples across water. Human beings hear those sound waves when they make our eardrums vibrate. The speed at which a sound makes the eardrum vibrate is the *frequency.* Frequency is measured in kilohertz (kHz), and one kHz equals one thousand vibrations per second. (You could say it really *hertz* when your eardrums vibrate . . . get it?) A lower-frequency sound is perceived as a lower pitch or tone, and a higher-frequency sound is perceived as a high pitch or tone. The volume or intensity of audio is measured in *decibels* (dB).

Understanding sampling rates

For over a century, humans have been using analog devices (ranging from wax cylinders to magnetic tapes) to record sound waves. As with video, digital audio recordings are all the rage today. Because a digital recording can only contain specific values, it can only approximate a continuous wave of sound; a digital recording device must "sample" a sound many times per second; the more samples per second, the more closely the recording can approximate the live sound (although a digital approximation of a "wave" actually looks more like the stairs on an Aztec pyramid). The number of samples per second is called the *sampling rate.* As you might expect, a higher sampling rate provides better recording quality. CD audio typically has a sampling rate of 44.1kHz — that's 44,100 samples per second — and most digital camcorders can record at a sampling rate of 48kHz. You will work with sampling rate when you adjust the settings on your camcorder, import audio into your computer, and export movie projects when they're done.

Delving into bit depth

Another term you'll hear bandied about in audio editing is *bit depth.* The quality of a digital audio recording is affected by the number of samples per second, as well as by how much information each sample contains. The amount of information that can be recorded per sample is the bit depth. More bits per sample mean more information — and generally richer sound.

Many digital recorders and camcorders offer a choice between 12-bit and 16-bit audio; choose the 16-bit setting whenever possible. For some reason, many digital camcorders come from the factory set to record 12-bit audio. There is no advantage to using the lower setting, so always check your camcorder's documentation and adjust the audio-recording bit depth up to 16-bit if it isn't there already.

Recording Audio

At some point, you'll probably want to record some sound or narration to go along with your movie. Recording great-quality audio is no simple matter.

Professional recording studios spend thousands or even millions of dollars to build acoustically superior sound rooms. You may not have that kind of budgetary firepower handy, but if you're recording your own sound, you can get nearly pro-sounding results by following these basic tips:

- **Use a good external microphone.** As described in Chapter 4, if you're recording on-scene with your camcorder, an external microphone positioned close to your subject almost always records better audio than the camcorder's built-in mic. When recording in your office, choose a high-quality microphone designed to record high-fidelity sound. A good mic isn't cheap, but it can make a huge difference in recording quality.

- **Control ambient noise.** True silence is a very rare thing in modern life. Before you start recording audio, carefully observe various sources of noise. These could include your neighbor's lawn mower, someone watching TV in another room, extra computers, and even the heating duct from your furnace or air conditioner. Noise from any (or all) of these things can reduce the quality of your recording.

- **Try to minimize sound reflection.** Audio waves reflect off any hard surface, which can cause echoing in a recording. Cover the walls, floor, and other hard surfaces with blankets to reduce sound reflection.

The easiest way to record audio is with a microphone connected to your computer, although some computers can make a lot of noise with their whirring hard drives, spinning fans, and buzzing monitors. The following sections show you how to record audio using a microphone connected to the microphone jack on computer.

Connecting a tape player to your computer

If you recorded audio onto an audio tape, you can connect the tape player directly to your computer and record from it just as if you were recording from a microphone. Buy a patch cable (available at most electronics stores) with two male minijacks (standard small audio connectors used by headphones, microphones, and computer speakers). Connect one end of the patch cable to the headphone jack on the tape player and connect the other end to your computer's microphone jack. The key, of course, is to have the right kind of cable. You can even buy cables that allow you to connect a turntable to your computer and record audio from your old LPs.

Once connected, you can record audio from the tape using the same steps described in the sections in this chapter on microphone recording. You'll have to coordinate your fingers to press Play on the tape player and click Record in the recording software at about the same time. If the recording levels are too high or too low, adjust the volume control on the tape player.

Recording audio with your Macintosh

You can record audio directly in iMovie. In fact, most new Macs have built-in microphones (the Mac Mini does not have a built-in microphone, but you can attach an external mic). The built-in mic works for very basic narration, but keep in mind that it does not record studio-quality sound. If you have a better mic, connect it to the computer's external microphone jack. The following sections show you how to set up your microphone and record audio.

Setting up an external microphone

Some microphones can connect to the USB port on your Mac. A USB microphone is easier to use because your Mac automatically recognizes it and selects the USB mic as your primary recording source. If your external microphone connects to the regular analog microphone jack — and your Mac already has a built-in mic — you may find that iMovie doesn't recognize your external microphone. To correct this problem, you must adjust your system's Sound settings:

1. **Open the System Preferences window by choosing Apple⇨ System Preferences.**

2. **Double-click the Sound icon to open the Sound preferences dialog box.**

3. **Click the Input tab to bring it to the front.**

4. **Open the Microphone pull-down menu and choose External Microphone/Line In.**

5. **Press ⌘+Q to close the Sound dialog box and System Preferences.**

Your external microphone should now be configured for use in iMovie.

Recording in iMovie

After you've decided which microphone to use and you've configured it as described in the previous section, you're ready to record audio using iMovie. As with most tasks in iMovie, recording is pretty easy:

1. **Open the project for which you want to record narration or other sounds, and switch to the timeline view if you're not there already.**

   For more on editing in the timeline, see Chapter 8. If you don't have a project yet and just want to record some audio, that's OK too.

2. **If you're working with a current movie project, move the play head to the spot where you want to begin recording.**

3. **Click the Audio button above the timeline to open the audio pane (as shown in Figure 7-1).**

4. **Say a few words to test the audio levels.**

As your microphone picks up sound, the audio meter in iMovie should indicate the recording level. If the meter doesn't move at all, your microphone probably isn't working. You'll notice that as sound levels rise, the meter changes from green to yellow and finally red. For best results, try to keep the sound levels close to the yellow part of the meter.

If the audio levels are too low, the recording may have a lot of unwanted noise relative to the recorded voice or sound. If levels are too high, the audio recording could pop and sound distorted. Unfortunately, iMovie doesn't offer an audio level adjustment for audio you record, so you'll have to fine-tune levels the old fashioned way, by changing the distance between the microphone and your subject.

5. **Click Record and begin your narration.**

   The movie project plays as you recite your narration.

6. **When you're done, click Stop.**

   An audio clip of your narration appears in the timeline, as shown in Figure 7-1.

For more on working with audio clips in your movie projects, see Chapter 10.

Figure 7-1: You can record audio directly in iMovie.

Audio meter

Recorded audio clip　　　Record/Stop

Recording voice-over tracks in Windows Movie Maker

Recording audio using Windows Movie Maker is pretty easy. Strangely, Adobe Premiere Elements is set up to do almost everything *but* record audio narration, so if you're using Premiere, you should temporarily switch over to Movie Maker for recording narration.

Before you can record audio with Movie Maker, your computer must have a sound card and a microphone. (If your computer has speakers, it has a sound card.) The sound card should have a connector for a microphone as well. Check the documentation for your computer if you can't find the microphone connector.

After your hardware is set up correctly, you're ready to record audio. To record audio in Windows Movie Maker, follow these steps:

1. **Open the movie project for which you want to record audio, and switch to the timeline view if you aren't there already.**

   For more on editing in the timeline, see Chapter 8. (If you don't have a project yet and just want to record some audio, that's okay too.)

2. **If you're working with a current movie project, move the play head to the spot where you want to begin recording.**

3. **Choose Tools⇨Narrate Timeline.**

   The Narrate Timeline screen appears, as shown in Figure 7-2.

4. **Say a few words to test the audio levels.**

   As your microphone picks up sound, the Input Level meter indicates the recording level. If the meter doesn't move at all, your microphone probably isn't working. You'll notice that as sound levels rise, the meter changes from green to yellow and finally red. For best results, try to keep the sound levels in or near the yellow part of the meter. You can fine-tune the levels by adjusting the Recording Volume slider.

5. **Click Start Narration.**

   The timeline starts to play. You're on! Start talking.

6. **When you're done, click Stop Narration.**

   Playback stops and a Save Windows Media File dialog box appears.

7. Enter a filename for the narration and click Save.

An audio clip of your narration appears in the Audio/Music track of the timeline, as shown in Figure 7-2.

You may need to record several cuts of your narration, adjusting the Input Level slider to get the audio levels just right. If the narration is too quiet, move the slider up. If the narration is distorted or has loud pops, move the slider down.

For more on working with audio clips in your movie projects, see Chapter 10. If you plan to use the recorded narration in another program (such as Premiere Elements), you can find the files in the folder My Documents\My Videos\Narration.

Adjust input level.

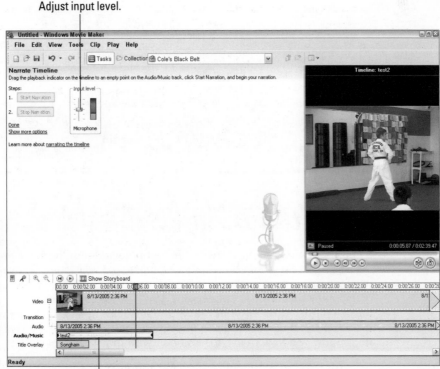

Figure 7-2:
Recording
narration in
Windows
Movie
Maker is
easy.

Recorded narration clip

Comprehending copyrights

As I show throughout this chapter, music can easily be imported into your computer for use in your movies. The tricky part is obtaining the rights to use that music legally. Realistically, if you're making a video of your daughter's birthday party, and you only plan to share that video with a grandparent or two, Kool and the Gang probably don't care if you use the song "Celebration" as a musical soundtrack. But if you start distributing that movie all over the Internet — or (even worse) start selling it — you could have a problem that involves the band, the record company, and lots and lots of lawyers.

The key to using music legally is licensing. You can license the right to use just about any music you want, but it can get expensive. Licensing "Celebration" for your movie project (for example) could cost hundreds of dollars or more. Fortunately, more affordable alternatives exist. Numerous companies offer CDs and online libraries of stock audio and music, which you can

license for as little as $30 or $40. You can find these resources by searching the Web for "royalty free music," or visit a site such as `www.royaltyfree.com` or `www.royaltyfreemusic.com`. You usually must pay a fee to download or purchase the music initially, but after you have purchased it, you can use the music however you'd like. If you use audio from such a resource, make sure you read the licensing agreement carefully. Even though the music is called "royalty free," you still may be restricted on how many copies you may distribute, how much money you can charge, or what formats you may offer.

Another — more affordable — alternative may be to use the stock audio that comes with some moviemaking software, or to use a third-party music generation program. Music generators automatically generate music in a variety of styles and moods, and some allow you to create your own compositions. See Chapter 18 for more on music-generating programs.

Working with CD Audio

If you're even remotely interested in technology — and because you're reading this book, I'll go out on a limb and guess that you are — you probably upgraded your music collection from Edison wax cylinders to compact discs (CDs) some time ago. At some point, you'll probably want to use some of the music on those CDs for your movie soundtracks. Most editing programs make it easy to use CD audio in your movie projects. The next couple of sections show you how to use CD audio in your movie projects.

Importing CD audio in iMovie

If you're using Apple iMovie, you can take audio directly from your iTunes library or import audio from an audio CD. Here's the basic drill:

1. **Put an audio CD in your CD-ROM drive, and then click the Audio button above the timeline on the right side of the iMovie screen.**

   The audio pane appears, as shown in Figure 7-3.

2. **If iMovie Sound Effects are currently shown, open the pull-down menu at the top of the audio pane and choose Audio CD.**

   A list of audio tracks appears, as shown in Figure 7-3.

3. **Select a track and click Play in the audio pane to preview the song.**

4. **Click Place at Playhead in the Audio panel to place the song in the timeline, beginning at the current position of the play head.**

Figure 7-3:
Songs from audio CDs can be imported directly into your movie projects using iMovie.

Ripping MP3 or AAC files with iTunes

You may find that it is more efficient to copy music to your hard drive using iTunes rather than iMovie. If you use iTunes, the files are always handy and ready to use on your hard drive, and, as an added bonus, you can listen to the songs while you work or copy them to your iPod.

The process of turning an audio file into an MP3 or AAC file is sometimes called *ripping* or *encoding.* iTunes can easily rip files from audio CDs in one of these formats. The AAC format offers smaller file sizes than MP3, but MP3 files are compatible with more MP3 players and video-editing programs. iMovie can use AAC or MP3 files, so if you're using iMovie, AAC is probably the better way to go. Copying audio onto your hard drive in AAC or MP3 format is quite simple:

1. **Insert an audio CD into your CD-ROM drive.**

2. **If iTunes doesn't launch automatically, open the program using the Dock or your Applications folder.**

3. **With the iTunes program window active as shown in Figure 7-4, choose iTunes⇨Preferences.**

    The iTunes Preferences dialog box opens.

Figure 7-4:
iTunes can rip CD audio onto your hard drive in MP3 format.

4. **Click the Importing button at the top of the Preferences dialog box.**

5. **Make sure that MP3 Encoder or AAC Encoder is selected in the Import Using menu, and then click OK.**

    The iTunes Preferences dialog box closes, and you are returned to the main iTunes window.

Working with AAC, MP3, and WMA audio

Unless you've been living under a rock for the last couple of years, you probably know that MP3 players are among the most popular new electronics gadgets. As the name implies, MP3 players play MP3 audio files. MP3 is an industry standard format for highly compressed audio files that provide good audio quality while using only a little bit of storage space. Most MP3 players can play other formats as well. Apple's popular iPods also support the AAC format, and many other MP3 players support the WMA format. AAC and WMA both offer even higher compression than MP3, which means that AAC and WMA files can be even smaller than MP3s, while maintaining the same quality.

If you have an MP3 player, you probably already have a lot of your music collection "ripped" into one or more of these three formats. Will they work with your video-editing program? That depends on your operating system:

- **Macintosh:** You can pull MP3 and AAC files directly from your iTunes library into iMovie, using the procedure described earlier in this chapter for importing CD Audio. Simply choose iTunes from the pull-down menu at the top of the audio pane. WMA files are not supported by iMovie.

- **Windows:** MP3 and WMA files can be imported into Premiere Elements, Windows Movie Maker, and most other Windows-based editing programs. I show you how to import audio files in the following section. Most Windows-based editing programs do not support AAC files.

6. **Place check marks next to the songs you want to import.**

   You can use the playback controls in the upper-left corner of the iTunes window to preview tracks.

7. **Click Import in the upper-right corner of the iTunes screen.**

   The songs are imported; the process may take several minutes. When it's done, the imported songs are available through your iTunes library for use in iMovie projects.

Importing CD audio in Windows

If you use Windows, the best way to import and manage CD audio is with Windows Media Player. If you prefer a different media player program, you can use it instead, so long as it can record audio in a common format such as MP3, WMA, or WAV. To copy music from a CD using Windows Media Player, follow these steps:

1. **Place an audio CD in your CD-ROM drive.**

   Open Windows Media Player if it does not open automatically.

2. **In Windows Media Player, click Copy from CD on the left side of the program window.**

3. **Place a check mark next to the songs you want to copy.**

4. **Click Copy Music at the top of the screen.**

   Windows Media Player copies the selected songs to your hard drive. As you can see in Figure 7-5, songs that are already copied to your hard drive have Copied to Library listed in the Copy Status column.

Figure 7-5:
Use Windows Media Player to copy songs to your computer.

By default, Windows Media Player copies music in WMA format. The default location for the files is the My Documents\My Music folder. Songs are usually organized into subfolders by artist and album. WMA files can be easily imported into almost any Windows-based video-editing program. To import the songs:

  ✔ **Adobe Premiere Elements:** Choose File⇨Add Media⇨From Files or Folders, and browse to the folder containing the song you want to import.

  ✔ **Windows Movie Maker:** Click Import Audio or Music in the Movie Tasks list on the left side of the screen. Browse to the folder containing the song you want to import.

Once imported, your songs can be added to your movie projects. See Chapter 10 for more on using music in your movies.

Part III
Editing Your Movie

The 5th Wave   By Rich Tennant

In this part . . .

Perhaps the best thing about digital video is the ease with which you can edit it. Just connect your digital camcorder to your computer's FireWire port, import the video (as described in Part II), and you're ready to edit.

When you edit video, you put scenes in the order you want them, remove unwanted material, add titles (words on the screen titles), and create special, visually appealing transitions between video clips. You can also add sound effects, a music soundtrack, and some still pictures or graphics if you like. And of course, special effects add a lot of excitement to your movie as well. This part shows you how to do these things using software that is available to you right now.

Chapter 8

Bringing Hollywood Home with Basic Editing

Digital is one of those buzz-words that we hear tossed around a lot these days. Like *high-definition* or *broadband,* when we hear the word *digital* associated with a product, we know that it's supposed to be better.

But what makes *digital* video better than what came before, really? Of course, digital video doesn't lose quality every time it is played or copied, and digital camcorders usually incorporate the best in modern lens technology. But what really makes digital video cool, in my opinion, is the ease with which it can be edited. Until recently, video editing was something you could do only if you were an industry professional with access to broadcast equipment or high-buck movie studios. Now, thanks to affordable digital camcorders and powerful personal computers, a complete video production operation can be yours for just a few hundred dollars.

In this chapter, I show you how to start editing video. In just a few minutes, you'll be trimming raw video clips and turning them into real movies. I start by showing you how to begin a project — a great movie has to start some-where — and then I show you how to work with video clips and assemble them into a movie.

Starting a New Movie Project

An ancient proverb by Confucius says, "A journey of a thousand miles begins with a single step." When you begin the thousand-mile journey of a movie project, your first step is to actually create a project in your editing program. Fortunately, this single first step is an easy one. When you open iMovie or Windows Movie Maker, simply choose File⇨New Project. In Premiere Elements, launch the program and click the New Project button.

After you have a new project started, your first step is usually to capture or import some video so you have something to edit. If you have some video to capture, see Chapter 5 (for digital video) or Chapter 6 (for analog video) for information on how to do that. Captured video appears as clips in the clips pane (in iMovie), the Collections window (in Movie Maker), or the Media window (in Premiere), where it is ready to use in your movies. Figure 8-1 shows a collection of captured clips in Windows Movie Maker.

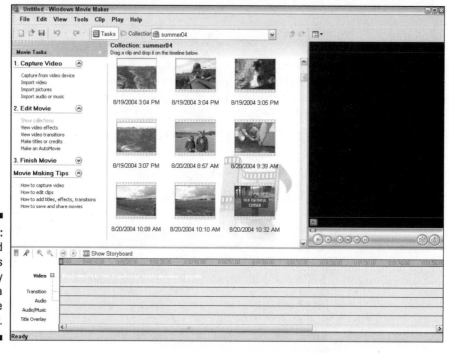

Figure 8-1: Captured video clips are ready to use in a new movie project.

Working with Video Clips

When you record an hour of video with your camcorder, that hour usually contains many different scenes. You probably stop and restart the camcorder many times as you record different video scenes. A *scene* most often starts when you press the Record button on your camcorder, and ends when you stop recording again, even if only for a second.

When you capture video into an editing program like iMovie or Movie Maker, those scenes are called clips. A *clip* is the basic denomination used in video editing. Most video-editing programs automatically detect scene breaks and divide your video up into clips during capture. As you edit and create your movies, you'll find this feature incredibly useful.

Organizing clips

Most video-editing programs store clips in a grid-like area called a *clip browser* or *collection album.* Apple iMovie (Figure 8-2) subdivides clips into video clips, still photos, and audio clips. You can access them using buttons at the bottom of the clip browser or *pane,* as Apple's documentation calls it.

Windows Movie Maker is a little different. It tosses video clips, songs, and still photos together on the same screen, but it organizes clips into collections. In Figure 8-3, I am viewing clips in a collection called "summer04." You can quickly switch between collections using the Collections menu on the Movie Maker toolbar, or click the Collections button on the toolbar to view a list of collections on the left. The collections list on the left side of the screen works like a folder browser in Windows Explorer. Simply click a collection on the left to view its contents on the right.

Whenever you capture or import video in Windows Movie Maker, a new collection is automatically created. You can also create new collections by choosing Tools⇨New Collection Folder. Like folders in Windows, collections can be used to organize clips by subject, media type, or any other criteria that you decide.

In iMovie's clip browser, you can manually rearrange clips by dragging them to new empty blocks in the grid. You can move the clips wherever you want. This handy feature allows you to sort clips on your own terms, rather than just have them listed alphabetically or in some other arbitrary order.

Clip browser

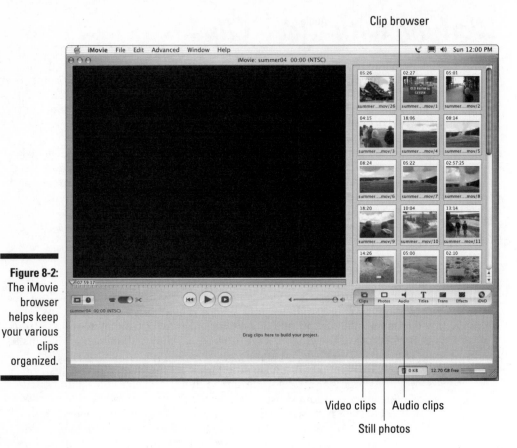

Figure 8-2:
The iMovie
browser
helps keep
your various
clips
organized.

Video clips | Audio clips

Still photos

Previewing clips

As you gaze at the clips in your clip browser, you'll notice that a thumbnail image is shown for each clip. This thumbnail usually shows the first frame of the clip; although it may suggest the clip's basic content, you won't really know exactly what the clip contains until you actually preview the whole thing. Previewing a clip is easy: Just click a clip in the browser, and then click the Play button in the playback controls of your software's preview window.

As the clip plays, notice that the play head under the preview window moves. You can move to any portion of a clip by clicking and dragging the play head with the mouse. Figure 8-4 shows Movie Maker's preview window and playback controls.

Audio clip   Still photo   Video clip

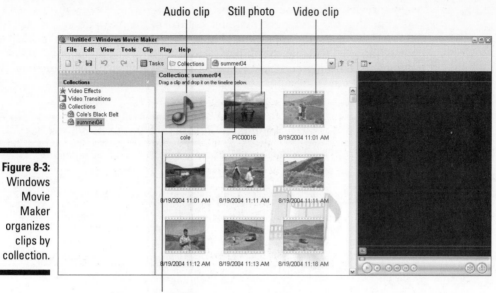

Figure 8-3:
Windows
Movie
Maker
organizes
clips by
collection.

Choose a collection

Figure 8-4:
Use
playback
controls and
the play
head to
preview
clips.

Play head

Playback controls

As you preview clips and identify portions you want to use in your movies, you'll find that precise, frame-by-frame control of the play head is crucial. The best way to get that precision is to use keyboard buttons instead of the mouse. Table 8-1 lists important keyboard controls for three popular video-editing programs. If you're using different editing software, check the manufacturer's documentation for keyboard controls.

Table 8-1	Keyboard Controls for Video Playback		
Command	*Apple iMovie*	*Microsoft Windows Movie Maker*	*Adobe Premiere Elements*
Play	Spacebar	Spacebar	Spacebar or L
Pause	Spacebar	Spacebar	Spacebar or K
Fast forward	⌘+]	Ctrl+Alt+→ (jumps to next clip)	L (press again to increase speed)
Rewind	⌘+[	Ctrl+Alt+← (jumps to previous clip)	J (press again to increase speed)
One frame forward	→	Alt+→	→
One frame back	←	Alt+←	←

As you can see, some controls are fairly standardized across many different video-editing applications. For example, almost all editing programs use the spacebar to play or pause video. Premiere Elements also uses the J, K, and L keys to control basic playback. The J-K-L combination is common in professional-style video-editing programs like Adobe Premiere and Apple Final Cut Pro.

If you don't like using the keyboard to move to just the right frame, you may want to invest in a multimedia controller such as the SpaceShuttle A/V from Contour A/V Solutions (www.contouravs.com). This device connects to your computer's USB port and features a knob and dial that you can use to precisely control video playback. It's so much easier than using the mouse or keyboard, you'll wonder how you ever got by without one! (I describe multimedia controllers in greater detail in Chapter 18.)

Trimming out unwanted parts

Professional Hollywood moviemakers typically shoot hundreds of hours of footage just to get enough acceptable material for a two-hour feature film. Because the pros shoot a lot of "waste" footage, don't feel so bad if every single frame of video you shot isn't totally perfect either. As you preview your clips, you'll no doubt find bits that you want to cut from the final movie.

Understanding timecode

A video image is actually a series of still frames that flash rapidly by onscreen. Every frame is uniquely identified with a number called a *timecode.* All stored locations and durations of all the edits you perform in a movie project use time-codes for reference points, so a basic under-standing of timecode is important. You'll see and use timecode almost every time you work in a video-editing program like Movie Maker or Apple iMovie. Timecode is often expressed like this:

```
hours : minutes : seconds :
    frames
```

The fourteenth frame of the third second of the twenty-eighth minute of the first hour of video is identified as:

```
01:28:03:13
```

You already know what hours, minutes, and sec-onds are. *Frames* aren't units of time measure-ment, but rather, the individual still images that make up your video. The frame portion of time-code starts with zero (00) and counts up to a number determined by the frame rate of the video. In PAL video, frames are counted from 00 to 24 because the frame rate of PAL is 25 frames per second (fps). In NTSC, frames are counted from 00 to 29. The NTSC and PAL video standards are described in greater detail in Chapter 3.

"Wait!" you exclaim. "Zero to 29 adds up to 30, not 29.97."

You're an observant one, aren't you? As men-tioned in Chapter 3, the frame rate of NTSC

video is 29.97 fps. NTSC timecode actually skips the frame codes 00 and 01 in the first second of every minute, except every tenth minute. Work it out (you may use a calculator), and you see that this system of reverse leap-frames adds up to 29.97 fps. This is called *drop-frame* timecode. In some video-editing systems, drop-frame timecode is expressed with semicolons (;) between the numbers instead of colons (:). Thus, in drop-frame timecode, the fourteenth frame of the third second of the twenty-eighth minute of the first hour of video is identified as

```
01;28;03;13
```

Why does NTSC video use drop-frame time-code? Back when everything was broadcast in black and white, NTSC video was an even 30 fps. For the conversion to color, more bandwidth was needed in the signal to broadcast color information. By dropping a couple of frames every minute, there was enough room left in the signal to broadcast color information, while at the same time keeping the video signals com-patible with older black-and-white TVs.

Although the punctuation (for example, colons or semicolons) for separating the numerals of time-code into hours, minutes, seconds and frames is fairly standardized, some video-editing programs still go their own way. But whether the numbers are separated by colons, decimals, or magic crystals, the basic concept of timecode is the same.

The solution is to trim the clip down to just the portion you want. The easiest way to trim a clip is to split it into smaller parts before you place it in your movie project:

1. **Open the clip you want to trim by clicking it in the browser, and move the play head to the exact spot where you want to split the clip.**

   Use the playback controls under the preview window to move the play head. Table 8-1 lists some keyboard shortcuts to help you move the play head more precisely.

2. **In Windows Movie Maker, click the Split Clip button in the preview controls, or choose Clip⇨Split. In Apple iMovie, choose Edit⇨Split Video Clip at Playhead.**

3. **Repeat step 2 to split the clip again.**

You now have multiple clips created from the one original clip. In Figure 8-5, I have split one clip into three. Splitting clips like I've shown here isn't the only way to edit out unwanted portions of video. You can also trim clips once they're placed in the timeline of your movie project (a process described later in this chapter). But splitting the clips before you add them to a project is often a much easier way to work because the unwanted parts are split off into separate clips that you can use (or not use) as you wish. In the next section, I show you how to add clips to the timeline or storyboard of your editing program to actually start turning your clips into a movie.

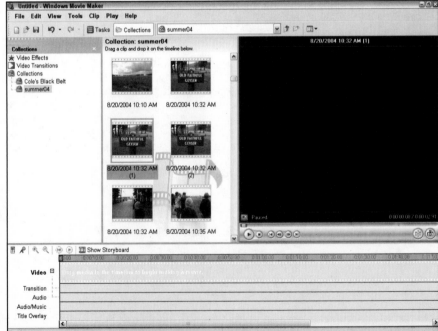

Figure 8-5:
Splitting clips is one way to trim out unwanted bits of video.

Don't worry! Trimming a clip doesn't delete the unused portions from your hard drive. When you trim a clip, you're actually setting what the video pros call *in points* and *out points*. The software uses virtual markers to remember which portions of the video you chose to use during a particular edit. If you want to use the remaining video later, it's still on your hard drive, ready for use.

If you want, you can usually unsplit your clips that you have split as well. In Windows Movie Maker, hold down the Ctrl key and click on each of the clips that you split earlier. When each clip is selected, right-click the clips and choose Combine. Unfortunately, Apple iMovie doesn't have a simple tool for recombining clips that you have split. If you just split a clip, you can undo that action by choosing Edit⇨Undo or pressing ⌘+Z.

Assembling Your Clips into a Movie

You're probably wondering when the fun begins. This is it! It's finally time to start assembling your various video clips into a movie. Most video-editing programs provide the same two basic tools to help you assemble a movie:

- ✔ **Storyboard:** This is where you throw clips together in a basic sequence from start to finish — think of it as a rough draft of your movie.
- ✔ **Timeline:** After your clips are assembled in the storyboard, you can switch over to the timeline to fine-tune the movie and make more advanced edits. The timeline is where you apply the final polish.

The storyboard and timeline are basically just two different ways of showing the same thing. In most editing programs — including iMovie and Windows Movie Maker — you can toggle back and forth between the storyboard and timeline whenever you want. Some people prefer to use one or the other exclusively; for now, starting with the storyboard will keep it simple.

Visualizing your project with storyboards

If you've ever watched a "making of" documentary for a movie, you've probably seen filmmakers working with a storyboard. It looks like a giant comic strip where each panel illustrates a new scene in the movie. The storyboard in your video-editing program works the same way. You can toss scenes in the storyboard, move them around, remove scenes again, and just generally put your clips into the basic order in which you want them to appear in the movie. The storyboard is a great place to visualize the overall concept and flow of your movie.

To add clips to the storyboard, simply drag them from the clip browser down to the storyboard at the bottom of the screen. As you can see in Figure 8-6, I have added five clips to the iMovie storyboard.

Click for storyboard view

Click for timeline view

Figure 8-6:
The storyboard is a good place to start assembling your project.

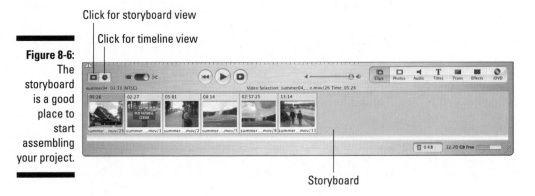

Storyboard

The storyboard should show a series of thumbnails, as shown in Figure 8-6. If your screen doesn't quite look like this, you may need to switch to the storyboard view. (Figure 8-6 shows the buttons for toggling between storyboard view and timeline view in iMovie; the equivalent buttons for Movie Maker are shown in Figure 8-7.)

Figure 8-7:
Windows Movie Maker's storyboard looks a lot like the storyboard in iMovie.

Click to toggle between storyboard and timeline.

The *storyboard* is possibly one of the most aptly named items in any video-editing program because the thumbnails actually do tell the basic story of your movie. The storyboard is pretty easy to manipulate. If you don't like the order of things, just click and drag clips to new locations. If you want to remove a clip from the storyboard in iMovie, Movie Maker, or most any other editing program, click the offending clip once to select it and then press Delete on your keyboard.

Using the timeline

Some experienced editors prefer to skip the storyboard and go straight to the timeline because it provides more information and precise control over your movie project. To switch to the timeline, click the timeline button. (See Figure 8-6 for the location of the button in iMovie; see Figure 8-7 to find where the button is located in Movie Maker.)

One of the first things you'll probably notice about the timeline is that not all clips are the same size. Consider Figure 8-8, which shows the timeline view of the same project shown in Figure 8-7. In the timeline view, the width of each clip represents the length (in time) of that clip, unlike in storyboard view, where each clip appears to be the same size. In timeline view, longer clips are wider, shorter clips are narrower.

Shorter clip   Timeline ruler

Figure 8-8:
The timeline provides a bit more information about your movie project.

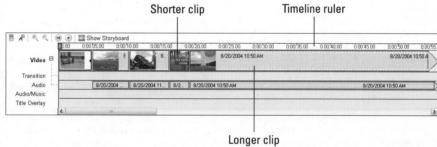

Longer clip

Adding clips to the timeline

Adding a clip to the timeline is a lot like placing clips in the storyboard. Just use drag-and-drop to move clips from the clip browser to the timeline. As you can see in Figure 8-9, I am inserting a clip between two existing clips on the timeline. Clips that fall after the insert are automatically shifted over to make room for the inserted clip.

Timeline ruler

Figure 8-9:
Use drag-and-drop to place your clips in the timeline.

Zoom control   Click and drag to insert clips on the timeline.

Zooming in and out on the timeline

Depending on how big your movie project is, you may find that clips on the timeline are often either too wide or too narrow to work with effectively. To rectify this situation, adjust the zoom level of the timeline. You can either zoom in and see more detail, or zoom out and see more of the movie. To adjust zoom, follow these steps:

- ✔ **Apple iMovie:** Adjust the Zoom control in the lower left corner of the timeline (refer to Figure 8-9).

- ✔ **Microsoft Windows Movie Maker:** Click the Zoom In or Zoom Out magnifying glass buttons above the timeline, or press Page Down to zoom in and Page Up to zoom out.

- ✔ **Adobe Premiere Elements:** Press the + key on your keyboard to zoom in, or press the key to zoom out. Alternatively, hover your mouse pointer over the zoom slider above the timeline ruler, and then click and drag left or right on the slider to adjust zoom.

Tracking timeline tracks

As you look at the timeline in your editing software, you'll notice that it displays several different tracks. Each track represents a different element of the movie — video resides on the video track; audio resides on the audio track. You may have additional tracks available as well, such as title tracks (see Chapter 9 for more on adding titles) or music tracks (see Chapter 10 for coverage on how to add music to your movie). Figure 8-10 shows the tracks used in the Windows Movie Maker timeline.

Video track

Figure 8-10:
Different
timeline
tracks
contain
different
kinds of
content.

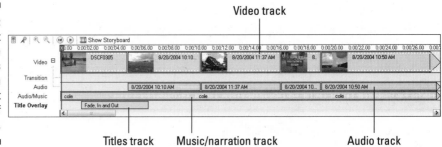

Titles track   Music/narration track   Audio track

Some advanced video-editing programs (such as Adobe Premiere Elements) allow you to have many separate video and audio tracks in a single project. This advanced capability is useful for layering many different elements and performing some advanced editing techniques (described in Chapters 11 and 17).

When you record and capture video, you usually capture audio along with it. When you place one of these video clips in the timeline (see Figure 8-10), the accompanying audio usually appears just underneath it in the audio track. Apple iMovie hides the accompanying audio by default, but you can reveal it as described in the next section.

What did iMovie do with my audio?

Apple iMovie is a very simple program. Unfortunately, sometimes it is a little too simple for its own good. For example, when you place video tracks in the timeline as shown in Figure 8-9, the accompanying audio is not displayed by default. If you ever want to edit the audio and video separately — and at some point, you probably will — you need to extract the audio clips out of the video clips. To do so, follow these steps:

1. **Click once on a clip in the timeline to select it.**

2. **Choose Advanced⇨Extract Audio, or press ⌘+J.**

   The audio now appears as a separate clip in the timeline, as shown in Figure 8-11.

3. **Repeat steps 1 and 2 for each clip in the timeline.**

Figure 8-11:
To work with audio and video separately in iMovie, extract audio clips from the video clips.

Extracted audio clips

It may be a good idea to wait until later (like, when you're done editing the video portion of the movie) to extract audio from your video clips. If you still need to trim the video clip (as described later in this chapter), you'll have to trim the audio clip separately if it has been extracted.

Fine-Tuning Your Movie in the Timeline

After you've plopped a few clips into your timeline or storyboard, you're ready to fine-tune your project. This fine-tuning is what turns a series of raw video clips into a real movie. Most of the edits described in this section require you to work in the timeline, although if you want to simply move clips around without making any edits or changes, you'll probably find that easiest in the storyboard. This is especially true if you're using iMovie. To move a clip, simply click-and-drag it to a new location as shown in Figure 8-12.

Figure 8-12:
Click and drag clips in the storyboard to move them to new locations in the movie.

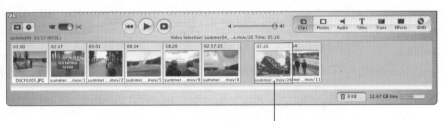

Drap and drop a clip to move it.

Trimming clips in the timeline

Dropping clips into the storyboard or timeline is a great way to assemble the movie, but a lot of those clips probably contain some material that you don't want to use. The simple solution is to trim the clips down to just the portions you want.

Trimming clips in Windows Movie Maker

If you look up "easy" in the dictionary, you'll see a picture of someone trimming clips in the Movie Maker timeline. (Well, OK, maybe not, but we are talking to the *Webster's Dictionary* people about making this change.)

To trim a clip in the Movie Maker timeline, first click the clip you want to trim to select it. Now simply hover your mouse pointer over the trim handle (the trim handle looks like a little black triangle) at the beginning or end of a clip in the timeline, and click-and-drag the handle to trim the clip. In Figure 8-13, you can see that I am trimming a clip down to just over three seconds in length.

You can only trim clips in timeline view, not storyboard view. If you don't see the trim handles as shown in Figure 8-13, click the Show Timeline button above the storyboard.

Figure 8-13:
Fine-tune
the in points
and out
points for
clips in the
timeline by
clicking and
dragging the
trim handle.

Click and drag to trim the clip.

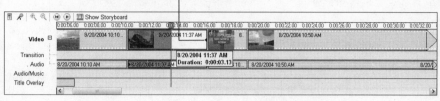

Trimming clips in Apple iMovie

In the previous section, I show how easy it is to trim clips in Movie Maker. iMovie makes trimming easy too, but in a different way. iMovie uses the preview window for clip-trimming operations. If you look closely at the lower-left corner of the preview window, you'll see two tiny little triangles, as shown in Figure 8-14. These are in-point and out-point markers; you can use them to trim clips in the timeline.

To trim a clip, follow these steps:

1. **Click a clip in the timeline to select it.**

   When you click the clip, it should load into the preview window. If it does not, make sure that the desired clip is actually selected in the timeline. The clip should turn blue when it is selected.

2. **Click and drag the out-point marker in the lower-left corner of the preview window to a new location along the playback ruler, as shown in Figure 8-14.**

3. **Click and drag the in-point marker to a new position if you wish.**

   The selected portion of the clip — that is, the portion between the in and out points — turns yellow in the preview window playback ruler.

4. **Choose Edit➪Crop as shown in Figure 8-14.**

   The clip is trimmed (*cropped*) down to just the portion you selected with the in and out points. Subsequent clips in the timeline automatically shifts to fill in the empty space on the timeline.

If you trim a video clip from which you have extracted the audio, only the video clip is trimmed; you have to trim the audio separately.

Figure 8-14:
Use the
iMovie
preview
window to
trim clips in
the timeline.

Selected portion   Out point marker

In point marker

Removing clips from the timeline

Changing your mind about some clips that you placed in the timeline is virtually inevitable, and fortunately removing clips is easy. Just click the offending
clip to select it and press the Delete key on your keyboard. Poof! The clip
disappears.

If you're using iMovie, you should know however that when you delete a clip
by pressing the Delete key, the clip goes to iMovie's trash bin. After the trash
is emptied (by double-clicking the trash icon at the bottom of the iMovie program window), the deleted clip is no longer be stored on your hard drive,
meaning that if you decide you want it back later, you'll have to re-capture it.
Thus, if you simply want to remove a clip from the timeline, I recommend
that you first switch to the storyboard, and then drag the unwanted clip back
up to the clip browser, just in case you decide that you want to use it later.

Undoing what you've done

Oops! If you didn't really *mean* to delete that clip, don't despair. Just like word processors (and many other computer programs), video-editing programs let you undo your actions. Simply press Ctrl+Z (Windows) or ⌘+Z (Macintosh) to undo your last action. Apple iMovie, Adobe Premiere Elements, and Windows Movie Maker all allow you to undo several actions, which is helpful if you've done a couple of other actions since making the "mistake" you want to undo. To redo an action that you just undid, press Ctrl+Y (Windows) or Shift+⌘+Z (Macintosh).

Another quick way to restore a clip in iMovie to its original state — regardless of how long ago you changed it — is to select the clip in the timeline and then choose Advanced⇨Restore Clip. The clip reverts to its original state.

Adjusting playback speed

One of the coolest yet most unappreciated capabilities of video-editing programs is the ability to change the speed of video clips. Changing the speed of a clip serves many useful purposes:

- ✔ Add drama to a scene by slowing down the speed to create a "slow-mo" effect.

- ✔ Make a scene appear fast-paced and action-oriented (or humorous, depending upon the subject matter) by speeding up the video.

- ✔ Help a given video clip better fit into a specific time frame by speeding it up or slowing it down slightly. For example, you may be trying to time a video clip to match beats in a musical soundtrack. Sometimes this synchronicity can be achieved by slightly adjusting the playback speed of the video clips.

Of course, you want to carefully preview any speed changes you make to a video clip. Depending on the software, you could encounter some jittery video images or other problems when you play around with speed adjustments.

Pay special attention to audio clips when you adjust playback speed. Even though a small speed adjustment might be barely perceptible in a video clip, even the tiniest speed changes have radical effects on the way audio sounds. Usually, when I adjust video speed, I discard the audio portion of that clip.

Adjusting playback speed in Apple iMovie

Changing playback speed in iMovie couldn't be easier. If you look closely, you'll see a slider adjustment for playback speed right on the timeline. To adjust speed, follow these steps:

1. **Switch to the timeline (if you aren't there already) by clicking the timeline view button (refer to Figure 8-6).**

2. **Click the clip that you want to adjust to select it.**

   The clip should turn blue when it is selected.

3. **Adjust the speed slider at the bottom of the timeline, as shown in Figure 8-15.**

   To speed up the clip, move the slider toward the hare. Move the slider toward the tortoise to (surprise) slow down the clip.

4. **Play the clip to preview your changes.**

5. **Giggle at the way the audio sounds after your changes.**

Giggle at preview here.

Figure 8-15: Use the speed slider at the bottom of the timeline to adjust playback speed.

Speed slider

Select clip

If you don't want to include the audio portion of the clip after you've made speed changes, choose Advanced⇨Extract Audio to extract the audio, and then delete the audio clip after it is extracted.

Another neat thing you can do to video clips in iMovie is reverse the playback direction. To do so, select the clip and choose Advanced⇨Reverse Clip Direction. The clip now plays backward in your movie. To reverse it back to normal, just choose Advanced⇨Reverse Clip Direction again.

Adjusting playback speed in Windows Movie Maker

Windows Movie Maker only gives you two speed adjustment options: You can slow a clip down by half, or speed it up to double-speed. This doesn't give you any fine-tuning speed adjustment, but at least these two options are better than nothing. To speed up or slow down a clip in Movie Maker

1. **Click View Video Effects in the task list on the left side of the screen.**

   If you don't see the task list, click the Tasks button on the Movie Maker toolbar, or choose View⇨Task Pane.

2. **Scroll down the list of effects to find the two speed-changing effects.**

3. **Click and drag an effect from the list of video effects, and drop it on the clip you want to change.**

   To speed the clip up, use the Speed Up, Double effect. To slow down a clip, use the Slow Down, Half effect. When you apply a video effect to a clip, a star appears on the clip in the timeline, as shown in Figure 8-16.

Use the preview window to preview your changes. If you don't like the speed change, you can simply remove the effect from the clip. To remove an effect, right-click the clip in the timeline and choose Video Effects from the menu that appears. In the Add or Remove Video Effects dialog box (Figure 8-17), select the effect you want to remove from the Displayed Effects list and click Remove. Click OK and your clip is restored back to normal speed.

Adjusting playback speed in Adobe Premiere Elements

Not surprisingly, more advanced video-editing programs like Adobe Premiere Elements give you more advanced controls over speed changes. Apple iMovie only lets you make minor speed adjustments on a short scale, and Windows Movie Maker gives just two options. But Premiere Elements lets you change speed along an infinitely adjustable scale.

Premiere's infinite range of speed adjustment gives you more editing power, but like a powerful sports car or a high-limit credit card, that power must be exercised with care. You may find that some speed adjustments cause your video playback to become jerky and uneven. To prevent this, you should only adjust speed to a percentage listed in Table 8-2.

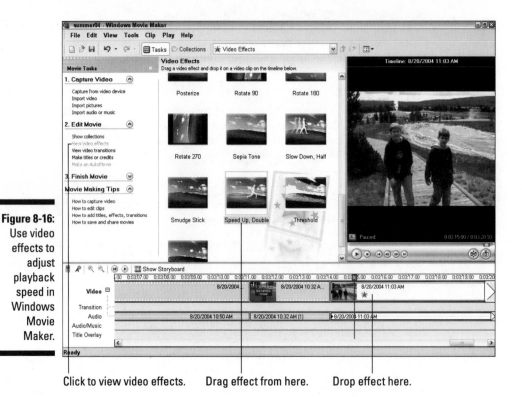

Figure 8-16: Use video effects to adjust playback speed in Windows Movie Maker.

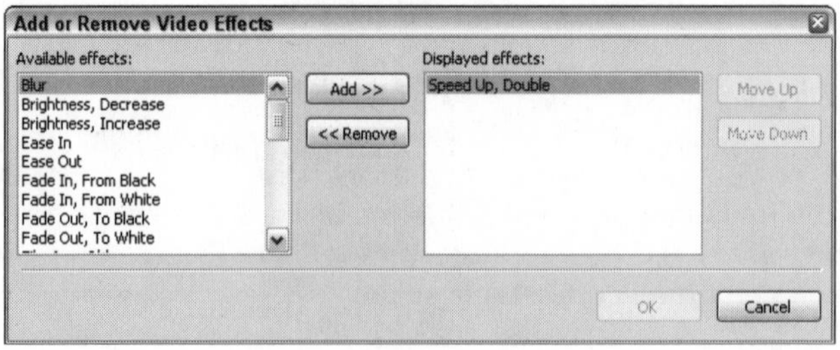

Click to view video effects.   Drag effect from here.   Drop effect here.

Figure 8-17: Use this dialog box to remove video effects in Windows Movie Maker.

Table 8-2	Adobe Premiere Elements Safe Speed-Change Percentages
Safe Slow-Motion Speeds	*Safe Fast-Motion Speeds*
50%	100%
33.33%	200%
25%	300%
20%	400%
16.67%	500%

If you do a little math, you can see a pattern in the safe speeds listed in Table 8-2. If you turn all of the Safe Slow-Motion percentages into ratios, you would see that they all start with the number one. The 50% speed gives a ratio of 1:2, which means that Premiere Elements slows the clip down by turning each single frame into *two* frames. With a speed change of 25% (1:4), each frame becomes four frames. Likewise, all of the Safe Fast-Motion percentages end with 1 when converted to ratios. The 200% speed gives a ratio of 2:1, and the 300% speed gives a ratio of 3:1. These ratios help Premiere Elements maintain smooth playback when adjusting speed.

To adjusting the speed of a clip in Premiere Elements

1. **Select a clip for which you want to adjust the speed.**

   You can choose a clip in the Media window, or one that has already been placed in the timeline.

2. **Choose Clip⇨Time Stretch.**

   The Time Stretch dialog box appears, as shown in Figure 8-18.

3. **Enter a new percentage number in the Speed field.**

   To make the clip play at double its original speed, enter **200** percent. To make the clip play at half speed, enter **50** percent. The duration of the clip is adjusted automatically, based on your percentage change. Again, I strongly recommend that you use a percentage from Table 8-2.

4. **If you want the clip to play in reverse, place a check mark next to the Reverse Speed option.**

   This option can be handy if you're going for a "fast rewind" look for the clip.

5. **Place a check mark next to Maintain Audio Pitch to, um, maintain the audio pitch of the clip.**

   If you maintain the audio pitch, you can make speed adjustments to video without making the accompanying audio sound like Alvin and the Chipmunks or Darth Vader. This feature is especially handy if you want to maintain ambient sounds such as crashing waves or chirping birds with a clip. Experiment with this setting, trying the clip with and without the Maintain Audio Pitch setting enabled. Play the clip each way and see how this option affects the audio.

6. **Click OK to close the Time Stretch dialog box.**

7. **Play the clip to preview your speed changes.**

Figure 8-18: Premiere Elements uses percentages to make speed changes.

Chapter 9

Using Transitions and Titles

Anyone with two VCRs can wire them together, dub the desirably scenes from tape to tape, and call it *editing*. But the results will be pretty sloppy, and even amateurish-looking compared to what you can do with your computer. Programs like Apple iMovie or Windows Movie Maker allow you to step up to the next level. For example, you can add a transition that allows one clip to gracefully fade into the next, and you can add your own onscreen credits and notations using titles.

This chapter shows you how to add titles and transitions to your movies. These are two of the most popular features in video-editing programs; unlike some of the more advanced (and obscure) effects and tools, transitions and titles are things you'll probably actually use in every single project.

Fading and Transitioning Between Clips

Any video-editing program worthy of its name allows you to add custom transitions between video clips. Most programs give you a catalog of transitions to choose from, ranging from simple fades to fancy star-patterns and 3-D boxes. Most transitions can be generally divided into a few basic categories:

✔ **Straight cut:** This is actually no transition at all. One clips ends, and the next begins, poof! Just like that.

✔ **Fade:** The outgoing clip fades out as the incoming clip fades in. Fades are also sometimes called *dissolves*.

- **Wipe:** The incoming clip wipes over the outgoing clip using one of many possible patterns. Alternatively, the outgoing clip may wipe away to reveal the incoming clip.

- **Push:** The outgoing clip is pushed off the screen by the incoming clip.

- **3-D:** Some more advanced editing programs provide transitions that seem to work three dimensionally. For example, the outgoing clip might wrap itself up into a 3-D ball, which then spins and rolls off the screen. Adobe Premiere Elements includes some 3-D transitions.

Whatever style of transition you want to use, modern video-editing programs make the process easy. But before you can use any transitions, you need a project that already has several clips in its timeline. If you haven't put together a project yet, see Chapter 8 to find out how. The following sections show you how to select and use transitions in your movie projects.

Choosing the best transition

Before you choose which transition to use, you need to decide *if* you should even use a transition at all. Transitions can really be a lot of fun to play around with, but for that reason, it's really easy to overuse transitions. Remember, the focus of your movie project is the video content, not your editing skills. More often than not, the best transition is a simple dissolve or none at all. For example, I usually only use transitions between major changes of setting or subject matter. If you use fancier transitions, I recommend using the same or similar transitions throughout the whole project. This makes the transitions fit more seamlessly into the movie.

Transitions are usually organized in their own window or palette. Transition windows usually vary slightly from program to program, but the basics are the same. The following sections show you how to review transitions in iMovie, Movie Maker, and Premiere Elements.

Reviewing iMovie's transitions

Apple iMovie offers a little more than a dozen transitions from which to choose. That may not sound like a lot of choices, but I think you'll find that iMovie's transitions cover the styles you're most likely to use anyway. You can also add transitions using plug-ins from third parties. In Figure 9-1, I am previewing a transition created by Gee Three and available as a free download from www.geethree.com. To view iMovie's transitions, click the Trans button above the Timeline. A list of transitions appears, as shown in Figure 9-1.

Transition preview window

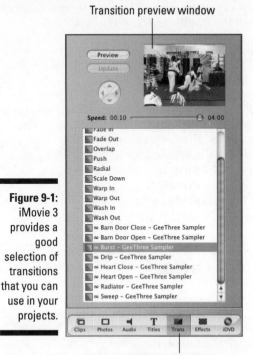

Preview
Update
Speed: 00:10   04:00
Fade In
Fade Out
Overlap
Push
Radial
Scale Down
Warp In
Warp Out
Wash In
Wash Out
∞ Barn Door Close – GeeThree Sampler
∞ Barn Door Open – GeeThree Sampler
∞ Burst – GeeThree Sampler
∞ Drip – GeeThree Sampler
∞ Heart Close – GeeThree Sampler
∞ Heart Open – GeeThree Sampler
∞ Radiator – GeeThree Sampler
∞ Sweep – GeeThree Sampler
Clips Photos Audio Titles Trans Effects iDVD

Figure 9-1: iMovie 3 provides a good selection of transitions that you can use in your projects.

Click to view transitions.

As you look at the list of transitions, most of the names probably look pretty foreign to you. Names like "Circle Closing," "Radial," and "Warp Out" are descriptive, but really the only way to know how each transition will look is to preview it. To do so, click the name of a transition in the list. A small preview of the transition briefly appears in the transition preview window.

Oops! You missed it. Click the transition's name again. Wow, it sure flashes by quickly, doesn't it? If you'd like to see a larger preview, click the Preview button. A full-size preview appears in iMovie's main viewer screen.

If your transition preview window shows nothing but a black screen when you click a transition, move the mouse pointer down and click a clip in the timeline or storyboard to select it. The selected clip should now appear when you preview a transition.

Previewing transitions in Windows Movie Maker

Windows Movie Maker comes with 60 (yes, 60) transitions. In fact, so many transitions are provided with Movie Maker that they don't all fit on one screen. To see a list of transitions, click View Video Transitions in the task list on the left side of the screen, or choose Tools➪Video Transitions. A list of transitions appears in the middle of the screen, as shown in Figure 9-2.

If your version of Windows Movie Maker doesn't have 60 or more transitions, you may have an older version of Movie Maker. See Appendix C for instructions on updating Windows Movie Maker.

To preview a transition, simply click it in the list of transitions, and then click the Play button in the video preview window on the right. A preview of the transition appears in the viewer window. The preview uses standard photographs from the Windows XP stock wallpaper library. In Figure 9-2, I am previewing the Zig Zag, Vertical transition.

Choosing transitions in Adobe Premiere Elements

When you step up to a more advanced editing program, you usually step up to more advanced transitions as well. And so it is with Adobe Premiere Elements, which offers 79 transitions ranging from simple fades to advanced 3-D spinning boxes. Premiere also gives you a lot of control over transitions, allowing you to extensively customize them.

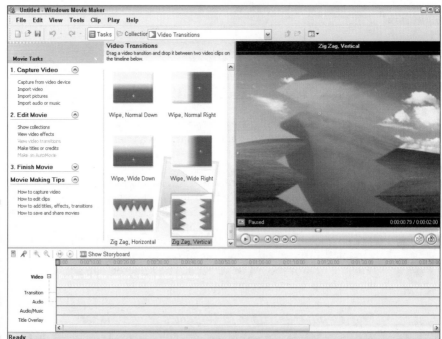

Figure 9-2: Windows Movie Maker offers an impressive selection of transitions.

Premiere's transitions are stored in the Effects and Transitions window. To preview transitions:

1. **Click the arrow to expand the Effects and Transitions window as shown in Figure 9-3.**

   The Effects and Transitions window is located on the left side of the screen under Media window.

2. **Click the Transitions button, and then click the arrow next to Video Transitions.**

   Premiere Elements organizes transitions into 11 categories.

3. **Click an arrow next to a category to reveal a list of video transitions, and then click a transition for a thumbnail preview.**

Click to expand window.

Click to expand category.

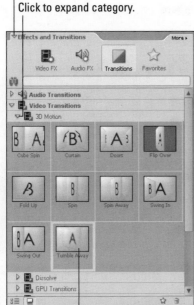

Figure 9-3:
Premiere
Elements
provides 79
transitions.

Click transition to preview.

Adding a transition to the timeline

Adding a transition to a project is pretty easy and works the same way in almost every video-editing program available. For now, add a simple dissolve (also called a fade) transition to a project. If your editing program currently shows the storyboard for your project, switch to the timeline (see Chapter 8 for more on the timeline and basic editing). Next, click and drag the Fade (in Windows Movie Maker) or Cross Dissolve (in iMovie) transition from the list of transitions and drop it between two clips on the timeline.

The appearance of the transition varies slightly depending on the editing program you are using. As you can see in Figure 9-4, Windows Movie Maker displays transitions in a special Transitions track in the timeline. Apple iMovie, on the other hand, uses a special transition icon that overlaps the adjacent clips as shown in Figure 9-5.

Drag transition from here.

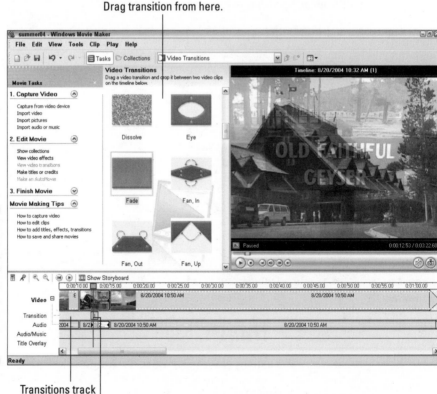

Figure 9-4:
Windows
Movie
Maker
places
transitions
in the
Transitions
track.

Transitions track

Drop transition here.

Figure 9-5:
iMovie uses
a special
transition
icon.

iMovie uses a special transition icon.

When you first apply a transition in iMovie, the program must render the transition before it can be viewed. *Rendering* is a process that allows the computer to play back the transition at full speed and quality. I explain rendering in more detail in Chapter 13.

To preview the transition, simply play the timeline by clicking Play under the preview window or pressing the spacebar on your keyboard. If you don't like the style of the transition, you can delete it by clicking the transition to select it, and then pressing Delete on your keyboard. If you think the transition just needs some fine-tuning, check out the next section.

Adjusting transitions

Video transitions usually have some features or attributes that can be adjusted. Most important, perhaps, is the length of the transition. The default length for most transitions is about two seconds. Sometimes a two-second transition is too long — or not long enough. The next two sections show you how to adjust the length of transitions and make other changes where possible.

Modifying iMovie transitions

The iMovie transition window doesn't just provide a place to store transitions; it also helps you to control them. To adjust the length of a transition, follow these steps:

1. **Click the transition in the timeline to select it.**

2. **Adjust the Speed slider in the transitions window.**

   The length of the transition is shown in the preview window, as shown in Figure 9-6.

3. **Click Update in the transitions window to update the length of the transition in the timeline.**

4. **Click the Play button under the preview window to preview your results.**

Click to update transition

Length of transition

Directional control   Speed slider

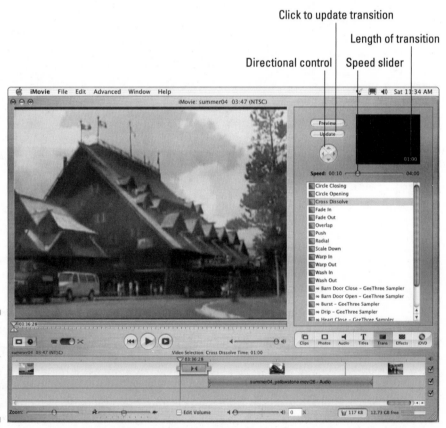

Figure 9-6:
Use the Speed slider to adjust the length of the clip.

Some iMovie transitions, such as Push, allow you to control the direction of travel for the transition. When you click the Push transition to select it in the transition window, the directional control (Figure 9-6) becomes active. Then you simply click the arrows in the directional control to change the direction in which the Push transition moves.

Adjusting transitions in Movie Maker

Windows Movie Maker gives you a good selection of transitions, but unfortunately the only change you can make to a transition is to adjust the duration. To change the duration of a transition in Windows Movie Maker, simply click and drag the edge of the transition in the Timeline, as shown in Figure 9-7. Click Play to preview your duration adjustment.

Figure 9-7: Click and drag the edge of a transition to change its duration.

Click and drag

Fine-tuning transitions in Premiere Elements

Transition adjustment is one feature where you really start to see the difference between a basic program like Windows Movie Maker and a more advanced program like Premiere Elements. Whereas Movie Maker only lets you control the duration of a transition, Premiere Elements allows you to customize virtually every aspect of a transition. Premiere even has a special window just for fine-tuning transitions. To reveal the transition control window, double-click the transition in the timeline. A transition control window appears in the lower-right as shown in Figure 9-8.

I could spend an entire chapter talking about all the transition control that Premiere Elements gives you. In fact, I do just that in my book *Adobe Premiere Elements For Dummies* (from Wiley Publishing, Inc.). I can't devote a whole chapter here to Premiere Elements, but I can give the highlights:

- Use arrows around the preview window to change the direction of directional transitions.

- Click Show Timeline to reveal a split timeline in the transition control window. This timeline allows you to precisely see and adjust the timing of the transition in relation to the outgoing and incoming clip. The large Start and End windows can also be used to fine-tune the beginning and ending points of the transition.

- Add and customize borders and backgrounds to some transitions. If you can apply a border to a transition, you'll see options to change the thickness and color of the border. Some transitions also have solid-colored backgrounds, in which case you can use a color-picker to adjust the color.

- Add anti-aliasing to smooth edges. In Figure 9-8, I have applied the Tumble Away transition. The outgoing clip tumbles away in a 3-D box. Anti-aliasing smoothes out the blockiness that can sometimes occur on the edges of boxes and other transition elements. If you see blockiness, try enabling anti-aliasing.

Other options may be available, depending on the transition. Whatever transition you choose, you'll probably need to experiment a bit with various features and adjustments to get just the right effect.

Preview window

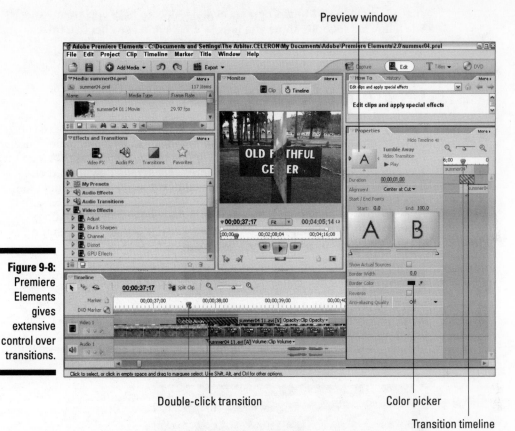

Figure 9-8:
Premiere
Elements
gives
extensive
control over
transitions.

Double-click transition

Color picker

Transition timeline

Giving Credit with Titles

Next to trimming out unwanted scenes, adding titles is probably one of the
most common edits that you will make to your movies. Titles — the words
that appear onscreen during a movie — can serve many important functions.
They can tell your audience the name of your movie, who made it, who
starred in it, who paid for it, and who baked cookies for the cast. Titles can
also clue the audience in to vital details — the story's location, the current
time and date, or the score of the game — with minimum fuss. And of course,
titles can reveal what the characters are saying if they're speaking a different
language.

Virtually all video-editing programs include tools to help you create titles. The following sections show you how to create and use effective titles in your movie projects.

Creating effective titles

It's easy to think of titles as just words on the screen. But think of the effects, both forceful and subtle, that well-designed titles can have. Consider the *Star Wars* movies, which all begin with a black screen and the phrase, "A long time ago, in a galaxy far, far away . . ." The simple title screen quickly and effectively sets the tone and tells the audience that the story is beginning. And then, of course, you get those scrolling words that float three-dimensionally off into space, immediately after that first title screen. A story floating through space is far more interesting than white text scrolling from the bottom to top of the screen, don't you think?

Titles can generally be put into two basic categories: full-screen and overlays. Full-screen titles like the one shown in Figure 9-9 are most often used at the beginning and end of a movie, where the title appears over a background image or a solid color (such as a plain black screen). The full-screen title functions as its own element in the movie, as does any video clip. An overlay title makes words appear right over a video image, as shown in Figure 9-10.

Figure 9-9:
A full-screen title stands alone and is often used at the beginning or end of a movie.

Figure 9-10:
An overlay title appears right on a video image.

When using titles in your movies, you should follow some basic guidelines to make them more effective. After all, funny or informative titles don't do much good if your audience can't read them. Follow these general rules when creating titles for your movies:

- **Less is more.** Try to keep your titles as brief and simple as possible.

- **White on black looks best.** When you read words on paper, black letters on white paper are easier to read. This rule does not carry over to video, however. In video images, light characters over a dark background are usually easier to read. An exception would be if you already have a relatively light background. For example, if the background of your winter video scene is a field of white snow, you may need to use a darker text color. I show you how to control title colors and styles in the next couple of sections.

Video displays such as TVs and computer monitors generate images using light. (You can think of a TV screen as a big light bulb.) Because TV displays emit light, full-screen titles almost never have black text on a white screen. Most people find staring at a mostly white TV screen about as pleasant as staring at a lit light bulb: If you watch viewers look at a white TV screen, you may even see them squint. Squinting is bad, so stick to the convention of light words over a dark background whenever possible.

✔ **Avoid very thin lines.** In Chapter 3, I described the difference between interlaced and non-interlaced video displays. In an interlaced display — such as a TV — every other horizontal resolution line of the video image is drawn in a separate pass or field. If the video image includes very thin lines — especially lines that are only one pixel thick — interlacing could cause the lines to flicker noticeably, giving your viewers a migraine headache in short order. To avoid this, choose fonts that have thicker lines. For smaller characters, avoid serif fonts such as Times New Roman. *Serifs* (the extra strokes at the ends of characters in some fonts, such as the one you're reading right now) often have very thin lines that flicker on an interlaced video display.

✔ **Think big.** Remember that the resolution on your computer screen is a lot finer than what you get on a typical TV screen. Also, TV viewers typically watch video from longer distances than do computer users — say, across the room while plopped on the sofa, compared to sitting just a few inches away in an office chair. This means the words that look pleasant and readable on your computer monitor may be tiny and unintelligible if your movie is output to tape for TV viewing. Never be afraid to increase the size of your titles.

✔ **Think safety.** Most TVs suffer from a malady called *overscan,* which is what happens when some of the video image is cut off at the edges of the screen. In this respect, TVs are a lot like computer printers. Most TVs can't display the far edges of the video image, just as most printers can't print all the way to the very edges of the paper. When you're working on a word-processing document, your page has margins to account for the shortcomings of printers as well as to make the page more readable. The same applies to video images, which have *title safe margins.* To ensure that your titles show up onscreen and are not cut off at the edges, make sure your titles remain within this margin (also sometimes called the *title safe boundary*).

Apple iMovie and Windows Movie Maker don't show these margins onscreen; instead, they automatically keeps your titles inside the margins. In iMovie, if you know your movie will be viewed only on computer screens, place a check mark next to the QT Margins option in the Titles window. This places the margins closer to the edge of the screen. Windows Movie Maker does not allow you to override the margins.

The Adobe Title Designer — which comes with Adobe Premiere Elements — actually displays the title safe margins onscreen, and it's up to you to keep your titles inside them. The margins appear in the Title Designer window as thin white lines, as shown in Figure 9-11.

The Adobe Title Designer also displays *action safe margins.* Ideally, important action in the video image should not go outside of the action safe margins. This doesn't really affect your titles, however, because as you can see in Figure 9-11 the action safe margins are outside of the title safe margins.

✔ **Play, play, play.** I cannot stress enough the importance of previewing your titles, especially overlays. Play your timeline after adding titles to see how they look. Make sure the title is readable, positioned well onscreen, and visible long enough to be read. If possible, preview the titles on an external video monitor (see Chapter 13 for more on using external monitors).

Figure 9-11: Don't let your titles fall outside the title safe margins.

Title safe margin   Action safe margin

You can use transitions between full-screen titles and other video clips. Dissolves (described earlier in this chapter) often look nice when used to transition from a full-screen title to the video.

Adding titles to your project

Throughout this book, I often say that most video-editing programs have a lot in common. Most of the time they do, but when it comes to creating and using titles in a movie project, most editing programs tend to go their own way. The next couple of sections show you the basics of how to create and insert titles in iMovie, Windows Movie Maker, and Adobe Premiere Elements.

Creating titles in iMovie

Apple prides itself — and rightfully so — on providing computers and software that are easy to use. Adding titles to your iMovie project could hardly be easier. To create a title, follow these steps:

1. **If you're creating an overlay title, click the video clip in the timeline that will appear behind the title.**

   This operation ensures that the proper clip appears in the preview window as you edit and preview your title. If you're currently working in storyboard mode, I recommend that you switch over to the timeline by clicking the Timeline button, which appears to the lower-left of the monitor. If you're creating a full-screen title (one that is over a black background instead of superimposed over a clip), don't worry about selecting a clip in the timeline: Just go straight to step 2.

2. **Click the Titles button above the timeline.**

   The iMovie title designer appears.

3. **Type the words for the title in the text boxes near the bottom of the title designer (as in Figure 9-12).**

4. **Choose a title style for your title from the Titles list (not to be confused with the brand of golf ball).**

   Most of the listed titles are for moving titles. When you click one, a preview of the motion appears in the preview window at the top of the title designer. If you want a static title that doesn't move, choose a Centered, Stripe, or Subtitle title.

5. **If the movie will be output to videotape or DVD for viewing on conventional TVs, make sure the QT Margins option is *not* checked.**

   The QT option allows titles in movies destined for the Web to use a little more screen space, but this isn't recommended for movies that will be shown on TVs. The problem is *overscan,* which I described earlier in the section, "Creating effective titles."

6. **If you want to create a standalone title with a black background, place a check mark next to the Over Black option.**

7. **Click the Color box to choose a new color for the title.**

8. **Use the Font menu to choose a new font face, and adjust the size of the title using the size slider.**

9. **When you're ready to add the title to the project, drag the title from the Titles list and drop it into the timeline, just before the clip over which you want the title to appear.**

   The title appears in the timeline. If you created an overlay title, it is automatically superimposed on the video clip before which you placed the title. If you choose the Over Black option in step 6, the title is a standalone clip in the timeline with a black background.

If you decide to edit a title you created earlier, select the title in the timeline, make your changes, and then click the Update button at the top of the title designer window.

Font Face menu

Preview window

Titles list

Color box

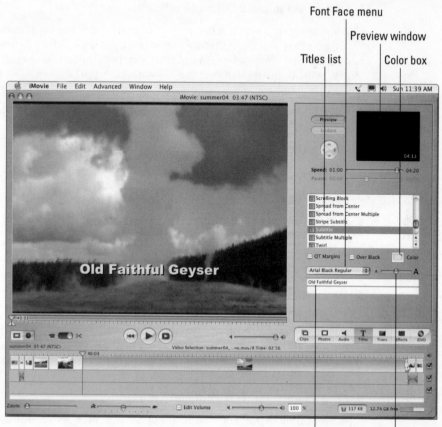

Figure 9-12:
iMovie's title
designer is
easy to use.

Type text here.

Size slider

Making titles in Windows Movie Maker

When Microsoft first released Windows Movie Maker back in 2000, its title
creation capabilities were severely stunted. Your only option was to go into
Microsoft Paint, create a title as a picture, and then import the picture into
Movie Maker.

Thankfully, Movie Maker has been through several important revisions over
the years, and it now provides a reasonable yet still basic title designer. To
start creating a title in Movie Maker, follow these steps:

1. **Click a clip in the timeline to select it.**

   If you want to insert a full-screen title in the middle of your movie, select the clip that will immediately follow the title. If you want to create an overlay title, select the clip upon which the title will be overlaid. If you just want to insert a title at the beginning or end of the movie, you can skip step 1.

2. **Click Make Titles or Credits in the task list on the left side of the screen, or choose Tools⇨Titles and Credits.**

3. **Click an option for where you want to insert the title.**

   The five options are self-explanatory and pertain to where you want to insert the title in the movie. If you want to create an overlay title, choose the Add Title on the Selected Clip in the Timeline option.

4. **Enter some text for the title.**

   You will notice two text boxes for entering text. The upper box is for the larger main text, and the lower box is for smaller text such as a subtitle. You may enter text in one or both boxes if you wish.

5. **Click Change the Title Animation.**

   A long list of animation options appears. These options let you create text that flies on or off the screen, fades in and out, and more. Scroll through the list and click options that interest you. When you click an animation option, a preview of the animation appears in the preview window on the right.

6. **Click Change the Text Font and Color.**

   A list of text appearance options appears as shown in Figure 9-13.

7. **Use the menus and options to adjust the appearance of the text.**

   Movie Maker allows you to change font, text appearance, alignment, size, transparency, and color. Experiment with the various settings to get a text appearance that looks good to you. A preview of your changes appears in the preview window on the right.

8. **When you are done, click Done, Add Title to Movie.**

   The title is added to your timeline at the location you specified in step 3.

Don't worry about getting the text perfect the first time. If you want to change a title later, simply double-click the title in the timeline to reopen the appearance and animation options.

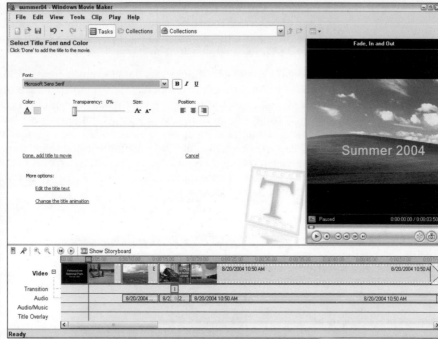

Figure 9-13:
Changing
the
appearance
of titles is
easy in
Windows
Movie
Maker.

Using the Adobe Title Designer

Adobe Premiere Elements includes a powerful title designer. You might assume that a more powerful title designer is more complex, and in some respects that is true in the case of Premiere. However, the Premiere Elements title designer does incorporate some useful features like templates and styles that make it really easy to quickly create stunning, high-quality titles. To create a title in Premiere Elements,

1. **Choose Title⇨New Title, and then choose the type of title you want to create.**

   The New Title submenu contains five options:

   • Default Still: Choose this if you just want to create a basic, static title.

   • Default Roll: Choose this if you want to create a title that rolls vertically up or down the screen.

   • Default Crawl: Choose this if you want to create a title that crawls horizontally across the screen.

- **Based on Current Title:** Select an existing title in the timeline, and then choose this to create a new title with the same appearance. This option is a helpful time-saver if you want all of the titles in a movie to have a similar look and feel.

- **Based on Template:** Choose this if you want to create a title based on one of Adobe's many templates. The templates have pre-designed text styles, and most of them have themed background graphics. For example, one of the Travel-themed templates has a background image of a map and compass. If you choose this option, a window appears as shown in Figure 9-14, listing various templates. Click the triangles in the list of templates on the left to expand the list, and click the name of a template to preview it on the right. Click OK when you have chosen a template.

Figure 9-14:
Adobe's title designer includes many attractive design templates.

2. **If you chose an option other than a title based on a template, enter a name for the title in the New Title dialog box and click OK.**

   The exact name isn't important, so long as it's something you'll remember later.

3. **Type some text for your title.**

   If your text runs off the edge of the screen, right-click the text and choose Word Wrap from the menu that appears. This helps your text fit on the screen a bit better.

   One of the really nice things about the Adobe title designer is that when you are creating overlay titles, the real video image from your project appears in the background of the designer window. To change the video image that appears in the title designer window, simply move the play head in the timeline to a different place. This helps ensure that your titles don't obscure important parts of the video image, or vice versa.

4. **Adjust the style, appearance, and alignment of the text.**

The Adobe title designer gives you many options. Figure 9-15 points out some of the most important and useful ones. To move text, first click the Selection tool. This allows you to click and drag text to a new location. If you want to make a background for your text, use the shape tools.

5. **When you are done creating the title, click and drag the title from the Media window and drop it on the timeline as shown in Figure 9-15.**

In Figure 9-15, you can see that I have dropped the title on the Video 2 track. This means the title will be an overlay title. To create a full-screen title, drop it on the Video 1 track.

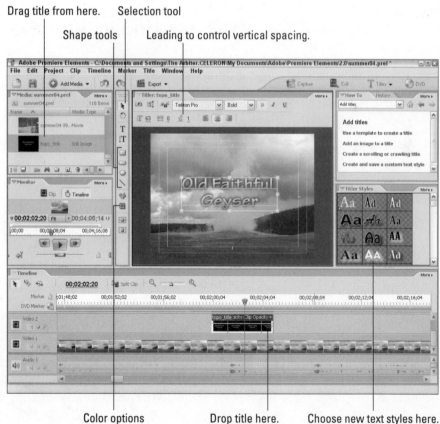

Drag title from here.   Selection tool

Shape tools   Leading to control vertical spacing.

Figure 9-15:
Text styles
help you
make
attractive
titles.

Color options   Drop title here.   Choose new text styles here.

Changing the length of titles

After you've added some titles to your movie project and previewed them a couple of times, you'll probably find that you need to change how long some of them appear. Does the title flash by so quickly that you don't have time to read it? Does the title seem to linger a few seconds too long? Changing the length for titles is pretty easy, but you must be viewing the timeline in your editing program, and not the storyboard. As I describe in Chapter 8, the time-line is where you perform "fine-tuning" edits such as changing the length of a title.

If you want to change the length of a title, you can do it in a couple of ways:

- In almost any video-editing program, hold the mouse pointer over an edge of the title in the timeline, and then click and drag the edge back and forth to make the title longer or shorter. This method is quick and easy but not very precise.
- In iMovie, move the Speed slider left or right in the title designer window.

In addition to altering the duration of your title, you can change which clip your overlay titles appear over. Just drag the titles left or right in the timeline if you want to change when they appear.

Chapter 10

Working with Audio

In This Chapter

▶ Working with audio tracks

▶ Adjusting volume

▶ Twanging audio rubberbands

▶ Using sound effects

▶ Adding a musical soundtrack

Sound is one of the most important yet most easily overlooked aspects of movie making. Good pictures are important, but if you want to make high-quality movies, you absolutely must give them a high-quality soundtrack.

In Chapter 7, I showed you how to record better audio. Now it's time to plug that audio into your movie project. In this chapter, I show you how to work with audio in a movie timeline. I show you how to fine-tune that audio, as well as add a musical soundtrack if you desire.

Basic video-editing programs like Apple iMovie and Windows Movie Maker don't provide much in the way of advanced audio-editing tools. If you want to see what kind of audio tools are available in a more advanced program like Adobe Premiere Elements, check out Chapter 17, where I show how to use Premiere's advanced audio tools to improve the sound quality of audio clips.

Using Audio in a Movie

Most video-editing programs share a lot in common. Virtually all of them have separate audio tracks in the timeline for background music, narration (or sound effects), and the audio that accompanies the video clips in the timeline. (Audio tracks are described in greater detail in the next section.)

Many movie-editing programs can also show audio waveforms. A *waveform* is a line that graphically represents the rising and falling level of sound in an audio clip. Figure 10-1 shows the waveform for an audio clip in Adobe Premiere Elements. Waveforms are useful because they allow you to edit your audio visually, often with pinpoint accuracy. By looking at the waveform, you can tell when loud sounds or extended periods of quiet occur.

Although many movie-editing programs use audio waveforms, Apple iMovie isn't one of them. You can still edit audio (as I show later in this chapter); you just won't be able to do it visually in iMovie. Fortunately, plenty of other programs *can* display audio waveforms — including Apple Final Cut (both the Express and Pro versions), Adobe Premiere (both Elements and Pro), Pinnacle Studio, and Windows Movie Maker.

Figure 10-1:
Waveforms
allow you to
see what
you're doing
as you work
with audio.

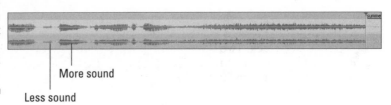

More sound

Less sound

Understanding audio tracks

A video-editing program can play several sources of audio at once. For example, while you hear the audio that was recorded with a video clip, you may also hear a musical soundtrack and some narration that was recorded later. When you're working on a movie project in your editing software, each of these unique bits of audio goes on its own separate audio track in the timeline.

Most editing programs provide audio tracks for main audio (the audio that was recorded with a video clip), music, and narration. More advanced editing programs offer many more audio tracks that can be used any way you wish. Adobe Premiere Elements, for example, lets you have up to 99 audio tracks in the timeline. It's hard to imagine why you might actually *need* that many audio tracks, but too many is probably better than not enough.

Windows Movie Maker has two separate audio tracks, as shown in Figure 10-2. The Audio track contains the audio portions of video clips in the Video track, and the Audio/Music track is where you can add narration or background music.

TIP

If you don't see the Transition and Audio tracks in the Movie Maker timeline, click the plus sign next to the Video track to expand it.

Figure 10-2:
Movie
Maker's
timeline
provides
two
separate
audio
tracks.

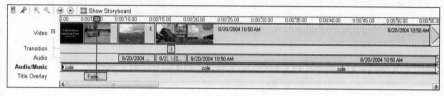

Apple iMovie handles audio tracks a little differently, but you still have essentially three audio tracks to work with. The main audio track is actually hidden inside the video track. Two other audio tracks handle sound effects and background music. You can extract audio from video clips if you want (simply select the clip in the timeline and choose Advanced⊅Extract Audio), but doing so causes the main audio to take up one of the other two audio tracks. Figure 10-3 shows iMovie's audio tracks. You can enable or disable audio tracks by using the check boxes on the right side of the timeline. This is helpful during editing when you want to hear just one or two audio tracks at a time.

Figure 10-3:
Apple
iMovie
provides
three audio
tracks,
although
one is
hidden most
of the time.

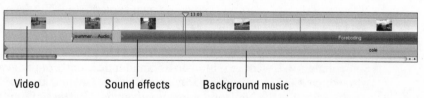

Video   Sound effects   Background music

Adding audio to the timeline

Adding audio to the timeline is pretty easy. Record and import your audio as described in Chapter 7, and then simply drag and drop it to an audio track. You can move clips by dragging them left or right in their respective tracks, and you can trim them by dragging on the edges. In fact, you'll find that editing audio tracks is a lot like editing video tracks — you can use the same basic editing techniques that I describe in Chapter 8.

One nice feature of iMovie is that it allows you to link audio clips to video clips. For example, suppose you've recorded some narration to go along with a video clip. If you decide to move that video clip to a different part of the timeline, you have to move the narration clip as well. If the two clips are linked, moving one also moves the other. To link an audio clip to a video clip in iMovie, follow these steps:

1. **Position the audio and video clips that you want to link in the timeline.**

2. **Move the play head to the beginning of the audio clip.**

3. **Click once on the audio clip to select it.**

4. **Choose Advanced⇨Lock Audio Clip at Playhead.**

A yellow pin appears on both the audio and video clips, as shown in Figure 10-4. If you move the video clip to a different place in the timeline, the linked audio clip moves with it. To unlink the clips, select the audio clip and choose Advanced⇨Unlock Audio Clip.

Figure 10-4:
Yellow pins
indicate that
the audio
and video
clips are
linked.

Pins

Editing audio and video separately

Sometimes you'll want to edit main audio independently of the video clip with which it is associated. In iMovie, first extract main audio from the video clip by selecting the clip and choosing Advanced⇨Extract Audio. In Adobe Premiere Elements, right-click a clip in the timeline and choose Unlink Audio and Video from the menu that appears.

Windows Movie Maker doesn't handle audio quite as effectively as Premiere and iMovie. It is not possible to unlink audio and video, so if you want to make changes to the audio portion of a clip independent of the video portion, you have to cheat a little. Here's how:

1. **Click and drag a video clip that includes audio from the Collections window to the timeline.**

   The video portion appears in the video track of the timeline, and the audio portion appears in the audio track.

2. **Right-click the audio clip in the timeline and choose Mute from the menu that appears.**

   You can't remove the audio portion of a clip from the timeline, but you can make it quiet!

3. **Click and drag the same clip from the Collections window to the Audio/Music track of the timeline, as shown in Figure 10-5.**

When you drop a clip on the Audio/Music track, only the audio is added to the timeline, not the video. You can now change the duration and position of this audio track by dragging it back and forth along the Audio/Music track. Of course, the disadvantage of doing this is that now you can't add a musical soundtrack or narration because the Audio/Music track is filled with the clip you just inserted. If you really need more control over audio tracks, consider stepping up to Adobe Premiere Elements or another more advanced program.

Figure 10-5:
Audio clips can be added to the Audio/ Music track.

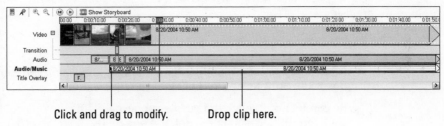

Click and drag to modify.   Drop clip here.

Adjusting volume

Perhaps the most common thing anyone does to audio tracks is adjust the volume. As you preview your project, you may notice that the background music seems a little too loud or the narration isn't loud enough. You may also have sounds in the main audio track that you want to get rid of altogether, without affecting the rest of the audio clip. Virtually all video-editing programs allow you to adjust volume in two different ways:

✔ You can adjust the overall volume of an entire clip or track.

✔ You can adjust volume dynamically within a clip, making some parts of the same clip louder and some parts quieter.

Many programs display audio rubberbands across audio clips. *Rubberbands* (see Figure 10-6) aren't just for holding together rolled up newspapers or your hairdo; in video programs, they show you the volume for an audio clip, and they allow you to make dynamic adjustments to the volume throughout the clip. Windows Movie Maker doesn't have audio rubberbands, but iMovie, Premiere Elements, and most other editing programs do.

Figure 10-6: Rubber-bands make it easy to adjust volume in your audio clips.

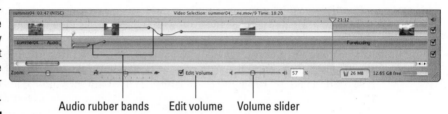

Audio rubber bands Edit volume Volume slider

Adjusting overall volume

Modifying the overall volume for an audio clip or a whole track is pretty simple, but the procedure varies a bit depending on which program you are using.

In Apple iMovie, follow these steps:

1. **Click a clip to select it. (To adjust multiple clips simultaneously, hold down the Shift key as you click each clip.)**

   Be careful not to click the purple rubberband line. If you accidentally click the rubberband and a dot appears on the line, press ⌘+Z to undo the change.

2. **With the desired clip(s) selected, adjust the Volume slider leftward to reduce volume or right to increase volume.**

   As you adjust the slider (shown in Figure 10-6), you see the rubberband lines move up or down.

In Windows Movie Maker, right-click an audio clip and choose Volume. A volume control dialog box appears. Adjust the slider control in the dialog box to adjust volume for that clip.

Windows Movie Maker also lets you balance audio levels from your video clips and your Audio/Music track. Choose Tools⇨Audio Levels to open the Audio Levels dialog box as shown in Figure 10-7. Adjust this slider to change whether the audio from your video or the audio from the Audio/Music track should be more prominent. This is a handy adjustment to have, although unfortunately you can only adjust the overall balance in the whole project rather than dynamically throughout the movie.

Figure 10-7:
This simple
dialog box
controls
audio levels
in Windows
Movie
Maker.

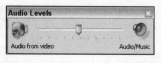

Adjusting volume dynamically

Believe it or not, I very seldom adjust the overall volume of an entire clip or track. Usually I prefer to adjust volume dynamically throughout the clip. Adjusting volume dynamically allows me to fine-tune audio to better match other things that are going on in the project. I adjust volume dynamically at times like these:

- **Narration is about to begin.** I may reduce the volume of background music a bit so that the spoken words are more easily heard.

- **The sound changes between video clips.** Such a change often sounds abrupt or harsh. I can reduce that by fading audio in at the beginning of the clip, and fading it out at the end.

- **I can eliminate unwanted sounds from a clip.** Sometimes your camera's microphone picks up unwanted noises such as chatting audience members or wind gusts.

Dynamic volume adjustment is where audio rubberbands really come in handy. In iMovie, click once on a rubberband for one of your audio clips. When you click the rubberband, a little dot appears. You can click and drag that dot up or down to adjust the volume of the clip. Not only can you place as many dots as you can squeeze onto a rubberband, but you can also move those dots around on the rubberband to make constant adjustments throughout the clip. Like real rubberbands, audio rubberbands are stretchy and can be moved quite a bit, but unlike real rubberbands, they don't snap back when you stop moving them. Play around a bit with the rubberbands to see just how fun volume adjustments can be!

Those little dots on audio rubberbands act like pins to hold the bands in place. If you want to get rid of a dot, click and drag it off the top or bottom of the clip. Twang! The dot disappears, and the rubberband snaps back into place.

The rubberbands in Premiere Elements are a little different. To place a dot on the rubberband, first move the timeline's play head to the spot where you want to place a dot. Click the Add/Remove Keyframe button on the track header to place a dot (see Figure 10-8). Move the play head and place additional dots, and then click and drag the dots up and down to adjust Premiere's audio rubberbands.

Play head

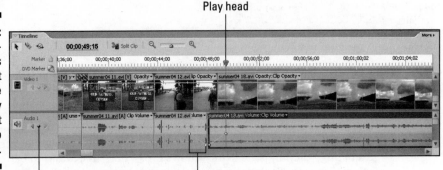

Figure 10-8: Use rubberbands to adjust volume dynamically throughout an audio clip.

Add/Remove Keyframes button   Rubberband dots

Windows Movie Maker doesn't offer rubberbands or other fancy methods of adjusting volume dynamically, but you can fade audio in or out. To make an audio clip fade in or out in Movie Maker, right-click the audio clip in the time-line and choose Fade In or Fade Out from the menu.

Using iMovie's sound effects

Sound effects can really separate a good movie from a great movie. In Chapter 7, I suggest that if a picture is worth a thousand words, sometimes a sound is worth a thousand pictures. Consider how various sound effects can affect the mood of a scene:

- ✔ A quiet room somehow seems even quieter if you can hear the subtle ticking of a clock.
- ✔ Applause, cheering, or laughter suggest how the viewer should feel about an event in the movie.
- ✔ Chirping birds suggest peace and serenity.
- ✔ Footsteps make movement seem more real, even when the feet are not shown in the video image.

Some programs come with pre-recorded sound effects that are ready to use in your movies. Windows Movie Maker and Premiere Elements don't offer any built-in sound effects, but Apple iMovie does. To view a list of sound effects in iMovie, click the Audio button above the timeline and choose iMovie Sound Effects from the menu at the top of the audio pane. A list of sound effects appears (as shown in Figure 10-9), including standard sound effects as well as special Skywalker Sound Effects. Skywalker Sound, as you may know, is the brainchild of George Lucas of *Star Wars* fame, and the sound effects included with iMovie are very high-quality.

To preview a sound effect, choose it from the list and click Play in the audio pane. To use a sound effect in your project, simply click and drag it to an audio track in the timeline. You can trim and adjust the volume of sound effects just as you would any other audio clip.

Figure 10-9:
Apple
iMovie
includes a
collection of
high-quality
Skywalker
Sound
Effects.

Adding a Musical Soundtrack

Background music for movies is nothing new. Even before the day of "talkies," silent movies were traditionally accompanied by musicians who played piano and other instruments in the theater as the movie was shown. I'm sure you're eager to use music in some of your movie projects as well. The next two sections show you how to add soundtrack music to your movies.

In Chapter 7, I show you how to import music from audio CDs or MP3 files. After you have inserted an audio file into your editing program, you can add the file to the music track in your timeline. The procedure varies depending on which editing program you are using:

✔ In Apple iMovie, use iTunes (described in Chapter 7) to import music from audio CDs into your iTunes library. Then click the Audio button in iMovie, choose iTunes from the menu at the top of the audio pane as shown in Figure 10-10, and click and drag a song from your iTunes library to an audio track on the iMovie timeline.

✔ In Windows Movie Maker, use Windows Media Player or another media player program to copy music from an audio CD to your hard drive. In Movie Maker, click Import Audio or Music in the task list on the left side of the screen, or choose File➪Import. Browse to the folder containing the music file you want to import, click the desired file to select it, and click Import. The song is imported into your current media collection. Windows Movie Maker supports music in WMA, MP3, WAV, and most other common audio formats.

Figure 10-10:
iMovie lets
you import
music
directly from
your iTunes
library.

Chapter 11

Advanced Video Editing

*I*f you're brand new to this whole movie-editing thing, having the capability to add transitions, titles, and musical soundtracks to your videos probably seems pretty cool. But transitions, titles, and sounds are just the beginning of what you can do. Even the most basic video-editing programs these days provide some special-effects features. Slightly more advanced programs — such as Adobe Premiere Elements or Apple Final Cut Express — offer truly astounding special-effects capabilities that even moviemaking professionals could barely afford to dream about just a few years ago.

Although Apple iMovie and Windows Movie Maker offer some basic effects, if you want to do truly advanced video editing, you need to step up to an advanced editing program. In this chapter, I focus solely on what can be done with an advanced editing program. I use Adobe Premiere Elements, but the techniques described here can be easily used with Final Cut Express or most other advanced video editors. Of course, I can't cover every single detail and aspect of video effects here, but this chapter gives you a crash course in how to use the most common effects.

Using Video Effects

When I mention "special effects," what's the first thing that pops into your mind? You're probably envisioning spaceships soaring between the stars, giant monsters destroying a city, or a superhero soaring unassisted through the sky. Such effects are indeed special, but they only scratch the surface of how effects can be used in movies. Special effects can

- ✔ Transport the viewer to a different place and time
- ✔ Show subjects that would be otherwise impossible or too expensive to photograph
- ✔ Change the mood or feel of a piece of video
- ✔ Add visual excitement or a sense of the exotic

Special effects aren't all about spaceships and monsters. Consider the scene in Figure 11-1. I have used the Find Edges effect to create an image that is exotic while at the same time fitting in with the martial arts visual theme of the clip. This clip would look good as the background for a DVD menu or a title screen.

Figure 11-1: Special effects can make regular clips seem more exotic.

Reviewing Premiere's effects

Adobe Premiere Elements comes with more than 70 video effects. You'll probably never use many of the effects: Some of them are rather obscure and puzzling. But you never know when the strangest effect may provide just the visual appeal that you are looking for, so familiarizing yourself with what Premiere has to offer is a good idea.

To view the selection of video effects, minimize the Media window and maximize the Effects and Transitions window, shown in Figure 11-2. If you don't see the Effects and Transitions window, choose Window➪Effects. Click the arrow next to Video Effects to expand the list, and then click an arrow next to a category to see what it holds inside. A thumbnail picture shows a basic preview of each effect. Video effects are organized into these 13 categories:

✔ **Adjust:** These effects tweak the color and light in your images. Some effects like Auto Color and Auto Contrast can be used to quickly improve poor video color, whereas others like Extract and Posterize can add an artistic look. I show how to use some of these effects later in this chapter.

✔ **Blur & Sharpen:** Use blur effects to soften a video image, or sharpen effects to improve slightly out-of-focus video images.

✔ **Channel:** The Invert effect sits all alone in the Channel category. As the name implies, the Invert effect inverts the colors in the video image, making it look like a photo negative.

✔ **Distort:** These effects bend, twist, warp, ripple, reflect, and otherwise distort the video image.

✔ **GPU Effects:** These provide advanced three-dimensional motion effects that take advantage of the graphics processing unit (GPU) in your computer's video card. Most modern PCI and AGP video cards have a GPU, but if your computer has a video card built-in to the motherboard, it may not have a GPU, meaning you won't be able to use Premiere's GPU Effects. Check your computer's documentation for more information.

✔ **Image Control:** Like the Adjust effects, these effects can be used to adjust and modify the light and color in your video images. I show how to use some of the Image Control effects to improve light and color later in this chapter.

✔ **Keying:** Keying effects can make some parts of your video image transparent. This is useful for bluescreening and other compositing effects. I show how to composite video later in this chapter.

✔ **Perspective:** These effects modify the apparent perspective of the video image. You can rotate the image on a three-dimensional plane, bevel the edges of the image, or raise the image and put a drop-shadow behind it.

✔ **Pixelate:** The lone effect in this group is named Facet, and it adds a pixilated texture to your video image.

✔ **Render:** The Lens Flare effect in this category adds a fake lens flare to the video image, whereas the Lightning effect adds fake lightning. Cool! Use the Ramp effect to cover your video image with a gradient.

✔ **Stylize:** If you've ever used a graphics program like Photoshop, the Stylize effects may look familiar. They add artistic color and texture effects to a video image, such as the Find Edges effect used in Figure 11-1.

✔ **Time:** The Time effects can be used to modify the relationship between your video frames and everyone's favorite fourth dimension, time. The Echo effect causes frames to echo across future frames, and the Posterize Time effect can be used to modify the frame rate of video clips.

✔ **Transform:** These effects transform the shape and position of your video images. You can change the camera view, crop the image, flip it upside-down, and more.

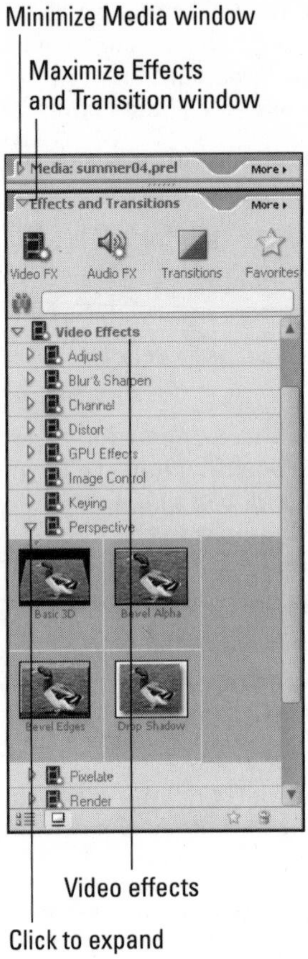

Minimize Media window

Maximize Effects
and Transition window

Figure 11-2:
Video
effects are
stored in the
Effects and
Transitions
window.

Video effects

Click to expand

Applying effects

Applying an effect to a video clip couldn't get much easier. Just click and drag
an effect from the Effects and Transitions window, and drop it on a video clip
in the timeline. A red bar at the top of the timeline means that at some point
your effect will have to be rendered (rendering is explained in Chapter 13).
Click Play in the preview window to see how it looks!

Of course, in most cases, applying the effect is just the beginning. Most
effects can be highly customized in Premiere Elements, and your preview of
the effect may reveal some details that you want to change.

A few effects cannot be modified, but most effects can be adjusted somewhat.
When you apply an effect to a clip, settings for the effect appear in the clip
Properties window on the right side of the screen. To adjust properties,
follow these steps:

1. **If you don't see the Properties window, choose Window⇨Properties.**

   The Properties window appears on the right side of the screen.

2. **Click the clip that has the effect you want to modify in the timeline.**

   When you select a clip in the timeline, properties for that clip appear in the Properties window, as shown in Figure 11-3. Along with Image Control, Motion, and Opacity — items found in the Properties window for every video clip — you should see the name of the effect you applied in the list.

Toggle Animation

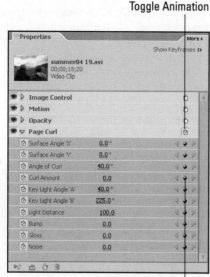

Figure 11-3:
Use the
Properties
window to
fine-tune
your effects.

Add/Remove Keyframe

3. **Click the arrow next to the name of the effect.**

   A list of options and settings for the effect appears. In Figure 11-3, I have applied the Page Curl effect (from the GPU Effects group) to a clip. The exact options you see vary depending on the effect. Settings are usually numbers or menus.

   Some effects don't have any settings that can be adjusted. In these cases, you don't see an arrow next to the name of the effect, or any options below it.

4. **To change a numeric setting, click and drag right or left on the number to scroll it up or down.**

   Alternatively, just click once on the number and type a new value.

I wish I could show you every setting for every effect, but unfortunately that would fill an entire book by itself. The best advice I can give is to play around with settings until you get an effect that you like. Later in this chapter, as well as in Chapter 17, I show you how to use specific settings to perform some popular special effects. In the next section, I show you how to use keyframes to control the timing of video effects and settings changes.

Controlling effects with keyframes

When you apply an effect to a clip, you may want the effect to appear only for part of the clip, or you may want the effect to change as the clip plays. Premiere Elements allows you to control the timing of effects by using *keyframes.* A keyframe is simply a frame of the movie that you set as a landmark (as you would the points you create and adjust on audio rubberbands when you edit audio, as described in Chapter 10). In advanced video-editing programs, you can set as many keyframes as you like, and you can change the properties of effects at each keyframe.

For example, suppose you use the Page Curl GPU effect on a video clip, as I did in Figure 11-3. You may notice that when you apply the Page Curl effect to a clip, it dog-ears the corner of the screen, rather than gradually peeling it away as the clip plays. You can make the Page Curl effect peel the page away, but you have to use keyframes to make it work. Here's how:

1. **Click and drag the Page Peel effect from the list of GPU Effects and drop it on a video clip in your timeline.**

2. **Place the timeline play head somewhere in the middle of the clip, and then press Page Up on your keyboard.**

   The play head moves to the very beginning of the clip.

3. **In the Properties window, click the arrow next to the Page Curl effect to expand the list of options.**

4. **Click and drag left on the number for the Curl Amount option until the number is set to zero.**

5. **Click the Toggle Animation button next to the Page Curl effect (Figure 11-3).**

   When you click the Toggle Animation button, keyframe control buttons appear, as shown in Figure 11-3.

6. **Click the Add/Remove Keyframe button next to the Curl Amount option (Figure 11-3).**

   A keyframe is set at the very beginning of the clip.

7. **Move the timeline play head to a spot about 3-5 seconds before the end of the clip.**

8. **Click the Add/Remove Keyframe button again.**

A second keyframe is added to the clip. If we don't change any settings at this second keyframe, the effect has no, uh, *effect* on the clip for the first portion of the clip.

9. **Press the Page Down key on your keyboard to move the play head to the very end of the clip.**

10. **Click the Add/Remove Keyframe button again, and then click and drag the Curl Amount number to the right until it gets to 100.**

Notice that the Page Curl is going to go from zero to 100% between the second and third keyframes. Play the timeline and you should see the image curl away. Keyframes can be used to animate and control many effects in this manner.

When using the Page Curl effect, put the clip you want to curl away in the Video 2 (or higher) track, and have it overlap another clip in track Video 1. When the clip in Video 2 peels away, it reveals the clip in Video 1.

Animating Video Clips

Now wait a minute; aren't these things called "movies" because the pictures are already *moving?* Why would a video clip need to be animated? You may not need to animate the actual *subjects* in the video, but you can move the video image across the screen. For example, a small picture-in-picture image could sail across the screen to give a hint of action that will happen later in the movie. You can move a clip across the screen along a fixed path or a zigzag pattern, you can rotate clips, and you can distort them. To animate a clip, follow these steps:

1. **Click the clip in the timeline that you want to animate to select it, and make sure that the play head is somewhere over the clip.**

   Just about any clip that you animate should be in track Video 2 or higher.

2. **Choose Window➪Properties to open the Properties window for the selected clip.**

3. **Click the arrow next to the Motion heading to expand the Motion controls as shown in Figure 11-4.**

4. **Click the clip's video image in the Monitor.**

   When you click the clip in the monitor, cross-hairs appear in the middle of the clip, and square handles appear on the sides and corners of the video image.

5. **Click and drag the square handles to change the size of the image.**

6. **Click and drag on the middle of the image to move the image to a new location on the screen.**

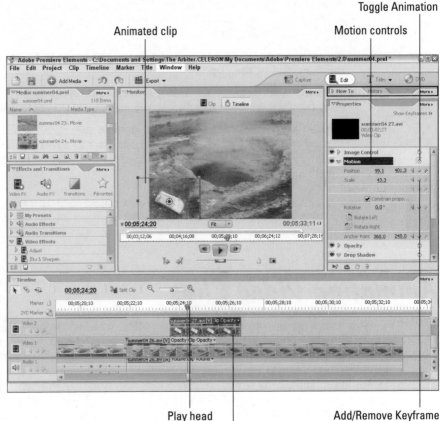

Toggle Animation

Animated clip

Motion controls

Play head

Add/Remove Keyframe

Select clip in video 2 track or higher

Figure 11-4:
Use the
Monitor to
resize and
animate
clips.

So far all you've done is resize a clip, not animate it. If you play the timeline to preview your change, you'll notice that your clip has been resized, but it doesn't go anywhere. To actually animate the clip and make it go somewhere, you just use keyframes. Effect keyframes are described in the previous section. To animate your resized clip,

1. **Click the Toggle Animation button next to Motion (see Figure 11-4).**

2. **Click the Add/Remove Keyframe button next to the Position control.**

   A keyframe is set at the current video frame for the current size and position of your clip.

3. **Move the play head in the timeline to a different location in the clip.**

4. Click and drag the resized clip in the monitor to a new location.

A new keyframe is automatically created. If you wish, you can even drag the clip completely off-screen. This causes the clip to appear to exit, stage left (or right, or up, or . . .).

Now play the timeline. You should see the resized clip move across the screen as it plays between the two keyframes you created. Unhappy with the results? Play around with it! Animation is one of those effects that you really need to fiddle around with to get just the right look.

Adjusting Color and Light

Great photographs are usually distinguished by perfect lighting and rich, stunning color. Some of this comes from photography skills and high-quality cameras, but these days, even the best photos usually share a secret: Photoshop. Advanced photo-editing programs like Adobe Photoshop offer tools to enhance and improve light and color in most pictures.

Just because you're working with videos doesn't mean you have to settle for inferior pictures. Yes, you need to use care when shooting video, and a high-end camcorder helps, but if you want pro-quality movie images, you should spend some time tweaking and improving those images in a program like Adobe Premiere Elements. Premiere includes some excellent Photoshop-style filters and effects that help you quickly and easily improve your video clips.

Improving video images is such a big subject that I spend an entire chapter talking about it in my book *Adobe Premiere Elements For Dummies* (Wiley Publishing, Inc.). I can't do that here, but I can provide an overview of the best tools that Premiere Elements puts at your disposal:

✓ **Image Controls:** Click any clip in the timeline and then open its Properties window (Window➪Properties). Click the arrow next to Image Control to reveal Brightness, Contrast, Hue, and Saturation settings. You can use these four settings to manually adjust the appearance of your images, but unless you really know what you're doing, you may find the results less than satisfactory.

✓ **Auto Color effect:** This effect in the Adjust category is one of the easiest, most effective tools for color correction. It quickly adjusts color levels and contrast in the clip to optimize color. This effect doesn't improve *every* clip, but it does improve *most* clips and takes only a moment to apply.

✔ **Auto Contrast effect:** Use this effect in the Adjust category to quickly enhance contrast without changing color.

✔ **Auto Levels effect:** Also in the Adjust category, use this effect to quickly enhance color without changing contrast.

✔ **Brightness and Contrast effect:** This Adjust effect does exactly what the name implies. If you just want to adjust the brightness or contrast of a clip, this effect can do the job.

✔ **Shadow/Highlight effect:** Use this Adjust category effect to improve the appearance of heavily shadowed subjects, or to soften extreme highlights in the image. Use this effect if you find that the Auto Levels or Auto Color effects unfavorably changes the color of the image.

✔ **Black & White effect:** This effect is in the Image Control category, and it removes color from your video image and turns it to grayscale. Use this effect during dream or flashback sequences.

✔ **Color Balance (HLS):** This Image Control effect allows you to adjust hue, saturation, and lightness in the image. It is similar to the Hue/Saturation controls in Adobe Photoshop.

✔ **Color Balance (RGB):** You can make direct changes to the levels of red, green, and blue in the image using this effect from the Image Control category.

✔ **Color Match:** This is one of the most powerful Image Control effects in Premiere Elements, and can match colors between video clips.

✔ **Color Pass:** This Image Control effect removes all but one color from a video image. Use this effect to place special emphasis on a particular object by making everything except that object grayscale. The Color Pass effect works best if the object contrasts strongly with the background. Say you have footage of a red balloon against a blue wall. Turn everything else grayscale to emphasize the colorful balloon.

✔ **Color Replace:** Use this Image Control effect to replace one color in a video image with another.

✔ **Gamma Correction:** This Image Control effect adjusts the brightness of midtones in an image without affecting shadows or highlights.

✔ **Tint:** This Image Control effect modifies only the color tint of the image. Use this to change the overall color cast of the image.

Don't be afraid to experiment. But remember, even the basic catch-all effects like Auto Color and Auto Levels don't work perfectly for every clip, so preview any clips you modify to make sure the color and light still look good. Also, remember that colors on your computer screen may look different on a TV. If possible preview your changes on an external video monitor, as described in Chapter 18.

Compositing Video

Compositing is one of the most common special effects used in modern movies and video. When you see an action hero battle a dinosaur, a damsel in distress cling to the fiftieth floor ledge by her fingertips, or the TV weatherman stand in front of a huge storm map, you're looking at a scene that was created by the magic of *compositing*. When you composite clips, you combine portions of two or more clips to make a video image that would otherwise be difficult or impossible to capture.

You don't need a Hollywood budget — or even a local Eyewitness News budget — to do compositing. Adobe Premiere Elements provides all the tools you need to do your own compositing effects, and in the next couple of sections, I show you how.

Understanding transparency

When you composite video, one video image is superimposed on top of another. Consider the TV weather forecast, where the image of the weatherman is superimposed over a moving weather map. To make this happen, portions of the video clip containing the weather man must be made transparent so that the weather map shows up in the background.

Compositing effects are also sometimes called *bluescreen* or *greenscreen* *effects*. This is because the weatherman (in the current example) is shot against a backdrop screen that is entirely blue or green. The exact shades of blue or green used are shades not normally found in clothing or skin tones. A program like Premiere Elements can look at that scene, recognize every part of the clip that is a certain color of green or blue, and make it transparent. To make part of the image transparent, Premiere uses effects called *keys*. A key effect keys out certain colors, which is just a fancy way of saying it removes them.

Consider the video clip shown in Figure 11-5. This clip shows a cat against a bright blue background. Premiere Elements can key out all the blue parts of this image to make them transparent, while leaving the cat in the image.

Premiere Elements allows you to make an entire video clip transparent or semi-transparent if you wish. Simply select a clip in the timeline, open the Properties window for that clip (Window➪Properties), and click the arrow next to Opacity to expand the Opacity controls. Click and drag left or right on the Clip Opacity control to decrease opacity (make it more transparent) or increase opacity (make it less transparent). You can also click Fade In or Fade Out to make the clip fade in at the beginning or out at the end.

Figure 11-5:
The solid-
colored
background
will be
transparent,
but the cat
will remain.

Shooting video against a bluescreen

Professional moviemakers shoot subjects against solid blue or solid green screens to make compositing easy. If you want to do some compositing, you need to shoot your subjects against a solid-colored background as well. Here are some tips for choosing a background and shooting the video:

- ✔ Try to pick a color that contrasts sharply with everything else in the video image. It's not absolutely mandatory that you use a blue or green screen, but if you use a solid-white background and then try to make the color white transparent, parts of your subject that are white or almost white will become transparent as well.

- ✔ Light the backdrop as brightly and evenly as possible. Even if you have slight lighting variations over the backdrop, the camcorder will pick up those variations as different colors, making it more difficult to control transparency.

- ✔ If you don't want to slather bright-blue paint all over your walls, consider buying a big roll of blue picnic table covering from your local party supply store. Party stores sell picnic table coverings in all kinds of bright, obnoxious colors. Picnic table covering can be stapled or glued to a simple wood frame or sheets of plywood. Another option is bright blue cloth from a local fabric store. Cloth is less likely to show unwanted reflections or form permanent wrinkles that cause reflections to get even worse over time.

- ✔ Frame the video image carefully. You may find that your bluescreen needs to cover the floor as well as the background wall. When you shoot, make sure the bluescreen fills the entire video frame. Also, plan your shoots carefully to ensure that subjects in the background and bluescreen clips don't overlap. For example, notice that, in Figure 11-5, I positioned the cat toward the left of the video frame, whereas, in Figure 11-6, my kids are to the right. This allows the scene to come together properly.

Compositing video tracks

Shooting video against a bluescreen is the hard part. After you have some good video footage to work with, actually putting the compositing effect together is easy. Follow these steps:

1. **Place the background clip in the Video 1 track of the timeline.**

   In Figure 11-6, I have placed a clip showing a typical Saturday morning scene from the local soccer fields. The scene is about to become a lot less typical.

2. **Place the bluescreen clip in track Video 2 or higher.**

   Of course, your clip may not have been shot against a bluescreen, but this should be whatever clip you want to superimpose over the background clip. I am placing the clip from Figure 11-5 in track Video 2.

3. **Open the Keying category under Video Effects in the Effects and Transitions window.**

   If you don't see the Effects and Transitions window, choose Window➪Effects. The Keying category contains several different keying effects.

Figure 11-6:
Another lovely day at the soccer field.

4. **Click and drag the Chroma key effect from the Transitions and Effects window and drop it on your clip in the Video 2 track.**

   Why not use the Blue Screen Key or the Green Screen Key if you shot your video against a blue or green screen? Unless you shot your video in a professional-quality studio, complete with professional-quality lighting, a professional-quality backdrop, and professional-quality catering, the Blue Screen and Green Screen Keys probably won't work. Those keys depend on there being an exact, perfectly uniform shade of blue or green in the background, something that is difficult to achieve on a limited budget. The Chroma Key is easier to use because it works with a broader color range.

5. **Click the clip in track Video 2 to select it, and then choose Window⇨Properties to open the Properties window for that clip.**

   You should see the Chroma Key effect listed in the clip's Properties window. Also, make sure that the timeline's play head is somewhere over the Video 2 clip.

6. **Click the arrow next to Chroma Key to expand its controls as shown in Figure 11-7.**

Figure 11-7: It's Catzilla! Run for your lives!!

Soccer field clip   Cat against bluescreen clip   Adjust Chroma Key settings

7. **Click the eyedropper button next to the Color control, and then move the mouse pointer over the video image in the Monitor window.**

   When you hover over the video image, the mouse pointer should become an eyedropper.

8. **Click an area of color that is typical of the background color that you want to key out.**

   The background may or may not disappear. If the whole background does instantly disappear, congratulations! You are done. However, it's more likely that only a few specs of the image became transparent.

9. **Click and drag right on the Similarity number to key out colors similar to the one you picked.**

   Increasing Similarity simply allows Premiere Elements to key out a greater range of color. If you keep increasing this number, eventually the whole image will disappear.

   If increasing Similarity doesn't key out enough of the background, try using the color eyedropper again and click on a different spot of the background. Try to click on a spot that is most similar to the rest of the background.

10. **Adjust the Blend, Threshold, and Cutoff controls.**

    The Blend control blends the overlaid image with the image underneath. The Threshold and Cutoff controls adjust how shadows appear in the superimposed image. By playing with these controls, you may be able to key out more of the background without further increasing the Similarity setting.

11. **Choose a Smoothing settling.**

    If the edges of your subject appear blocky after keying out the background, choose a Smoothing option. Smoothing uses anti-aliasing to smooth the edges of your subject.

12. **Play the timeline to preview your composite effect.**

No children, soccer balls, or stunt cats were harmed in the making of this movie.

Chapter 12

Working with Still Photos and Graphics

In This Chapter

▶ Getting still photos ready for use in your movies

▶ Importing stills into your video-editing program

▶ Using stills in a project

▶ Making still photos from frames of video

According to *Webster's New World Dictionary,* the word *movie* is actually a contraction of the term "moving picture." A series of still frames flash by so fast that they give the illusion that onscreen subjects are moving. Cool!

Sometimes, however, you may want to stop the illusion of motion and just show a still photo for a few seconds. You can do this easily, and in this chapter I show you how. I also show how to take single frames of video and turn them into still images that you can print out or use on a Web page. In the next section, I get you started by showing how to prepare still photos for use in movies.

Preparing Still Photos for Video

If you have a still photo that you want to use in your movie, you may be tempted to quickly import it and drop it in the timeline. I don't recommend this: There's a good chance that the still photo won't look very good. If you don't take the time to prepare your stills properly, two main problems can result:

✔ Images may become distorted and look unnaturally stretched or squeezed.

✔ Colors might not display properly.

The following sections help you prepare and use still graphics in your movies.

Adjusting the image size

In Chapter 3, I mention the concept of aspect ratios in video. To briefly recap, the *aspect ratio* describes the basic shape of the video image. (Figure 3-3 in Chapter 3 shows the difference between two common aspect ratios.) Most video images have an aspect ratio of 4:3, which means the width and height of the image can be divided into a 4:3 ratio.

When you take a picture using a digital still camera, that picture usually has an aspect ratio of 4:3 as well. Image sizes that have a 4:3 aspect ratio include 640 x 480, 800 x 600, and 1024 x 768. Your computer's monitor also probably has a 4:3 aspect ratio unless you have a newer widescreen monitor. Most TVs still have a 4:3 aspect ratio as well. Because the 4:3 aspect ratio is so common, dropping an 800 x 600 digital photo into a DV-based video project should be easy, right?

Unfortunately, it's not always that easy.

Digital images are made up of *pixels,* which are tiny little blocks of color that, when arranged in a grid, make up a picture. Pixels can have different aspect ratios too. Digital graphics usually have square pixels, whereas video usually has rectangular pixels. The frame size of NTSC video is usually listed as 720 x 480 pixels. This does not work out to 4:3; it's actually 3:2. However, it still *appears* to have a 4:3 aspect ratio because NTSC video pixels are slightly taller than they are wide.

What does all this mean? Suppose you place an uncorrected digital picture into a video program, and then you export that program back to tape. When you view the movie on a TV, the still image appears distorted. To correct this, you need to start with a digital photo that has an aspect ratio of 4:3, and then (depending on your local broadcast video standard) change the image size to

- ✔ 720 x 534 pixels (NTSC)
- ✔ 768 x 576 pixels (PAL)

Use the size that matches your local broadcast video standard (see Chapter 3 for more on video standards). Before you convert an image to one of these sizes, it should have an aspect ratio of 4:3. Common 4:3 image sizes include 800 x 600, 1024 x 768, and 1600 x 1200.

Again, you only need to convert the still image sizes if you plan to export the movie back to tape or DVD. If your movie will only be watched over the Web, you don't need to convert the image. The exact steps you should use to adjust the image size vary depending on the image-editing program you are using, but in most programs, they work something like this:

1. **Open the picture in your picture-editing program.**

   In this example, I use Adobe Photoshop.

2. **Open the dialog box that controls the image size in your software.**

   In Adobe Photoshop, choose Image➪Image Size.

3. **Remove the check mark next to the Constrain Proportions option.**

   Most editing programs have a similar constraining option (such as Constrain Size). Make sure it's disabled.

4. **Change the image size to 720 x 534 if you're working with NTSC video, or 768 x 576 if you're working with PAL video.**

   In Figure 12-1, I have changed the image size to 720 x 534 for NTSC video.

5. **Click OK and save the image as a JPEG image file.**

   Save the image using the JPEG format because it can then be used in just about any video-editing program. If your picture-editing software gives you a quality option when you save an image as a JPEG, choose the highest quality possible if the image will be used in a movie program. Other versatile formats include BMP, PICT, and TIFF, but you should check the help system for your video-editing program to see which formats are supported.

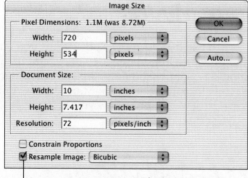

Figure 12-1:
Use image-editing software to adjust the size of your picture.

Deselect this check box

Although the image may look slightly distorted after you change the size, don't worry: It will look right when viewed with the rest of your video. Just remember that you only have to perform this modification if you plan to export the movie back to tape. If you plan to use your movie only on computer screens (or share it over the Internet), you don't need to change the aspect ratio of the image.

Getting the colors just right

In Chapter 3, I describe how TV screens and computer monitors don't show colors exactly the same way. The biggest problem is that some colors in computer graphics simply cannot appear on a TV. These colors are often called *illegal* or *out-of-gamut* colors. Although this isn't a super-serious problem, you should still fix any out-of-gamut colors in your images before using them in video programs.

Unfortunately, the ability to easily fix out of gamut colors is usually only found in more advanced, expensive video-editing programs. Adobe Photoshop, which retails for about $600, is one such program. To fix the colors in an image, simply open the picture in Photoshop and choose Filter⇨Video⇨NTSC Colors. This filter removes all colors from the image that are out of gamut for NTSC TVs. A lower-cost option that also enables you to fix out-of-gamut colors is Photoshop Elements, which is available for a much more affordable price of about $100. You might even be able to get it for free with some digital cameras.

If your image-editing program doesn't have a video color filter, I wouldn't lose too much sleep over it. But if it does, fix those out-of-gamut colors so that the image looks better in the final video program.

Using Stills in Your Movie

Still images are pretty easy to use in your movies. Basically, you import the image file, drop it into the timeline (just like a video clip), and then decide how long the still clip should remain onscreen. A lot of video programs use five seconds as a default time for still-image display, but you can easily change that yourself. The next few sections show you how to use stills in iMovie and Studio.

Using pictures in Apple iMovie

Apple's iMovie makes it easy to quickly use almost any picture on your computer in a movie project. Supported still-image formats include GIF, JPEG, PICT, TIFF, and BMP. The following sections show you how to import and use stills in your movies. I start by showing you how to use iPhoto — an important step because iMovie uses iPhoto for organizing stills.

Organizing photos with iPhoto

In the interest of simplification, iMovie uses Apple iPhoto for organizing still photos. This makes a lot of sense if you think about it; these two programs work together pretty seamlessly. If you already use iPhoto to organize your still images, you can move on to the next section. But if you haven't used iPhoto yet, you'll need to before you can use stills in iMovie. For more on using iPhoto, check out *iLife All-in-One Desk Reference For Dummies* by Tony Bove and Cheryl Rhodes, published by Wiley Publishing, Inc. In iPhoto, you can begin organizing your stills:

1. **Launch iPhoto by clicking its icon on the OS X Dock.**

   Alternatively, you can open it from the Applications folder on your hard drive.

2. **Choose File⇨Import.**

   The Import Photos dialog box appears, as shown in Figure 12-2.

3. **Browse to the folder that contains the picture or pictures that you want to import.**

4. **Select the picture and click Import.**

   To select multiple pictures, hold down the ⌘ key while clicking each picture file you want to import.

5. **The picture appears in the iPhoto library, as shown in Figure 12-2.**

   After the picture is imported into iPhoto, it's ready for use in iMovie as well.

6. **You can now quit iPhoto if you want by pressing ⌘+Q.**

Figure 12-2:
Locate the picture file that you want to import into iPhoto.

Using images in your movie project

iMovie can use any picture that has been imported into iPhoto. It's not mandatory that you import the photo into iPhoto first, but I recommend it because iPhoto is such a great way to organize your images. To use images from your iPhoto library in iMovie:

1. **Open iMovie and the movie project in which you want to use a still image.**

2. **Click the Photos button.**

   A collection of pictures that looks eerily similar to your iPhoto library appears in the iMovie window, as shown in Figure 12-3. If you've gone to the trouble of organizing photos into different albums in iPhoto, you can switch between those albums using the menu above the image browser.

3. **Click the clip that you want to use in the movie to select it.**

4. **Adjust the duration of the clip using the duration slider, which bears the images of a little tortoise and hare.**

   The default duration for a still clip is five seconds, but if you want it to display for less time, move the slider toward the bunny, er, I mean hare. If you want the clip to appear slow and steady, move the slider toward the tortoise.

   At about this time, you'll probably notice that your still graphic is moving in that little preview window in the upper-right corner of the screen. You'll also notice the Ken Burns Effect option just above. No, the Ken Burns Effect doesn't make Ken's smiling mug appear in your movie. It makes the camera appear to slowly zoom in or out on the still image, providing a visual continuity of movement that is otherwise broken by using a still image amongst moving video clips. (Ken Burns, the well-known documentary filmmaker responsible for such films as *The Civil War*, uses this trademark effect in a lot of his films.) If you don't want to use the Ken Burns Effect, remove the check mark next to this option.

5. **Click the Start radio button near the top of the screen.**

   This allows you to adjust the zoom level at the beginning of the clip.

6. **Adjust the Zoom slider.**

   If you don't want to zoom in on the image at all, drag the slider all the way to the left so that the zoom factor says 1.00.

7. **Click the Finish radio button near the top of the screen.**

   This allows you to adjust the zoom level at the end of the clip.

8. **Adjust the Zoom slider again.**

9. **Click Preview to preview the results of the effect.**

   If you aren't happy with the effect, continue tweaking the zoom settings and previewing the results.

10. **When you're done making adjustments, drag the clip and drop it down on the timeline or storyboard to insert it in your movie.**

You can still adjust clips after they have been dropped into the timeline or storyboard. Select the clip, click the Photos button, and then adjust the duration or other attributes in the Photos panel. Click Apply when you're done making changes.

Using pictures in Windows Movie Maker

Windows Movie Maker treats still pictures much like any other piece of media, such as video and audio clips. Before you import a still clip into Movie Maker, however, I recommend that you create a new collection just for stills. This will help you keep your media better organized. To create a new collection in Movie Maker,

Figure 12-3: The iMovie Ken Burns Effect lets you add some apparent motion to your still pictures.

Drop still image here

1. **Choose View➪Collections.**

   The Collections pane appears on the left side of the screen.

2. **Right-click Collections in the Collections pane and choose New Collection as shown in Figure 12-4.**

   A new collection named New Collection is added to your list of collections.

3. **Right-click the new collection and choose Rename.**

4. **Type a new name for your collection.**

   I recommend that you name it Still Photos or something similar.

Right-click here.

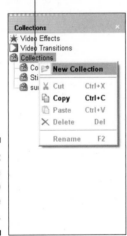

Figure 12-4:
Create a collection to organize your stills.

After you've created a new collection to house your still images, you can import some pictures. Choose View➪Task Pane to open the Tasks list on the left side of the screen, and then click Import Pictures. Use the Import File dialog box to find and import pictures. After they are imported, pictures can be added to the timeline or storyboard by a simple drag-and-drop operation, as shown in Figure 12-5.

As with most video-editing programs, the default duration for a still photo in Windows Movie Maker is five seconds. You can change the duration by clicking and dragging an edge of the still image in the timeline.

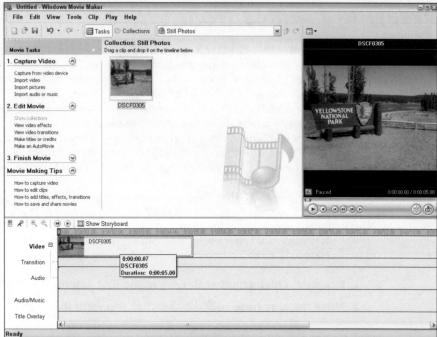

Figure 12-5:
Drag and
drop stills to
the timeline
in Movie
Maker.

Using pictures in Premiere Elements

Importing and using still pictures in Adobe Premiere Elements couldn't get much easier. To import a still picture, choose File➪Add Media➪From Files or Folders. Browse to the file you want to add and double-click it to import the picture into the Premiere Elements Media window. Simply click and drag the clip to add it to the timeline.

Premiere Elements gives you a handy way to control the duration of a still image. The default duration is five seconds. To change the duration, right-click the still image in the timeline and choose Time Stretch from the menu that appears. In the Time Stretch dialog box (Figure 12-6), click and drag left to shorten the duration, or drag right to lengthen the duration.

Figure 12-6:
Use this
dialog box
to change
the duration
of still
images.

Freezing Frames from Video

In the first half of this chapter, I showed you how to turn still photos into movies. Now I'm going to show you how to turn movies into still photos. There are a lot of good reasons to do this. For example, still images from scenes in your movie — also called *frame grabs* — work great on DVD menus, disc labels, or a Web site promoting your movie. And of course, sometimes a video clip is the only visual record you have of an event. In Figure 12-7, for example, I am grabbing a frame of video I shot of a bison. I had the camcorder in my hand when I shot this, not my still camera, so this is the only good close-up that I have of a bison.

Keep in mind, however, that the resolution of video images is really, really low compared to even the cheapest digital cameras, so frame grabs from video will always offer relatively low quality. The lower quality is especially apparent if you print the frame grab because image details will look blocky and pixelated. To freeze a frame of video and turn it into a still picture,

1. **Open the video clip that has the frame that you want to freeze.**

2. **Move the play head to the frame that you want to freeze.**

Figure 12-7: Locate the frame that you want to freeze.

Use the arrow keys (Alt+Arrow in Windows Movie Maker) to move forward or back a single frame at a time. You may have to hunt around a bit to find a good frame; you may find that one frame is blurry, but the next frame looks great.

3. **Grab the frame.**

   In Apple iMovie, choose File⇨Save Frame As.

   In Windows Movie Maker, choose Tools⇨Take Picture from Preview.

   In Premiere Elements, choose File⇨Export⇨Frame.

4. **Save the frame.**

   In iMovie, name the picture and choose a format in the Format menu. The available formats are JPEG and PICT, but if you're not sure which format to choose, I recommend JPEG.

   In Movie Maker, name and save the file. JPEG is the only format offered by Movie Maker.

   In Premiere Elements, click Settings in the Export Frame dialog box. The Export Frame Settings dialog box appears. Choose a format from the File Type menu (I recommend JPEG). Now click Video on the left side of the dialog box, and choose quality settings. As you can see in Figure 12-8, I am exporting a JPEG and I have changed the Quality slider to 100% because I don't want to lose any more quality than is necessary. Click OK to close the Export Frame Settings dialog box, and then name and save your file.

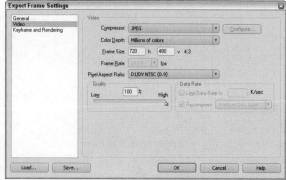

Figure 12-8: Choose an export format for the frame grab.

Chapter 13

Wrapping Up Your Movie

George Lucas once said, "Movies are never finished, they are abandoned." Video editing is addictive, and you may find that after you start working on your movie, it is hard to stop. But eventually other people are going to want to see what you've done, and that means you have to stop sometime.

Will your finished movie be perfect? No, probably not. Perfection is rarely achieved. But you can get close, and this chapter shows you how to best preview your movie to figure out just how close to perfect it really is. I also show you how to export your movie in AVI format from Movie Maker, and in MPEG format from Movie Maker, just in case you want to keep a high-quality archive of the movie or you want to edit it in another program.

Previewing the Movie

To preview your movie, click Play in the preview window of your editing program. The End.

Okay, you've probably guessed that there's a little more to previewing than just clicking Play, because we still have a whole chapter to go. First of all, you probably want to see a bigger preview than what is shown in the tiny little preview monitor of your editing program. If you want to see a bigger preview,

✔ **Apple iMovie:** Click the Play Movie Fullscreen button shown in Figure 13-1.

✔ **Adobe Premiere Elements:** Premiere doesn't make it easy to get a full-screen preview. You can choose 100% from the View Zoom Level menu under the preview screen in the Monitor window, but all this does is zoom in on the image. You have to manually click and drag the edges of the Monitor window to make it bigger so that you can actually see the larger view.

✔ **Windows Movie Maker:** Click Play and then press Alt+Enter to switch to a full-screen preview. Press Alt+Enter again to return to the regular editing window.

Of course, truly previewing a movie means a whole lot more than just clicking the Play button. To perform a truly effective preview, you must

✔ Draw a properly critical eye on the movie.

✔ Decide whether just previewing the movie on your computer screen is sufficient, or whether you need to preview it on a TV monitor.

Figure 13-1:
Click the Play Movie Fullscreen button in iMovie for an even bigger preview.

Click to play movie fullscreen.

The next two sections address both of these subjects. Brew that coffee, sit back in your director's chair, and get ready to see what kind of movie magic you hath wrought.

You should also make sure that you preview your movie on the same type of equipment that your audience will use. This includes testing it in the player software that your audience will use if you plan to share your movie on the Internet or a recordable CD.

Casting a critical eye on your project

Clicking Play and watching your movie may sound easy, but it's easy to get sidetracked in the wrong direction as you preview. To ensure that you get the most out of your preview, pop yourself some popcorn and follow these tips:

- **Watch the whole program from start to finish.** You may be tempted to periodically stop playback, reverse, and repeat sections, or perhaps even make tweaks to the project as you run it. This is fine, but to get a really good "feeling" for the flow of the movie, watch the whole thing start to finish — just as your audience will. Keep a notepad handy and jot down quick notes if you must.

- **Watch the program on an external TV.** If you plan to record your movie on videotape or DVD, previewing on an external monitor is very helpful. (See the next section in this chapter for a more detailed explanation.)

- **Have trusted third parties review the project.** Moviemakers and writers are often too close to their creations to be totally objective; an "outside" point of view can help a lot. Although I worked hard to write this book (for example), my work was reviewed by various editors, and their feedback was invaluable. Movie projects benefit from a similar review process. Even if you want to maintain strict creative control over your project, feedback from people who were not involved with creating it can help you see it afresh.

Previewing on an external monitor

Your editing software has a preview window, and at first glance it probably seems to work well enough. But if you plan to record your movie on videotape or DVD, just previewing it on the computer screen can cause a couple of problems:

- **TVs usually provide a bigger view.** A larger TV screen reveals camera movements and other flaws that might not be obvious in the tiny preview window on your computer screen.

✔ **Computer monitors and TVs show color differently.** Colors that look right on your computer may not look the same on a TV.

✔ **Most TVs are interlaced.** As I described in Chapter 3, TVs are usually interlaced, whereas computer monitors are progressively scanned, or non-interlaced. Titles or other graphics that have very thin lines may look fine on your computer monitor, but when viewed on a TV, those thin lines may flicker or appear to shimmer or crawl.

In Chapter 2, I show you how to connect a TV to your computer for previewing video. The cheapest option is to connect your digital camcorder to your FireWire port, and then connect the TV to the analog output on your camcorder. If you have an analog video capture card in your computer, you can connect your TV (and VCR) to the analog outputs for the card.

Apple iMovie makes previewing your work on an external TV monitor very easy. In iMovie, choose iMovie➪Preferences. The iMovie Preferences dialog box appears as shown in Figure 13-2. Place a check mark next to Play Video Through to Camera under Advanced options. Now that this option is enabled, whenever you play the timeline, the video is sent out to your camcorder if it is connected to your FireWire port and turned on in Player or VTR mode. If you have a TV monitor hooked up to the camcorder's analog outputs, the video image should appear there as well.

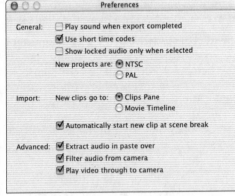

Figure 13-2:
Enable the
Play Video
Through to
Camera
option in
iMovie's
preferences.

Windows Movie Maker doesn't allow you to preview your movie on an external TV monitor, but Premiere Elements does. In fact, in Premiere Elements, there are no settings or special buttons to worry about. If your camcorder or monitor is connected to your computer's FireWire or USB 2.0 port and the device's power is turned on, your movie automatically plays on the external device when you play the timeline.

Exporting Your Movie

After about the millionth preview, you'll probably come to the realization that your movie is about as good as it's ever going to get. If you come up with some bright ideas later, you can always release a "Director's Cut," but for now it's time to wrap up your movie and export it.

When you decide that it's time to finish your project, you must export the movie so that others can view it. Before you export your movie, you must decide in which format you wish to export. After you've edited your movie in a program like Movie Maker or iMovie, you aren't limited to showing your work to others on your computer. You have many options with which to share your movie:

- ✔ **Videotape:** Almost everyone you know probably has a VCR that plays VHS tapes. Sure, the quality and gee-whiz factor of VHS tapes isn't as high as DVD, but most of your audience really won't care. In fact, you may find that VHS tapes are still preferred by some of your, uh, "technology-challenged" friends and family. If you have an analog capture card, you can connect a VCR directly to your computer and export your movie directly to a VHS tape. Otherwise export the movie back to a tape in your digital camcorder, and then dub the movie from the camcorder tape to a VCR. (Chapter 15 explains the process of exporting to tape in greater detail.)

- ✔ **DVD:** The DVD (Digital Versatile Disc) player has supplanted the VCR as the home video player of choice for many people. Tens of millions of households have DVD players in their home entertainment systems, and many modern computers can play DVD movies as well. DVD recorders are now affordable and widely available, so making your own DVDs is pretty easy. See Chapter 16 for details.

- ✔ **Internet:** The Internet is a popular place to share video, but remember that video files are usually very big and a majority of people still have relatively slow Internet connections. If you plan to export your movie for use on the Internet, use a Web-friendly format such as Apple QuickTime, RealNetworks RealVideo, or Windows Media Video. These formats usually have fairly low quality, but the trade-off is much smaller file sizes. When choosing one of these formats, make sure that your intended audience has software that can play your movies. See Chapter 14 for more on exporting your movie for Internet use.

- ✔ **Video file:** Some programs allow you to simply save the movie as a file. Common video file formats include AVI and MPEG. These files can be stored on your computer, or burned onto a CD so that others can watch your movie on their computers as well. Just remember that the AVI and MPEG formats are generally too big for anyone but broadband users to access online. AVI or MPEG files are useful, however, if you plan to edit the movie further using another editing program.

Decoding codecs

Digital video contains a lot of data. If you were to copy uncompressed digital video onto your hard drive, it would consume 20MB (megabytes) for every second of video. Simple arithmetic tells us that every minute of uncompressed video would use over 1GB. Dire though this may seem, storage isn't even the biggest problem with uncompressed video. Typical hard drive busses and other components in your computer simply can't handle a transfer rate of 20MB per second, meaning that some video frames will be dropped from the video. Dropped frames are described in greater detail in Chapter 5.

To deal with the massive bandwidth requirements of video, digital video is compressed using compression schemes called *codecs* (*compressor/decompressor*). The DV codec, which is used by most digital camcorders, compresses video down to 3.6MB per second. This data rate is far more manageable than uncompressed video,

and most modern computer hardware can handle it without trouble. When you capture DV video from a camcorder using a FireWire interface, a minute of video consumes just over 200MB of hard drive space. Again, most modern computers can manage that.

Why do codecs matter to you? When you choose a file format for exporting your movie, you're also usually choosing a codec to compress your movie (whether you realize it or not). Usually your export software automatically chooses a codec for you, such as when you export AVI or MPEG files. Sometimes you can choose and adjust codecs as well. Some codecs compress video more than others. Generally speaking, the more video is compressed, the more quality you lose. In most cases, I recommend you use the default codec chosen by Premiere (or whatever program you are using) when you select an export format.

If you're using Apple iMovie, QuickTime is the only file format available for export. In Chapter 14, I show you how to export your movie in QuickTime format.

When you export your movie, your editing program renders any edits that you made to the project. *Rendering* is the process of creating full-quality preview files of your edits. Simple edits like titles and basic dissolve transitions render in mere seconds, whereas more advanced edits such as picture-in-picture effects or 3-D transitions may take longer. Likewise, if you export your movie in a different format — for example, a smaller, lower-quality QuickTime movie for viewing on the Internet — the editing program must render a version of your movie in that format. You don't have to do anything special during the rendering process but wait.

The next couple of sections show how to export video from Windows Movie Maker and Adobe Premiere Elements.

Exporting AVI files from Movie Maker

If you're using Windows Movie Maker, you can export in AVI or Windows Media Video formats. AVI files are useful if you want to export your video in another program, or if you just want to keep a high-quality digital archive of your movie. To export your movie to an AVI file:

1. **Choose View⇨Task Pane to reveal the task pane on the left side of the screen.**

2. **Under Finish Movie in the task pane, click Save to My Computer.**

   The Save Movie Wizard appears.

3. **Type a name for your movie file in step 1, choose a location in which to save the file in step 2, and click Next.**

   If you're not sure where to save the file just use the default location, which is the My Videos folder in your My Documents folder.

4. **Click Show More Choices under Movie Settings.**

5. **Choose the Other Settings radio button, and then choose DV-AVI in the Other Settings menu.**

   As you can see in Figure 13-3, the Setting Details and Movie File Size boxes at the bottom of the Save Movie Wizard show you details about your file. The DV-AVI option saves video at maximum quality.

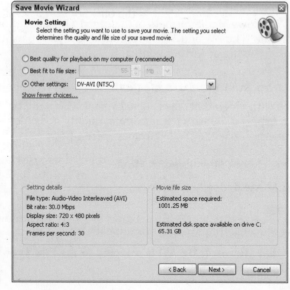

Figure 13-3:
Use the
Save Movie
Wizard to
save movies
as AVI files.

6. **When you are satisfied with the settings, click Next.**

    The export process begins as Movie Maker saves your movie. It will probably take a few minutes, depending on the length of your movie.

AVI is a good format to use if you want to export video for many Windows-based video-editing programs, including Adobe Premiere Elements, but you may find that some editing programs prefer MPEG. Pinnacle's Hollywood FX Pro, for example, works better with MPEG-format video. And of course, if you plan to use the exported file on a Mac, you'll find that the MPEG format is much more compatible with Mac multimedia software. Windows Movie Maker cannot export MPEG video, but Adobe Premiere Elements can. I show how later in this chapter.

If you aren't sure whether you have a specific need for one format or the other, it probably doesn't matter very much which one you choose. AVI files are usually a little bigger than MPEG files, but as I said earlier, if you're concerned about file sizes — say, for example, you plan to share the movie on the Internet — you really ought to be exporting the movie in a Web-friendly format like Windows Media Video. See Chapter 14 for more on exporting for the Web.

Exporting video from Premiere Elements

Advanced editing programs like Adobe Premiere Elements usually give you many export options. Premiere Elements can export video in AVI, MPEG, QuickTime, Windows Media Video, and several other formats. I cover the QuickTime and Windows Media formats in Chapter 14 because those are Web-friendly formats. The AVI and MPEG formats allow you to export high-quality video for archiving or further editing.

Exporting AVI files from Premiere Elements

If you're working with video that was originally shot with a digital camcorder and you want to export a file with the maximum quality possible — and file size is not a concern — use the DV-AVI format. Here's how:

1. **In Premiere, choose File➪Export➪Movie.**

    The Export Movie dialog box appears.

2. **Click Settings.**

    The Export Movie Settings dialog box appears.

3. **Make sure that Microsoft DV AVI is selected in the File Type menu, and then click Compile Settings.**

4. **In the AVI Compile Options dialog box (Figure 13-4), choose which timeline markers you want to export with the movie, and then click OK to close the dialog box.**

   If you created any timeline markers in your project, you can choose whether you want them to be exported with the movie here. Your markers may come in handy later. For more on working with markers, check out my book *Adobe Premiere Elements For Dummies* (Wiley Publishing, Inc.).

Figure 13-4: Choose whether you want to export markers.

5. **Select Video on the left side of the Export Movie Settings dialog box, and review video settings for your movie file.**

   The video settings should match the original source video that you were working with. For example, if you shot 4:3 "full-screen" video with a DV camcorder using the NTSC video format (see Chapter 3 for more on video formats, frame rates, and aspect ratios), your settings should look like those in Figure 13-5.

   I recommend that you leave the Keyframe and Rendering settings alone for now. Generally speaking, it is safest to just use the default Keyframe and Rendering settings provided by Premiere Elements.

Figure 13-5: Review video export settings for your movie.

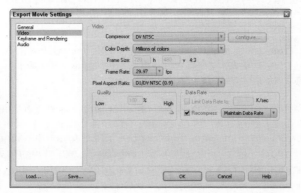

6. **Click Audio on the left side of the Export Movie Settings dialog box, and review audio settings for your movie file.**

   Audio has a huge effect on the size of file you export, but I recommend that you use the highest-possible settings here. This means exporting with a sample rate of 48,000Hz, a 16-bit sample type, and Stereo audio. Alternatively, if you don't want to export audio at all with your movie, click General on the left side of the Export Movie Settings dialog box and remove the check mark next to Export Audio.

7. **Click OK to close the Export Movie Settings dialog box.**

8. **In the Export Movie dialog box, enter a name for your movie file and select a location in which to save it.**

9. **Click Save.**

   Premiere Elements renders and exports your movie. The process may take a few minutes, depending on the size of your movie.

Exporting MPEGs from Premiere Elements

Adobe Premiere Elements can export your movies in many formats, including MPEG. I like the MPEG format because it is easy to use and — most importantly — widely supported among Mac and PC users. MPEG is actually a family of multimedia file standards. There are currently four MPEG standards:

- ✔ **MPEG-1:** This is the oldest version of the standard. A drawback of MPEG-1 is that it has a maximum picture size of 352 x 240 pixels.

- ✔ **MPEG-2:** This standard offers much higher video quality and full-size video. In fact, MPEG-2 is the format used by DVD movies, so if you burn your movies onto DVD, this is the format you'll use. (I cover burning your own DVDs in Chapter 16.) MPEG-2 files require special MPEG-2 player software, such as a DVD player program.

- ✔ **MPEG-3:** Usually abbreviated MP3 (you may have heard of it), this file format only contains audio and is a popular file format for music files today.

- ✔ **MPEG-4:** This newer standard is a cross of MPEG video and Apple QuickTime to produce video with very, very small file sizes. Support for this format is still limited.

Premiere Elements simplifies the MPEG creation process by offering export presets tailored to various kinds of media. To view the presets, click Export on the Premiere Elements toolbar and choose MPEG from the menu that appears. The Export MPEG dialog box appears as shown in Figure 13-6. The presets are divided into four categories:

- ✔ **DVD Compatible:** This is the highest-quality option, and it creates DVD-quality video. The settings in this preset roughly mirror the specifications for DV-quality video shot with a digital camcorder. Choose the

NTSC or PAL preset based on the type of video you are working with. Keep in mind that if you export a movie using this preset, Premiere Elements only creates a DVD-compatible file; it does not actually burn a DVD. If you want to record your movie to a DVD, see Chapter 16.

✔ **Multimedia Compatible:** These two presets create smaller, lower-quality MPEG files. The MPEG1 preset gives video quality similar that recorded by a standard, low-quality VHS VCR. MPEG2 video is a little better and more closely matches professionally-recorded VHS movies, but it is still well below DVD quality.

✔ **SVCD Compatible:** The SVCD (short for Super Video CD) presets create a file in NTSC or PAL format that is about halfway between the Multimedia and DVD presets in terms of quality. If you burn an SVCD movie onto a recordable CD, it will play in some — but not all — DVD players. An SVCD can hold about 20 minutes of video.

✔ **VCD Compatible:** Like SVCD, video that is burned onto a recordable CD in VCD (Video CD) format can play in some DVD players. VCD video quality is closer to the Multimedia presets, but a CD can hold up to an hour of video. VCD presets are available for NTSC and PAL video.

Although VCDs and SVCDs may sound like an exciting and affordable way to share video with your friends and family, keep in mind that many DVD players cannot play VCDs or SVCDs. Visit VideoHelp.com (`www.videohelp.com`) for compatibility lists that show which DVD players can and cannot play VCDs and SVCDs.

When you have chosen a preset for your MPEG, click OK in the Export MPEG dialog box. Give your file a filename and choose a location in which to save it in the Save File dialog box, and then click Save.

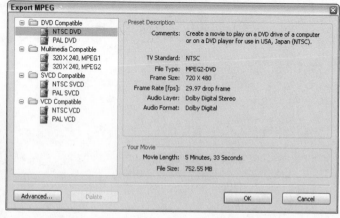

Figure 13-6:
Presets make it easy to export MPEG files.

Part IV
Sharing Your Video

The 5th Wave   By Rich Tennant

THE LEVINES EDIT THEIR AFRICAN SAFARI VIDEO

"Do you think the 'Hidden Rhino' clip should come before or after the 'Waving Hello' video clip?"

In this part . . .

When you are done editing your movie, it's time to share it with others. With digital video, sharing your movies has never been easier! This part shows you how to share your movies over the Internet, on videotape, or on DVD.

Chapter 14

Putting Your Movies on the Internet

Amateur moviemakers have been putting their friends and family to sleep with home movies for more than half a century now. Now thanks to the Internet, you no longer need to invite people over and feed them dinner before showing them your movies. You can now bore, er, I mean *entertain* a much broader audience than ever before by putting your movies online for all to see.

Of course, there are special challenges and considerations involved with sharing your movies online. The most important consideration is file size. Movie files are usually really big, and (believe it or not) a significant portion of Internet users still have slow dial-up modem connections. This means that big movie files take a long time to download, and the long download time might discourage your audience members from trying in the first place.

Fortunately, Apple iMovie, Adobe Premiere Elements, Windows Movie Maker, and most other modern video-editing programs help you export movies in small, Internet-friendly files. This chapter helps you prepare your movies for online use. I show you how to use the most efficient file formats so that your video files aren't too big, and I show you how to find an online home for your movies when they're ready to share.

Choosing a Video Format

Many different video formats are available for the movies you edit on your computer. Each format uses a different codec. (I explain codecs in greater detail in Chapter 13, but a codec, short for *compressor/decompressor,* is a software tool used for making multimedia files smaller.) Common video file formats include MPEG and AVI, but these two formats usually produce files that are too big to use online. Three other popular formats, however, are perfectly suited to the online world:

- ✔ **QuickTime (.QT):** Many Windows users and all Macintosh users have the QuickTime Player program from Apple. QuickTime is the only export format available with iMovie. Windows Movie Maker cannot export QuickTime movies, but Adobe Premiere Elements and many other advanced editing programs can.

- ✔ **RealMedia (.RM):** This is the format used by the RealNetworks RealPlayer, available for Windows and Macintosh systems, among others. RealMedia has declined in popularity in recent years, but many people still have and use RealPlayer. Pinnacle Studio and a few other editing programs can export RealMedia-format video, but iMovie, Premiere Elements and Windows Movie Maker cannot.

- ✔ **Windows Media Video (.WMV):** This format requires Windows Media Player. Virtually all Windows users and some Macintosh users already have it. Both Premiere Elements and Windows Movie Maker can export Windows Media Video.

Each of these three video formats has strengths and weaknesses. Ultimately the format you choose probably depends mainly on the editing software you're using — for example, if you're using iMovie on a Mac, QuickTime is your only option. Later in this chapter, I introduce you to the various software programs that are used to play these Web-friendly video formats.

Streaming your video

Doing stuff on the Internet usually means downloading files. For example, when you visit a Web page, files containing all the text and pictures on that Web page are first downloaded to your computer, and then your Web-browser program opens them. Likewise, if someone e-mails you a picture or a document with yucky work stuff, your e-mail program actually downloads a file before you open it.

Downloading files takes time, especially if they're big video files. You sit there and you wait. And wait. And wait. Finally the movie file is done downloading and starts to play, but by then you've left the room for a cup of coffee again. But software designers are crafty folk, and they've devised methods of getting around the problem of waiting a long time for downloads. They've come up with two basic solutions:

- ✔ **Streaming media:** Rather than downloading a file to your hard drive, streaming files can be played as the data streams through your modem. It works kind of like a radio, where "data" streams through in the form of radio waves, and that data is immediately played through the radio's speakers as it is received.

  With streaming audio or video, no file is ever saved on your hard drive. To truly stream your movies to other people, your movie files need to be on a special *streaming server* on the Web. There is a remote possibility that your Internet service provider offers a streaming media server, but most service providers do not.

- ✔ **Progressive download:** Newer video-player programs can "fake" streaming pretty effectively. Rather than receiving a movie signal broadcast over the Internet like a radio wave, viewers simply click a link to open the movie as if they were downloading the file. In fact, they *are* downloading the file — but as soon as enough of the file has been received (or *buffered,* as some programs call the process), the player program can start to play. The program doesn't need to wait for the whole file to download before it starts. Current versions of QuickTime, RealPlayer, and Windows Media Player all support progressive download.

  The really cool thing about progressive download is that you don't need any special kind of server to host the files. Just upload the video file to any server that has enough room to hold it.

I'm actually being kind of picky about terminology here. Many people now refer to progressive download video files as "streaming video," and because they basically function the same way, why not? The good news is that you don't need to do anything special to stream (or *progressively download,* or whatever you want to call it) your movies to your audience. Just output your movie in QuickTime, RealVideo, or Windows Media Video format, and let the player programs do the rest.

Comparing player programs

When you share your movie over the Internet, you're actually sharing a file. It is important that your intended audience can actually open that file, and that means your audience must have the right kind of software. The following sections introduce you to three common programs used for playing movies from the Internet.

QuickTime

Apple QuickTime (see Figure 14-1) is one of the most popular media players and has been around the longest, making it a good overall choice for your audience. QuickTime is available for Macintosh and Windows systems and is included with Mac OS X. QuickTime can play MPEG and QuickTime media. The QuickTime Player also supports progressive download, where files begin playing as soon as enough has been downloaded to allow continuous play-back. The free QuickTime Player is available for download at

www.apple.com/quicktime/download/

Figure 14-1:
Apple's
QuickTime is
one of the
most
common
and best
media
players
available.

Apple also offers an upgraded version of QuickTime called QuickTime Pro. QuickTime Pro costs about $30 (the regular QuickTime Player is free). Key features of QuickTime Pro include

✔ Full-screen playback

✔ Additional media management features

✔ Simple audio and video creation and export tools

✔ Advanced import/export options

If you already have iMovie (and therefore regular QuickTime), you don't absolutely need the extra features of QuickTime Pro. Your audience really doesn't need QuickTime Pro either (unless of course they want to watch movies in full screen). The standard QuickTime Player should suffice in most cases. Apple iMovie exports QuickTime-format files. If you're a Windows user, QuickTime Pro allows you to convert MPEG files to QuickTime format. Adobe Premiere Elements and some other advanced Windows video-editing pro-grams can also export files in QuickTime format.

RealPlayer

Another media player is RealPlayer from RealNetworks, shown in Figure 14-2. RealPlayer is available for Macintosh, Windows, and even Unix-based systems. The free RealPlayer software is most often used for RealMedia streaming media over the Internet, although it can also play MPEG-format media as well. More significantly, RealPlayer can play Windows Media and QuickTime video in addition to the RealMedia formats. This means that if you want to be able to use just one media player program for all movies — regardless of format — RealPlayer is probably the best choice.

Figure 14-2:
RealPlayer is another popular media player, often used for streaming media.

None of the programs featured in this book can export video in RealPlayer format, but Pinnacle Studio and a few others can. To download the free RealPlayer, visit

```
www.real.com/
```

RealNetworks offers other programs as well — and although they're not free, they offer additional features. RealNetworks has specialized in the delivery of streaming content, and they offer a variety of delivery options. You can use their software to run your own RealMedia streaming server, or you can outsource such "broadcast" duties to RealNetworks.

A complaint often heard about RealPlayer is that the software tends to be intrusive and resource-hungry once installed — and that the program itself collects information about your media-usage habits and sends that information to RealNetworks. These problems partially explain the decreasing popularity of RealPlayer in recent years. Although RealPlayer is still popular, consider that some folks out there simply refuse to install RealNetworks software on their computers. RealMedia is an excellent format, but I recommend that you offer your audience a choice of formats if you plan to use it; include (for example) QuickTime or Windows Media Video as well.

Windows Media Player

Microsoft's Windows Media Player (version 7 or newer) can play many common media formats. Windows Media Player comes pre-installed on modern computers that run Windows. Although the name says "Windows," versions of Windows Media Player are also available for Macintosh computers that run OS 8 or higher. Figure 14-3 shows Windows Media Player running in OS X. WMP is even available for Pocket PCs and countless other devices. WMP is available for free download at

`www.microsoft.com/windows/windowsmedia/download/`

Windows Media Player can play video in MPEG and AVI formats as well as the proprietary Windows Media formats. Windows Movie Maker and Adobe Premiere Elements are both capable of exporting Windows Media Video movies. I like the WMV format because it provides decent quality (for Web movies) with remarkably small file sizes.

Figure 14-3:
Windows
Media
Player is
required for
viewing
Windows
Media-
format
movies.

What are the compelling reasons for choosing Windows Media Video over other formats? Choose Windows Media as your format if

- ✔ **Most or all of your audience members use Windows.** Most Windows users already have Windows Media Player installed on their systems, so they won't have to download or install new software before viewing your Windows Media Video movie.

- ✔ **You want the look, but not the expense and complexity, of streaming media.** If you don't want to deal with the hassle of setting up and maintaining a streaming-media server, Windows Media format files can provide a workable compromise in the form of *progressive downloadable video:* When downloading files, Windows Media Player begins playing the movie as soon as enough of it is downloaded to ensure uninterrupted playback.

> ✔ **You're distributing your movie online and extremely small file size is more important than quality.** The Windows Media format can offer some very small file sizes, which is good if your audience will be downloading your movie over slow dial-up Internet connections. I recently placed a 3:23-long movie online in Windows Media format and the file size was only 5.5MB (megabytes). Of course, the movie was not broadcast quality, but because most of my friends and family still have slow dial-up modem connections to the Internet, they appreciated the relatively small download size.

Exporting Movies for the Online World

The Internet has been a place of rapidly shifting standards during the last couple of years, but QuickTime and Windows Media Video are emerging as the most popular formats for online video. Even if you like to be different, this is one instance where you probably want to follow the crowds. If you want people to watch your movie, you need to offer it in a format they can and will use. The following sections show how to export QuickTime movies using iMovie and Premiere Elements, and how to make Windows Media Video with Premiere and Windows Movie Maker.

Making QuickTime movies with iMovie

If you're using Apple iMovie and you want to make movies in QuickTime format, you're in luck. QuickTime is the only movie file format that iMovie can produce. QuickTime movies can be played using the QuickTime Player program, which is available for free for Windows and Macintosh systems. If you want to output in a different format, such as RealMedia, you'll need to use more advanced software such as Final Cut Express.

Exporting a QuickTime movie from iMovie is pretty simple. The QuickTime format offers a variety of quality and output settings that you can adjust, and iMovie provides several easy-to-use presets. You can also customize export settings if you wish. To export a QuickTime movie:

1. **When you're done editing your movie in iMovie, choose File➪Export.**

   The iMovie: Export dialog box appears, as shown in Figure 14-4.

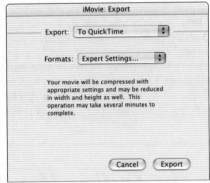

Figure 14-4:
Choose a
QuickTime
preset from
the Formats
menu, or
choose
Expert
Settings.

2. **Choose To QuickTime from the Export menu.**

3. **Choose the best preset for the way you plan to distribute your movie from the Formats menu.**

   iMovie provides three preset formats for export: Email, Web, and Web Streaming. Table 14-1 lists the specifications for each preset, as well as the CD-ROM and Full Quality DV presets. Unless your movie is very short, the CD-ROM and Full Quality DV presets generally produce files that are too big for online use. If you want to fine-tune your own settings, choose Expert Settings from the Formats menu.

4. **Click Export.**

   A Save Exported File As dialog box appears.

E-mailing your movies

The World Wide Web seems to get all the attention these days, but I think that e-mail, more than anything else, revolutionized the way we communicated during the last decade. Most of your friends, relatives, and business associates probably have e-mail addresses, and you probably exchange e-mail messages with those folks on a regular basis.

E-mail is already a great way to quickly share stories and pictures with others, and now that you're making your own movies, it only seems natural to start e-mailing your movie projects to friends as well. Before you do, keep in mind that movie files tend to be really big. Most e-mail accounts have file-size limitations for e-mail attachments, sometimes as low as 2MB. Other e-mail accounts don't allow any file attachments at all. And of course, many people still have slow dial-up modem connections to the Internet, meaning it will take them a long time to download a movie you send them.

If you want to e-mail a movie to someone, first ask the person whether it's okay to do so. Send an initial e-mail that says something like, "Hi there! I just finished a really awesome movie and I want to send it to you. The movie is in QuickTime format and the file is 1.3MB. Can I e-mail it to you?" Most people will probably say yes, and they'll appreciate that you took the time to ask.

5. **If you chose a preset format, give your movie a filename, choose a folder in which to save it, and click Save to save your movie to a file and finish the export process.**

   If you chose a preset format in step 3, you're done! But if you choose Expert Settings in the Formats menu, you still have a few more steps to complete in the export process. Your Save Exported File As dialog box looks like Figure 14-5, and you have some additional settings to adjust. At the bottom of the dialog box, you can choose presets from the Use menu, or click Options. If you click Options, the Movie Settings dialog box appears.

Figure 14-5: Name and save your movie file.

6. **(Optional) In the Movie Settings dialog box, leave the check marks next to Video and Sound if you want to include both in your movie.**

7. **(Optional) In the Movie Settings dialog box, click the Settings button under Video in the Movie Settings dialog box and adjust video settings.**

   The Compression Settings dialog box appears, as shown in Figure 14-6. Start by choosing a codec from the menu at the top of the dialog box. The Sorenson or H.263 codecs are pretty good for most movies, and the Motion JPEG A codec works well for movies that will be played on older computers. MPEG-4 — which I've chosen in Figure 14-6 — provides a superior balance of quality and compression, but viewers must have QuickTime 6 (or later) to play it.

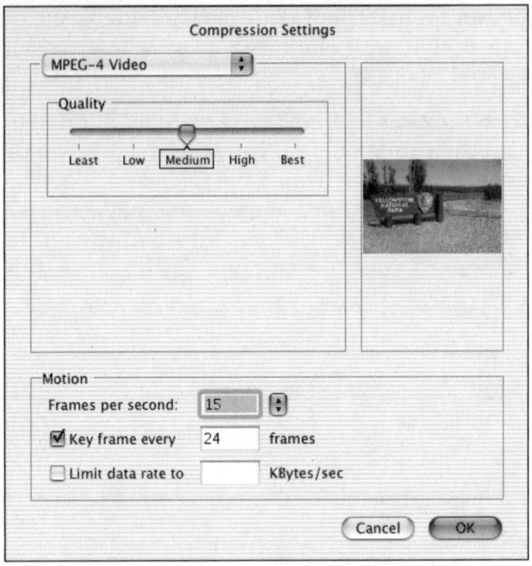

Figure 14-6:
Adjust video
compression
settings
here.

Adjust the Quality slider and preview how your video image will be affected. The Best quality setting provides better picture quality, but also increases the file size.

In the Frames Per Second field, you can choose a frame rate (in Figure 14-6, I've chosen 15 frames per second), or just choose Best from the menu to let iMovie automatically determine a good frame rate. More frames per second increase file size.

I recommend that you leave the Key Frame Every x Frames setting alone. (The default value is 24 — that is, a key frame occurs once every 24 frames — and a smaller number means *more* key frames.) Key frames help QuickTime compress and decompress the movie. More key frames provide better quality, but they also increase file size.

Click OK when you're done adjusting Compression Settings.

8. (Optional) In the Movie Settings dialog box, click the Filter button.

The Choose Video Filter dialog box appears. Here you can apply filters to your video image that can blur, sharpen, recolor, brighten, or perform a variety of other changes to the picture. Most filters also have adjustments that you can make using slider controls. A preview of your video image appears in the Choose Video Filter dialog box so that you can see the effects of the various filters. I don't usually find these filters very useful because normally I've already applied filters or effects to my video during the editing process. After making your selections, click OK to close the Choose Video Filter dialog box.

9. **(Optional) In the Movie Settings dialog box, click the Size button.**

   The Export Size Settings dialog box appears. Choose either Use Current Size, or choose Use Custom Size and enter a custom width and height in pixels. As shown in Table 14-1, a common frame size for Web movies is 240 pixels wide by 180 pixels high. Click OK to close the Export Size Settings dialog box.

10. **(Optional) In the Movie Settings dialog box, click the Settings button under Sound.**

    The Sound Settings dialog box appears as shown in Figure 14-7. For online movies, choose QDesign Music 2 in the Compressor menu. Reduce the sampling rate using the Rate box (for online use I recommend 22.050kHz or lower). Switching from Stereo to Mono also reduces the file size. Click OK to close the Sound Settings dialog box.

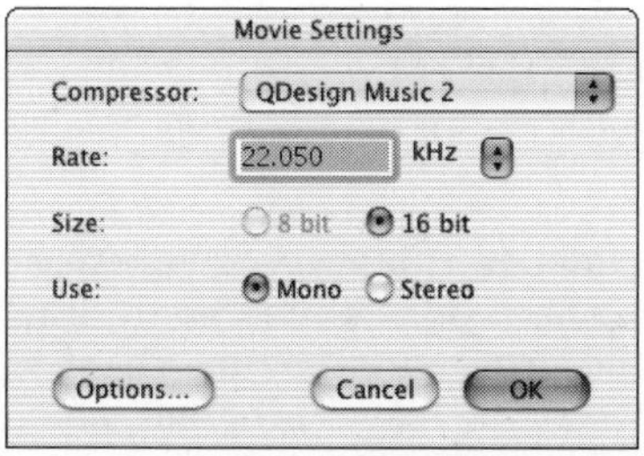

Figure 14-7:
Make sound
settings
here.

Movie Settings	
Compressor:	QDesign Music 2
Rate:	22.050 kHz
Size:	○ 8 bit ● 16 bit
Use:	● Mono ○ Stereo
Options...	Cancel OK

11. **(Optional) In the Movie Settings dialog box, leave the Prepare for Internet Streaming option checked if you want to take advantage of streaming or progressive download for this movie, and choose the Fast Start option in the Streaming menu.**

12. **Click OK to close the Movie Settings dialog box, and then click Save in the Save Exported File As dialog box.**

    The movie is exported using the settings you provided.

When the export process is complete, preview your movie in QuickTime, and check the file size of the movie. If the movie file is too big, re-export it using the lower quality settings (such as a smaller frame size, lower frame rate, or lower sample rate for the audio). If the movie is smaller than you expected, you may want to re-export it using slightly higher quality settings. When you're done, you can share your QuickTime movie file online by attaching it to an e-mail or placing it on a Web site. (Later in this chapter, I show you how to find and establish an online screening room for your movie.)

Table 14-1	iMovie QuickTime Export Presets		
Preset	*Frame Size (Pixels)*	*Frame Rate (Frames per Second)*	*Audio (Channels, Sample Rate)*
E-mail	160 x 120	9.99	Mono, 22.05kHz
Web	240 x 180	11.99	Stereo, 22.05kHz
Web streaming	240 x 180	11.99	Stereo, 22.05kHz
CD-ROM	320 x 240	14.99	Stereo, 44.1kHz
Full-Quality DV (NTSC)	720 x 480	29.97	Stereo, 32kHz

Exporting Windows Media from Movie Maker

Windows Movie Maker can export video in either AVI or Windows Media Video (WMV) format. If you want to share your movies on the Internet, WMV is the format you want to use. As I describe earlier in this chapter, WMV files must be watched using the Windows Media Player program, which is available for Windows and Macintosh PCs.

Exporting WMV movies from Windows Movie Maker is easy and versatile. You can choose from one of several basic export quality presets, or you can fine-tune the quality. You can even specify a file size. For example, if you want your movie to be no larger than 5MB, you can tell Movie Maker to make a file this size, and the program automagically adjusts settings to create a 5MB file with the best possible quality. Cool!

To turn your Movie Maker project into a WMV movie, follow these steps:

1. **In the Movie Tasks list, click Send to the Web under Finish Movie.**

   If the Movie Tasks list isn't open, choose View⇨Task Pane. The Save Movie Wizard appears when you click Send to the Web.

2. **Type a filename for your movie, and then click Next in the Save Movie Wizard.**

3. **On the Movie Setting screen of the Save Movie Wizard, click Show More Choices.**

When you first open the Movie Settings screen, you are presented with three basic options: Dial-up modem, ISDN, and DSL. In theory, you should use the Dial-up setting for dial-up users, and the DSL setting for broadband users. In reality, these are just settings presets and the names are rather superfluous. As you can see in Figure 14-8, when you click Show More Choices, you get (oddly enough) more choices. The two additional choices are

- **Best fit to file size:** This option is really cool because it allows you to tell Movie Maker how big you want the final file size to be. Only 10MB of server space available to store your movie? Click the up or down arrows to set the size to 10MB, as I have done in Figure 14-8. As you adjust the file size, note the Setting Details at the bottom of the Save Movie Wizard window.

- **Other settings:** This menu contains over 15 additional quality presets, allowing you to choose from a greater range of quality settings. The data rate is listed next to each preset in the menu. Lower bit rates mean lower-quality video.

Whatever preset or file size you choose, pay attention to the Setting Details box at the bottom of the Save Movie Wizard window. This box lists quality settings for the preset or file size you have chosen. Lower bit rates, smaller display sizes, and slower frame rates mean lower quality.

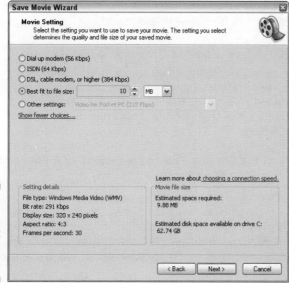

Figure 14-8:
Choose an export preset or file size here.

4. **After you've chosen a preset or export file size, click Next.**

   The Save Movie Wizard exports your movie. A progress bar gives you an estimate of the amount of time remaining. It usually takes a few minutes to export your movie, so this is a good time to go top-off your cup of coffee. When export is complete, the Save Movie Wizard shows a screen asking if you want to upload your movie to a Microsoft-partnered online media server. If you happen to have an account with one of the listed providers, enter your account name and password and click Next to upload your movie. Otherwise, just click Cancel to exit the Save Movie Wizard. I show how to find an online media server later in this chapter.

Exporting from Premiere Elements

It probably comes as no surprise that the video-editing programs created by Apple and Microsoft only allow you to export video in the formats created by those respective companies. Adobe has the advantage of being a third party, meaning that Premiere Elements can export video in many formats, including QuickTime and Windows Media Video.

If you want to offer your movies to Internet users in more than one format — and it's a good idea to do so — you owe it to yourself to step up to an advanced, versatile program like Premiere Elements. With just a few mouse clicks, you can export the same exact movie project in a multitude of formats. In the next couple of sections, I show you how to export Windows Media and QuickTime movies from Premiere Elements.

Creating Windows Media Video in Premiere Elements

Windows Media Player is pre-installed on all computers running modern versions of Windows, meaning that it is almost certainly the most popular media player available today. This makes the Windows Media export feature in Premiere Elements very handy, indeed. To export a movie project as Windows Media, follow these steps:

1. **Click Export on the Premiere Elements toolbar, and then choose Windows Media from the menu that appears.**

   The Export Windows Media dialog box appears. You are presented with a selection of eight presets, with names like "Pocket PC" and "128K Dual ISDN." Click a preset to see its description and specifications on the right side of the Export Windows Media dialog box. I don't find these presets terribly useful and prefer to fine-tune the export settings myself.

2. Click Advanced in the lower-left corner of the Export Windows Media dialog box.

A long Export Settings dialog box appears, as shown in Figure 14-9. The top section of this dialog box allows you to choose presets, and the bottom section lets you fine-tune export settings. Notice that the bottom section of the Export Settings dialog box has tabs named Video, Audio, and Audiences. As you adjust settings, keep an eye on the Estimated File Size in the lower-left corner of the Export Settings dialog box.

3. Review and adjust settings on the Video tab.

I won't cover every setting, but some of the more important video settings include

- **Video Codec:** The codec (see Chapter 13 for an explanation of codecs) is the scheme that will be used to compress and later play back your movie. This menu allows you to choose a codec that is compatible with older versions of Windows Media Player, which may broaden your audience. However, you will probably find that most of your audience already has Windows Media Player 9 or newer.

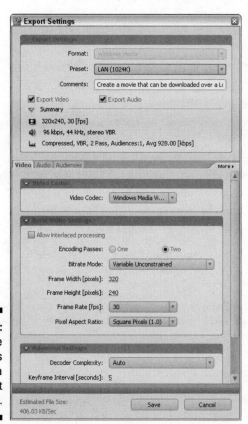

Figure 14-9:
Peruse
Windows
Media
export
settings.

- **Encoding Passes:** One encoding pass greatly speeds up the export process. If you choose two encoding passes, Premiere Elements takes about twice as long to export your movie. However, the final file size is smaller because two passes helps Premiere compress the video more efficiently.

- **Frame Width and Frame Height:** Click and drag left or right on either of these numbers to increase or decrease the size of your video image. Remember, the numbers should match the aspect ratio (see Chapter 3 for more on aspect ratios) of your video, so if your video has an aspect ratio of 4:3 and you choose a width of 640 pixels, the height should be 480 pixels.

- **Frame Rate:** Choose a lower frame rate to dramatically reduce file size.

- **Average Video Bitrate:** Move this slider left to reduce quality and file size, or move it right to increase quality and size.

4. **Click the Audio tab to review and adjust audio settings.**

   Good quality audio is extremely important, but audio settings can drastically affect the file size of your movie. In the Audio Format menu, choose different settings to see how the Estimated File Size changes for each one. If you don't see much of a change, choose a higher audio quality setting.

5. **When you are happy with your changes, click Save at the bottom of the Export Settings dialog box.**

   A Choose Name dialog box appears.

6. **Enter a name for your new preset — try to name it something descriptive so you'll remember it later — and click OK.**

   Your custom preset now appears in the Export Windows Media dialog box, and you can use it again in the future if you wish by selecting it in this dialog box.

Take a close look at the file size estimate that is now listed in the Export Windows Media dialog box. You may find that it differs wildly from the estimate shown in the Export Settings dialog box. The estimate in the Export Windows Media dialog box is a lot more trustworthy. If it looks like the file will be too big, go back and fine-tune your settings again to trim the file size down a bit.

7. **Click OK to close the Export Windows Media dialog box, type a filename for your movie (and choose a location in which to save it, if you wish), and click Save.**

   Premiere Elements starts to export your movie. A Rendering dialog box appears as shown in Figure 14-10. The progress bar provides shows you approximately how much time is left. Click the arrow next to Render Details to view additional export details as shown in Figure 14-10.

Figure 14-10:
Premiere
Elements
exports the
WMV
movie.

Exporting QuickTime movies from Premiere Elements

Windows Media Player may be a very popular video player program these days, but Apple's QuickTime has been around for many years and continues to be very popular as well. QuickTime is one of the most widely supported formats available, making it a great choice for export. Here's how to do it:

1. **Click Export on the Premiere Elements toolbar, and then choose QuickTime from the menu that appears.**

   The Export QuickTime dialog box appears. You are presented with a selection of eight presets with the same unhelpful names used for the Windows Media presets.

2. **Click Advanced in the lower-left corner of the Export QuickTime dialog box.**

   The Export Settings dialog box appears. If you have exported Windows Media from Premiere Elements, this Export Settings dialog box should look familiar. It's very similar to the WMV Export Settings dialog box shown in Figure 14-9, except that this one offers settings specific to QuickTime.

3. **Review and adjust settings on the Video tab.**

   I won't cover every setting, but some of the more important video settings include

   • **Video Codec:** The codec (see Chapter 13 for an explanation of codecs) is the scheme that is used to compress and later play back your movie. QuickTime presents a bunch of codecs, and I can't possibly explain them all here. Unless you already know that one of the other codecs is going to work better for you, I recommend that you stick with the Sorenson Video 3 Compressor.

   The remaining options on the video tab may change if you select a different codec. Here, I assume you are using the Sorenson codec, which is the default choice.

- **Spatial Quality:** This option controls the basic quality of the video. A higher number means higher quality video and a larger file size.

- **Frame Width and Frame Height:** Click and drag left or right on either of these numbers to increase or decrease the size of your video image. Remember, the numbers should match the aspect ratio (see Chapter 3 for more on aspect ratios) of your video, so if your video has an aspect ratio of 4:3 and you choose a width of 640 pixels, the height should be 480 pixels.

- **Frame Rate:** Choose a lower frame rate to dramatically reduce file size.

- **Field Order:** As described in Chapter 3, broadcast video frames are usually broadcast in two fields. This menu controls how fields are handled in your QuickTime file. Most of the time you should accept the default setting, but if you see visual glitches like interlacing jaggies (see Figure 3-2), try using a different setting in the Field Order menu.

- **Pixel Aspect Ratio:** If your QuickTime movie appears stretched or squeezed, choose one of the NTSC or PAL (as appropriate for your equipment) options from this menu. Otherwise, just use the default setting.

- **Bitrate:** Move this slider left to reduce quality and file size, or move it right to increase quality and size.

- **Video Hinter Track:** These settings are only for movies that will be placed on a streaming media server.

4. **Click the Audio tab to review and adjust audio settings.**

   As you can see in Figure 14-11, QuickTime provides several audio options that you can adjust. You can choose an audio codec (if you're not sure just accept the default), choose mono or stereo sound, and choose a different audio frequency. Stereo audio and higher frequencies increase file size.

5. **When you are happy with your changes, click Save at the bottom of the Export Settings dialog box.**

   A Choose Name dialog box appears.

6. **Enter a name for your new preset — try to name it something descriptive so you'll remember it later — and click OK.**

   Your custom preset now appears in the Export QuickTime dialog box, and you can use it again in the future if you wish by selecting it in this dialog box.

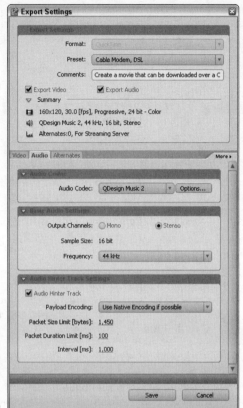

Figure 14-11:
Adjust audio settings for QuickTime export.

7. **Click OK to close the Export QuickTime dialog box, type a filename for your movie (and choose a location in which to save it, if you wish), and click Save.**

   Premiere Elements starts to export your movie. A Rendering dialog box appears as shown in Figure 14-10. The progress bar provides shows you approximately how much time is left. Click the arrow next to Render Details to view additional export details as shown in Figure 14-10.

Putting Your Movie on the Web

After your movies are exported in a Web-friendly format, it's time to actually make those movies available *on* the Web. This means you'll have to upload your movies to a *Web server* (basically a big hard drive that is connected to the Internet, set up so anyone with a Web browser can access files kept on it). The next two sections help you find a Web server on which to store your movie files, and I show you how to make a simple Web page that can serve as your online theater.

Finding an online home for your movies

If you want other people to be able to download and watch your movies, you'll need to put the movie files on a Web server. Your Internet service provider (ISP) might actually provide some free Web server space with your Internet account. This free space is usually limited to about 10MB, but the exact amount varies greatly. You can use your Web server space to publish pictures, movies, and Web pages that anyone on the Internet can see. Check with your ISP to find out whether you have some available Web server space — and, if you do, get instructions for uploading your files to its Web server.

If your ISP doesn't provide Web server space, or if it isn't enough space to hold all of your movie files, don't worry. Plenty of other resources are available. Several companies specialize in selling server space that you can use to store your movies. Three services include

- ✔ **.Mac (www.mac.com):** This service from Apple includes e-mail tools, an address book, antivirus service, and most importantly, 1GB of storage space on its Web server. Uploading movie files to .Mac is just as easy as copying files to different disks on your computer. The .Mac service costs approximately $100 per year, and provides many more features than I can list here.

- ✔ **HugeHost.com (www.hugehost.com):** As the name implies, HugeHost .com lets you put huge files online. The service is quite affordable, as well. For example, 500MB is just $7 per month, and it includes e-mail accounts and other services. See its Web site for other pricing plans.

- ✔ **GoDaddy.com (www.godaddy.com):** GoDaddy.com is very similar to HugeHost.com, but its basic 500MB service is just $4 per month, or about $38 per year.

Whatever you use as a Web server for your movie files, make sure you get specific instructions for uploading. You'll also need to know what the Web address is for the files that you upload. You can then send that address to other people so that they can find and download your movie.

Creating a (very) simple Web page

Yes, you read that heading correctly, I'm going to show you how to create a simple little Web page. Yes, this is still *Digital Video For Dummies,* and no, I'm not going to tell you *everything* you need to know about designing and managing a Web site. But making a simple little Web page is actually pretty, um, simple. To make a Web page, open a text-editing program:

▸ **Macintosh:** Open the Apple Tools folder in your Applications folder, and then double-click the TextEdit icon.

▸ **Windows:** Choose Start⇨All Programs⇨Accessories⇨Notepad.

After you have your text-editing program open, type the following exactly as shown here:

```
<html>
<head>
<title>My Online Theater</title>
</head>
<body>
<center>
<h1>My Online Theater</h1>
<p><a href="yellowstone.wmv">Yellowstone National Park</a>
        5.8 MB, Windows Media Video</p>
</center>
</body>
</html>
```

You'll notice that the line that starts with `<p>` refers to the name of a movie that I created. The text between the quotation marks (`yellowstone.wmv`, in my example) is the filename of the movie file. Change that text to match the filename of your own movie. Filenames on Web sites are usually case-sensitive, so make sure you use upper- and lowercase letters exactly as they are used by the movie file. Also change the descriptive text part (`Yellowstone National Park`, in my example) to match your own movie. I've also listed the file size and format, just so people who visit the page will know what to expect. You can change that information on your own file as well. When you're done typing all these lines, save the file and give it the following file-name:

```
index.html
```

Upload this file to the same directory on your Web server that contains your movie file. (You should get upload instructions from your ISP or Web server provider.) Make sure that both this `index.html` file and your movie file are in the exact same directory on the Web server. If the address to your movie file is

```
www.webserver.com/myaccount/yellowstone.wmv
```

simply provide your audience with this address instead:

```
www.webserver.com/myaccount/
```

When people visit that page, they'll see something similar to Figure 14-12. If you have several movies on your Web server, you can list them all on a single page. Just copy that line that starts with <p>, and then enter the filename and other information for each movie in each respective line.

There's a lot more to Web-page creation and management than what I have described here. Web design is a big subject, and if you're interested in creating more complex Web pages, I recommend that you obtain a book that covers the subject more thoroughly, such as *HTML 4 For Dummies,* Fourth Edition, by Ed Tittel and Natanya Pitts, or *Creating Web Pages For Dummies,* 6th Edition, by Bud E. Smith and Arthur Bebak, both published by Wiley Publishing, Inc.

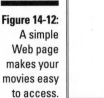

Figure 14-12:
A simple Web page makes your movies easy to access.

My Online Theater - Mozilla Firefox

File   Edit   View   Go   Bookmarks   Tools   Help

file:///c:/Document   Go

My Online Theater

Yellowstone National Park 5.8 MB, Windows Media Video

Done

Chapter 15

Exporting Movies to Tape

· ·

· ·

Most of the people you know probably own a DVD player by now. DVDs are a great way to share high-quality movies with your friends and family. Blank DVDs are cheap, they're easy to mail, and the discs don't have any moving parts to break or a tape to stretch and wear out. DVD is the way of the future.

Why not just forget about videotapes and head straight to Chapter 16 to start burning DVDs? DVDs have many advantages, but simplicity isn't one of them. Your non-tech savvy relatives may not be able to program the clocks on their VCRs, but they probably know how to insert a tape and press Play. With DVDs, there are menus to navigate, weird connectors to hook up on the back of the TV, and remote controls to lose under the sofa. Furthermore, many DVD players are finicky about what kinds of discs they'll play; some will play your home-made discs, and some won't. VCRs have no such problems. If a VHS tape plays in one VCR, it will probably play in all of them.

So don't stick that VCR up in the attic with the Betamax and the eight-track player just yet. You may need it to record your movies onto videotapes. This chapter shows you how to prepare your movie for viewing on TVs with VCRs, and how to export your movies from your video-editing program.

Prepping Your Movie for TV Playback

I often mention in this book that although computer monitors and TVs look similar, they are very difference devices. They display video differently, meaning that the video that looks just peachy in the preview window of your editing software may not look all that great when it's viewed on a regular TV. Computer monitors and TVs differ in three important ways:

- **Color:** Computer monitors and television screens generate colors differently. This means that colors that look fine on your computer may not look so hot when viewed on a TV.

- **Pixel shape:** Video images are made up of a grid of tiny little blocks called *pixels*. Pixels on computer monitors are square, but the pixels in TV images are slightly rectangular. Pixel shape is discussed in greater detail in Chapter 3, but basically this means that some images that look okay on your computer may appear slightly stretched or squeezed on a TV. This usually isn't a problem for video captured from your camcorder, but still images and graphics generated on your computer could be a problem. (See Chapter 12 for more on preparing still graphics for your movie.)

- **Interlacing:** As I describe in Chapter 3, TV video images are usually interlaced, whereas computer monitors draw images by using progressive scanning. The main problem you encounter when you export a project to tape is that the very thin lines that show up on the screen may flicker or appear to crawl. Pay special attention to titles, where thin lines are likely to appear in some letters. (See Chapter 9 for tips on avoiding this problem.)

In view (so to speak) of these issues, I strongly recommend that you try to preview your movie on an external monitor first. Check out Chapter 13 for instructions.

If you use the LCD display on your camcorder to preview your movie, keep in mind that the LCD panel probably isn't interlaced. However, the camcorder's viewfinder probably *is* interlaced. This means that flickering thin lines (for example) may show up in the viewfinder but not on the LCD panel. Preview the movie using *both* the LCD display and the viewfinder before you actually export it.

Setting Up Your Hardware

Getting your hardware ready for exporting movies to tape isn't so difficult, really. The easiest thing to do is connect your digital camcorder to your FireWire port and turn on your camcorder to VTR or Player mode. (Oh yeah, and insert a blank tape into the camcorder.) After your movie is recorded onto the tape in your camcorder, you can connect the camcorder to a regular VCR and dub your movie onto a standard VHS tape if you want.

I strongly urge you to use a fresh tape when exporting video to your camcorder. This prevents errors in communication between your digital camcorder and your computer. See the sidebar "Blacking and coding your tapes" in Chapter 4 for instructions on how to prepare a digital videotape for use.

If your master plan is to eventually record your movie on a VHS tape, you may want to skip the middleman — that would be your digital camcorder — and record straight from your computer to a regular VCR. If you want to do this, you basically have three options:

✔ **Use an analog video-capture card.** Analog capture cards (such as the Pinnacle AV/DV board) can usually export to an analog source as well as import from one. When you export video using an analog card, I strongly recommend you use the software that came with that card. Most analog capture cards come with special utilities to help you import and export video.

✔ **Use a video converter.** Chapter 6 describes how to capture analog video using a converter that connects to your computer's FireWire port. The converters listed in Chapter 6 also have analog outputs to which you can connect a VCR.

✔ **Use your digital camcorder as a converter.** I know, I know, I said I was going to show you how to *avoid* using your camcorder as the middleman when you export to VHS tape. But if you don't have an analog-capture card or a video converter, you might be able to connect your digital camcorder to your FireWire port, and then connect a VCR to the camcorder's analog outputs. If nothing else, this arrangement reduces wear and tear on your camcorder's expensive tape-drive mechanism. Some digital camcorders won't allow you to make this connection because some models can't send video out the analog ports at the same time they're taking video in through the FireWire cable. Experiment with your own camcorder and VCR and see whether this arrangement works for you.

If you are exporting to a VCR, make sure that a new, blank tape is inserted and ready to use, and make sure the VCR is set to the right channel. (Many VCRs have to be set to a special "AV" channel to accept video from composite video cables.) As a last step before you begin your export, preview your movie on a TV connected to the VCR (see Chapter 13) to make sure that the VCR is picking up the signal.

Exporting the Movie

After your hardware is set up properly and you're sure that your movie will look good on a regular TV, you're ready to export the movie. Regardless of what software you are using, keep in mind that — like video capture — video export uses a lot of memory and computer resources. To make sure that your system is ready for export

- ✔ **Turn off unnecessary programs.** If you're like me, you probably feel like you can't live without your e-mail program, Internet messaging program, Web browser, and music jukebox all running at once. Maybe *you* can't live without these things, but your video-editing software will get along just fine without them. In fact, the export process works much better if these things are closed, and you're less likely to have dropped frames or other quality problems during export.

- ✔ **Disable power-management settings.** If you're exporting a movie that's 30 minutes long, and your hard drive is set to go into power-saving mode after 15 minutes, you could have a problem during export because the computer mistakenly decides that exporting a movie is the same thing as inactivity. Power management is usually a good thing, but if your hard drive or other system components go into sleep mode during export, the video export will fail. Pay special attention to this if you're working on a laptop, which probably has pretty aggressive power-management settings right now.

  - On a Mac, use the Energy Saver icon in System Preferences to adjust power settings. Crank all the sliders in the Energy Saver window up to Never before you export your movie.

  - In Windows, open the Control Panel, click the Performance and Maintenance category if you see it, and then open the Power Options icon. Set all of the pull-down menus to Never before exporting your movie.

- ✔ **Disable screen savers.** Screen savers aren't quite as likely to ruin a movie export as power-management settings, but it's better to be safe than sorry.

- In Windows, right-click a blank area of the Windows desktop and choose Properties. Click the Screen Saver tab of the Display Properties dialog box, and choose the None screen saver. (That's my favorite one, personally.)

- On your Mac, open the Screen Saver icon in System Preferences and choose Never on the Activation tab of the Screen Saver dialog box.

Whenever you export a movie to tape, I always recommend that you place some black video at the beginning and end of the movie. Black video at the beginning of the tape gives your audience some time to sit down and relax between the time they push Play and the movie actually starts. Black video at the end of the movie also gives your viewers some time to press Stop before that loud, bright static comes on and puts out someone's eye. Some editing programs — like Apple iMovie — have tools that allow you to automatically insert black video during the export process. I'll show you how to insert black video using iMovie in the next section. But if you're using some other software that doesn't have this feature — like Adobe Premiere Elements or Windows Movie Maker — you'll need to add a clip of black video to the beginning and end of the project's timeline. You can usually do this by creating a blank full-screen title, and I'll show you how later in this chapter.

The most common failures encountered on VHS tapes are mangling or breakage at the very beginning of the tapes. Employees at video rental stores are quite skilled in the art of VHS tape repair, and they often repair beginning-of-tape problems by cutting off the damaged tape, and then re-attaching the remaining good tape to the reel. If you put 30 seconds of black video at the beginning of your VHS tapes, about three feet of tape can be cut off before any of your movie is trimmed away. And if you ever need such a repair performed, head down to your local video store. You should be able to find someone there to do the job for a couple of dollars.

Exporting to tape in Apple iMovie

Like most software from Apple, iMovie is entirely functional and to-the-point. And at no time is this more evident than when you want to export your movie to tape. iMovie doesn't have the ability to export directly to an analog capture card, but it definitely can export video at full quality to your digital camcorder. To export your finished movie to tape, follow these steps:

1. **Connect your digital camcorder to the FireWire port on your computer, and turn the camera on to VTR or Player mode.**

   Make sure that you have a new, blank videotape cued up and ready in the camcorder.

2. **In iMovie, choose File➪Export.**

   The iMovie Export dialog box appears as shown in Figure 15-1.

3. **Choose To Camera from the Export menu.**

4. **Adjust the Wait field if you want.**

   The Wait field controls how long iMovie waits for the camera to get ready before it begins export. I recommend leaving the Wait field set at five seconds unless you're exporting to a video converter (such as the Dazzle Hollywood DV Bridge) connected to your FireWire port. In that case, you may want to increase the wait to about ten seconds or so to ensure that you have enough time to press the Record button manually on your VCR.

   Whatever you do, *don't* reduce the Wait field to less than five seconds. Virtually all camcorders need some time to bring their tape-drive mechanisms up to the proper speed, and the Wait gives the camcorder time to get ready.

5. **Adjust the two Add fields to determine the amount of black video that will be recorded at the beginning and end of the tape.**

   I recommend putting at least 30 seconds of black video at the beginning and end of the movie.

6. **Click Export.**

   iMovie automatically exports your movie to the tape in your camcorder. If you're exporting directly to a digital camcorder, iMovie automatically controls the camera for you; there's no need to press the Record button on the camcorder. But if you are exporting through a video converter, you'll need to manually press Record on your analog VCR.

Figure 15-1:
Set your export options here.

Exporting to tape in Windows Movie Maker

Exporting movies to tape from Windows Movie Maker is pretty easy, but sometimes the quality isn't very good. The problems can start when you capture video into Movie Maker way back at the beginning of your project.

In Chapter 5, I recommend that you use the Digital Device Format (DV-AVI) video quality setting when you capture video into Movie Maker. If you use the Best Quality for Playback on My Computer — which Microsoft claims is the "recommended" setting — or some other setting, your video quality when you export back to tape may be poor. The next sections show you how to prepare and export your video to tape from Movie Maker.

Adding black video to your timeline

Earlier in this chapter, I described the importance of placing black video at the beginning and end of a movie that will be recorded onto tape. If you plan to export your Movie Maker movie project to tape in a digital camcorder, you'll need to add some black video clips to the beginning and end of the timeline. To add a black video clip to the beginning of your project, follow these steps:

1. **In the Movie Tasks pane on the left side of the screen, click Make Titles or Credits.**

   If the Tasks pane isn't visible, choose View⇨Task Pane.

2. **Click Add Title at the Beginning of the Movie.**

   Boxes appear where you would normally enter text (see Chapter 9 for more on creating titles), but we're not going to enter any text right now. Instead, we're going to use a text-less title as our black video clip.

3. **Place the cursor in the first text box and press the spacebar on your keyboard.**

   You have just created a "title" that consists of nothing but a space. Pretty clever, eh?

4. **Click Change the Text Font and Color.**

5. **Click the Change the Background Color button as shown in Figure 15-2.**

   A color picker dialog box appears.

6. **Click the black square, and then click OK to close the color picker dialog box.**

   The black color square is in the lower-left corner of the color picker. The preview window should now show a black background, rather than the default blue.

7. **Click Done, Add Title to Movie.**

   A black clip is inserted at the very beginning of your movie. By default, the clip is only a couple of seconds long, but I recommend that you increase the duration up to 30 seconds.

8. **Zoom in on the timeline so that you can see the black clip at the beginning of the timeline, and click the black clip once to select it.**

9. **Hover your mouse pointer over the edge of the black clip so that your pointer becomes a red two-headed arrow.**

10. **Click and drag the edge of the black clip right to increase the duration to about 30 seconds.**

    The exact duration isn't important, but 30 seconds is a good time for movies on videotape.

Repeat the steps above to add a black video clip to the end of your movie as well. In step 2, click Add Credits at the End of the Movie and follow the remaining steps to add black video to the end of your movie. I recommend 15 to 30 seconds of black video at the end of the movie.

Double-check all of the transitions, effects, titles, and other edits on your timeline. In some cases, adjusting the duration of the black video clip causes some of your edits to be misaligned. You may need to adjust some things to make sure they all still line up.

Click to change background color.

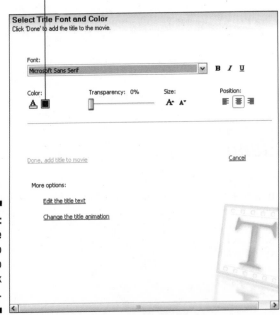

Figure 15-2:
Use the title editor to create a clip of black video.

Exporting the movie

Export a movie from Movie Maker to a tape in your digital camcorder is a mere three-click process. First, connect your camcorder to your computer's FireWire port, and place a blank tape in the camcorder. Turn the camcorder on to VTR/Player mode and follow these steps:

1. **In the Movie Tasks pane on the left side of the screen, click Send to DV Camera.**

   If the Tasks pane isn't visible, choose View➪Task Pane.

   If the Video Capture Wizard automatically appears when you turn on your camcorder, click Cancel to close the wizard. If you click Send to DV Camera and you see an error message stating that your camcorder isn't connected, double-check the connection to your camcorder and make sure it's turned on. You may need to turn the camera off and then back on.

2. **In the Save Movie Wizard, click Next.**

   A warning message appears as shown in Figure 15-3. Make sure that the tape in your camcorder is blank, or is cued past any video that you want to preserve. If the tape already contains video, Movie Maker is about to overwrite it.

3. **Click Yes.**

   Windows Movie Maker exports your movie and automatically records it to tape.

Figure 15-3:
Click Yes to
start
recording.

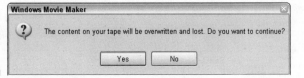

Exporting to tape in Adobe Premiere Elements

As DVDs have risen in popularity, companies like Adobe have rushed to add DVD-creation features to their video-editing programs. The latest version of Premiere Elements has powerful DVD creation tools, but the ability to record your movies to tape is still there as well. In the next couple of sections, I show you how to add black video to the beginning and end of your project, and then how to export your movie to tape.

Adding black video to the beginning and end of your movie

As mentioned earlier in this chapter, it's important to add at least 30 seconds black video to the beginning of any movie that you plan to record to tape. This "dead air" ensures that the beginning of your actual movie doesn't get cut off, especially if the tape gets damaged in the future.

Of course, the black video clip doesn't *have* to be plain black video. If you wish, you could use a clip that displays your logo, name, or copyright notice. Whatever you use should be non-critical to the movie itself.

To add a 30-second black video clip to the beginning of your movie, follow these steps:

1. **Click the New Item button at the bottom of the Media window, as shown in Figure 15-4.**

2. **Choose Black Video from the menu that appears.**

   A clip named Black Video is added to your Media window.

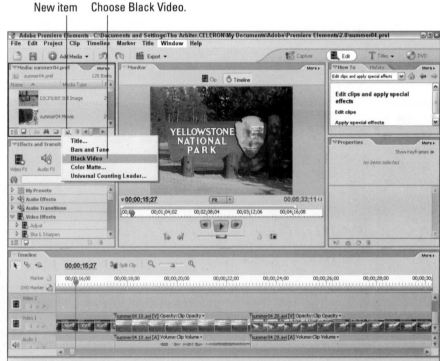

Figure 15-4: Create black video clips in the Media window.

3. **Right-click the Black Video clip in the Media window and choose Time Stretch.**

   A Time Stretch dialog box appears, as shown in Figure 15-5.

4. **Change the duration to 30 seconds, as shown in Figure 15-5, and then click OK to close the dialog box.**

5. **Click and drag the Black Video clip from the Media window to the beginning of your movie in the timeline.**

   The clip is added to the beginning of your movie, and everything else in the timeline automatically shifts right to make room for the clip. Repeat the steps above to add a 15-30–second black video clip to the end of your movie as well.

Figure 15-5: Change the duration to 30 seconds.

If you want the black video clip to fade into the beginning of your movie, add a Dissolve transition between the black video clip and the first clip of your movie. See Chapter 9 for more on working with transitions.

Exporting to tape from Premiere Elements

To export your movie from Premiere Elements to a tape in your DV camcorder, simply click Export on the Premiere Elements toolbar and choose To Tape from the Export menu. The Export to Tape dialog box appears as shown in Figure 15-6. Options to check in this dialog box include

✔ **Activate Recording Device:** Leave this option checked if you are exporting to a DV camcorder attached to your FireWire or USB 2.0 port. This option allows Premiere to take control of your camcorder using device control. See Chapter 3 for more on digital camcorders and device control.

If you are exporting to an analog camcorder or VCR using a video converter that is plugged in to your computer's FireWire or USB 2.0 port, you won't be able to use device control. Uncheck the Activate Recording Device option, and juggle your hands to press play on the camcorder or VCR a few seconds before clicking Record in Premiere Elements.

✔ **Assemble at Timecode:** If you check this option, you can then specify a timecode on the camcorder tape where you want Premiere to start recording the movie. Only use this option if you are working with a tape that has been blacked and coded (see Chapter 4 for more on blacking and coding videotapes).

✔ **Delay Movie Start:** Use this setting to delay the start of recording several frames. This allows the tape drive mechanism in your camcorder to get up to proper operating speed, thus avoiding video glitches at the start of recording. However, if you added 30 seconds of black video to the beginning of your movie as described in the previous section, you shouldn't need to delay the movie start.

✔ **Preroll:** This setting is similar to the Delay Movie Start setting, except that Premiere Elements rewinds the tape slightly and starts it rolling before the designated starting time of recording. Although this setting can be used in conjunction with the Assemble at Timecode option, if you put black video at the beginning of the movie, you shouldn't need any preroll.

✔ **Abort after Dropped Frames:** Dropped frames create serious video quality problems, and I recommend that you check this option. However, if your computer seems incapable of exporting the movie without dropping some frames, uncheck this option or set a higher number. I show how to prevent dropped frames — video frames that are lost because the computer can't keep up — in Chapter 5.

✔ **Report Dropped Frames:** If Premiere Elements drops any frames during export, you will definitely want to know about it. Leave this option checked.

When you are ready to start recording, click Record. Premiere Elements records your movie to tape.

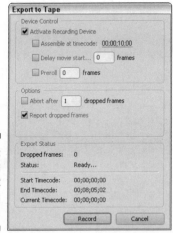

Figure 15-6:
Adjust tape export settings here.

Chapter 16

Making DVDs

*I*n November 1996, the first DVD — short for *digital versatile disc* — players came on the market. Like most new technologies, DVD players were expensive, and the format got off to a slow start. But players gradually became more affordable, and more and more movies were released on DVD. Sometime in 2002 or 2003 (depending on which industry expert you ask), DVD sales and rentals exceeded VHS, and today, DVD is the most popular format for sharing and watching movies.

Most new computers sold in the last couple of years have DVD-ROM drives, and many now have DVD recording drives as well. If you have a DVD burner on your computer, you can record your movie projects onto DVD, complete with navigation menus just like the discs that come from Hollywood. This chapter shows you how to record your own DVDs. But first, I explore some of the complex terminology and various formats of DVD burners and discs.

Understanding DVD Basics

DVDs provide higher quality and are physically smaller than VHS tapes, and unlike tapes, they don't have moving parts that break after a number of uses. Best of all, your local video-rental store never charges you a fee if you forget to rewind a DVD.

If DVDs have one disadvantage compared to videotapes, it's that the process of recording a movie onto DVD is a little more complicated. The following sections help you prepare to make your own DVDs by showing you what you need — and translating some terms and acronyms used in the DVD world.

Getting ready to record DVDs

Because video-editing programs and digital camcorders communicate so easily with each other, putting your movie on tape is pretty easy. If you have all the gear you need to capture and edit video, you also have everything you need to put your finished movies on tape. But if you want to record your finished movies on DVD, you'll need a couple more things:

- ✔ **A DVD burner:** Drives that can record DVDs are now widely available for less than a hundred dollars, and many new computers already have DVD burners built-in. If your computer doesn't already have a DVD burner, you can buy either an internal drive that replaces your current CD-ROM or CD-R drive, or an external drive that connects to your computer's FireWire or USB 2.0 port. Installing internal drives requires some level of computer hardware expertise, so the external solution is probably easier. The easiest solution of all (but also the most expensive) is to buy a new computer with a DVD burner already installed. Many new Macintosh computers — even some of the affordable eMacs and Mac Minis — come with the SuperDrive, which is Apple's DVD burner. Many Windows PCs come with built-in DVD burners as well. Look for "DVD-R" or "DVD+R" in the tech specs before you buy.

- ✔ **Blank DVDs:** Blank recordable DVDs look like blank recordable CDs, but they are different. Make sure you buy blank DVDs that are compatible with your particular DVD burner. For example, some blank discs may be compatible with DVD-R drives, but not DVD+R drives. I explain the differences in the next section.

- ✔ **DVD recording software:** Also called *mastering software* or *authoring software,* you need software on your computer that can properly format your video and record it onto a DVD. If you have a DVD burner, it probably came with recording software. Apple offers its own DVD recording program called iDVD (iDVD only works with Apple's SuperDrive). On the Windows side, Windows Movie Maker cannot record movies directly to DVD as of this writing; however, Adobe Premiere Elements, Pinnacle Studio, and many others can.

  DVD recording software usually includes tools to help you create DVD menus for your discs. Menus allow viewers to find and use the various features of your DVD movie. Figure 16-1 shows a menu that I made for one of my DVDs.

Comprehending DVD standards

One of the nice things about VHS tapes is that after you record a movie onto a tape, it'll play in just about any VCR. Likewise, you can usually look at the tape and immediately know how much video it will hold. For example, a tape labeled T-120 is going to hold about 120 minutes of video. Alas, DVDs are a little more complicated. Although many DVD players can play the DVDs that you record yourself, some players have trouble with them. And of course, the amount of space on a blank DVD is usually listed computer-style (gigabytes) rather than human-style (minutes). If a blank DVD says it can hold 4.7GB, how many minutes of video is that, exactly? The next few sections answer the most common questions about recording DVDs.

Figure 16-1: DVD-authoring software helps you create DVD menus such as this.

Choosing external DVD burners

If you don't feel like tearing into the innards of your computer to install a DVD burner, you may want to consider an external DVD burner. External DVD recording drives typically connect to either a FireWire or USB 2.0 port. If your computer already has a FireWire port, a FireWire DVD burner is the safer choice. External FireWire DVD burners are available for both Windows PCs and Macintosh computers.

Some external DVD burners can use a USB 2.0 port instead of a FireWire port. To use a USB 2.0 DVD burner, your computer must have a USB

version 2.0 port. If your computer was made in the spring of 2002 or earlier, there is a good chance that it only has USB 1.1. USB 1.1 isn't fast enough to effectively burn DVDs. Check the documentation for your computer if you aren't sure. You can add USB 2.0 ports to your computer using a USB 2.0 expansion card. But if you're going to go to that much trouble, you might as well add an internal DVD burner instead. Consult a computer hardware professional about upgrading any internal parts of your computer.

How much video can I cram onto a DVD?

Recordable DVDs are now available in two capacities. Single-layer DVDs, — which have been around longer — can hold up to 4.7GB of video or other data. Double-layer recordable DVDs — which are relatively new — can hold up to 8.5GB. The 4.7GB discs can hold roughly two hours of video, and the 8.5GB discs can hold about four hours. These times are very rough approximations; as I show later in this chapter, quality settings greatly affect how much video you can actually squeeze onto a disc. Some professionally manufactured DVDs can hold more because they are double-sided. Table 16-1 lists the most common DVD capacities.

Table 16-1		DVD Capacities
Type	*Capacity*	*Approximate Video Time*
Single-sided, single-layer	4.7GB	More than two hours
Single-sided, double-layer	8.5GB	Four hours
Double-sided, single-layer	9.4GB	Four and a half hours
Double-sided, double-layer	16GB	More than eight hours

You've probably seen double-sided DVDs before. They're often used to put the widescreen version of a movie on one side of the disc, and the full-screen version on the other. Unfortunately, there is currently no easy way for you to make double-sided DVDs in your home or office. These types of discs require special manufacturing processes, so (for now) you're limited to single-sided DVDs for your own movies.

What is the deal with the DVD-R/RW+R/RW alphabet soup?

When it comes to buying a drive to record DVDs, you're going to see a lot of similar yet slightly different acronyms thrown around to describe the various formats that are available. The basic terms you'll encounter are

- ✔ **DVD-R (DVD-Recordable):** Like a CD-R, you can only record onto this type of disc once.

- ✔ **DVD-RW (DVD-ReWritable):** You can record onto a DVD-RW disc, erase it later, and record something else onto it.

- ✔ **DVD-RAM (DVD-Random Access Memory):** These discs can also be recorded to and erased repeatedly. DVD-RAM discs are only compatible with DVD-RAM drives, which pretty much makes this format useless for movies because most DVD players cannot play DVD-RAM discs.

The difference between DVD-R and DVD-RW is simple enough. But as you peruse advertisements for various DVD burners, you'll notice that some drives say they record DVD-R/RW, whereas others record DVD+R/RW. The dash (-) and the plus (+) aren't simply a case of catalog editors using different grammar. The -R and +R formats are unique standards. If you have a DVD-R drive, you must make sure that you buy DVD-R blank discs. Likewise, if you have a DVD+R drive, you must buy DVD+R blank discs.

The differences between the -R and +R formats are not major. Either type of disc can be played in most DVD-ROM drives and DVD players. And as of this writing, both formats are widely available. Fortunately, most DVD burner manufacturers now offer "dual-format" drives that accommodate both -R and +R discs. If you're buying a new DVD burner, try to get one that accommodates both formats.

One more thing: When you buy DVD-R discs (that's *-R*, not +R), make sure you buy discs that are labeled for General use, and not for Authoring. Not only are the DVD-R for Authoring discs more expensive, but they're also not compatible with most consumer DVD-R drives. This shouldn't be a huge problem because most retailers only sell DVD-R for General discs, but it's something to double-check when you buy blank media.

How many layers do I need?

Until recently, DVDs that you could record yourself were limited to the single-layer, 4.7GB variety. Double-layer, 8.5GB discs could only be made in professional manufacturing facilities where (I'm not making this up) the two data layers would actually be glued together to make the final disc. Obviously, this process was out of reach to the average computer user like you and me.

Fortunately, new technologies have brought double-layer recordable DVDs to the masses. In fact, most new DVD burners being released today are double-layer drives. If you still need to buy a DVD burner, I strongly recommend a double-layer drive. Double-layer drives can record movies onto single- and double-layer recordable discs, and there will probably come a time when you'll be glad you have the extra storage capacity that a double-layer disc provides.

If you buy 4.7GB recordable DVDs, they only hold up to 4.7GB even if you have a double-layer drive. To record 8.5GB discs, you must buy special double-layer recordable discs. Double-layer discs are a little more expensive than single-layer discs, but they are available.

What are VCDs and SVCDs?

You can still make DVD movies even if you don't have a DVD burner.

Yes, you read that correctly. Okay, technically you can't make *real* DVDs without a DVD burner, but you can make discs that have menus just like DVDs and play in some DVD players. All you need is a regular old CD burner and some blank CD-Rs to make one of two types of discs:

✓ **VCD (Video CD):** These can hold 60 minutes of video, but the quality is about half that of a DVD.

✓ **SVCD (Super VCD):** These hold only 20 minutes of video, but the quality is closer to (although still a little less than) DVD quality.

These two formats are usually options you can choose in some DVD-burning programs, including Premiere Elements. You create VCDs and SVCDs just as you would DVDs. (Later in this chapter, I show you how to create a VCD or SVCD instead of a regular DVD.)

The advantage of VCDs and SVCDs is that you can make them right now if you already have a CD burner. Just keep in mind that VCDs and SVCDs are not compatible with all DVD players.

A great resource for compatibility information is a Web site called VideoHelp. com (`www.videohelp.com`). Check out the Compatibility Lists section for compatibility information on specific brands and models of DVD players.

Making Effective Menus

If you've ever watched a movie on DVD, you're probably familiar with DVD menus. When you first put a movie disc into a DVD player, a screen usually appears and offers help with navigating the various features of the disc. This menu screen usually includes links that play the movie from the beginning, jump to a specific scene, show you the special features, or change languages and other settings. Menus are an important part of any DVD, and DVD *authoring software* includes tools to help you make your own menus. When you make a menu, you need to

✓ Design the general appearance of the menu.

✓ Create buttons for the menu.

✓ Link menu buttons to parts of your movie.

In the next couple of sections, I show you how to make effective menus.

Creating a menu

The exact steps for making a menu vary (depending on the program you're using), but the basic process is the same. In Premiere Elements, for example, you start by choosing a template for your menu, which you can then customize. To create a menu in Premiere Elements, follow these steps:

1. **When you are done editing your movie, click the DVD button on the Premiere Elements toolbar to open the DVD workspace.**

   When you first click the DVD button, the DVD Templates dialog box appears as shown in Figure 16-2.

2. **Choose whether you want to have a menu.**

   It is possible to create a DVD that just plays automatically, with no menus. Simply choose Auto-Play DVD with No Menus and click OK to close the DVD Templates dialog box. A menu-less DVD may be okay for very short movies, but, for longer movies, menus are very useful. And besides, DVD menus are fun. Choose Apply a Template for a DVD with Menus if you want to include a menu.

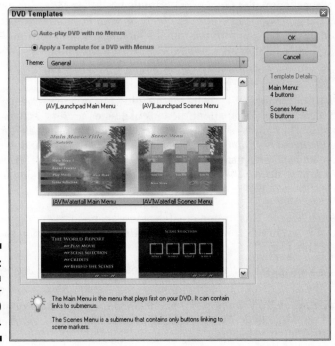

Figure 16-2: Choose a template for your DVD menu.

3. **If you are using a menu template, choose a category in the Theme drop-down list.**

   Premiere Elements divides templates up into various themes. Most of them have descriptive names.

4. **Scroll through the list of templates, and click one to view details about the template or to select it.**

   When you click a template, a few details about that template appear under Template Details on the right. The details aren't terribly, uh, *detailed,* but they do tell you how many buttons the template has in the main menu and scenes menu. This is kind of important because Premiere Elements doesn't let you change the number of buttons once you've selected a template.

   Take your time and browse through the various templates that are available. Premiere Elements comes with a lot of really nice templates, and you're bound to find one that matches the theme of your movie. Remember, you can customize the menu later. For example, one of the New Baby templates shows a picture of a baby. The stock photo is simply there as a placeholder; if your own baby is cuter, you can insert a picture of her into the menu later.

   Whatever template you choose, keep in mind that TV screens won't display the graphics and colors as nicely as your computer screen. Try to avoid menu designs with too much white, and make sure that buttons and other text contrast strongly with the background.

5. **When you've found a template that you like, click OK.**

If you have not created DVD scene markers in your movie's timeline, you'll see a message warning you about the lack of scene markers. I cover DVD markers and other kinds of markers in greater detail in my book *Adobe Premiere Elements For Dummies* (Wiley Publishing, Inc.). If you don't know how to create markers, just click Yes in the Automatically Set DVD Scene Markers warning dialog box. When you click Yes, you see a dialog box similar to the one shown in Figure 16-3. You have several choices:

✔ **At Each Scene:** This option creates a new scene marker every time there is a new clip in the Timeline. If you're not sure which option to choose, select this one.

✔ **Every *x* minutes:** Use this option to create DVD markers at specific time intervals.

✔ **Total Markers:** If you choose this option and enter a number such as five, Premiere Elements automatically creates five scene markers evenly placed along the timeline.

✔ **Clear Existing DVD Markers:** Check this option only if you want to delete DVD markers that you created before.

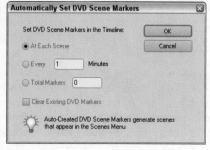

Figure 16-3:
Let
Premiere
Elements
create
scene
markers for
you.

When you've made a choice, click OK. Premiere Elements creates your DVD markers for you. In Figure 16-4, I chose to have Premiere create markers at each new scene. Markers appear as green arrows on the timeline ruler, and they are really easy to work with. If you want to move a marker, simply click and drag it left or right in the timeline. If you want to delete a marker, simply right-click it and choose Clear DVD Marker from the menu that appears.

If you created markers at each new scene, I definitely recommend that you delete some of the markers. If your movie has a lot of small clips, you may find that the scene breaks are packed too close to each other.

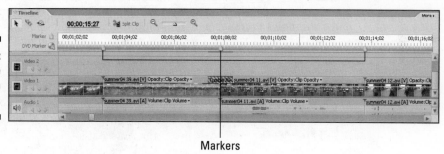

Figure 16-4:
Markers are
identified in
the timeline.

Markers

Customizing the menu

When you work in Premiere's DVD workspace, the monitor changes to the DVD Layout window as shown in Figure 16-5. This is the most important part of the process because this is where you customize the appearance and function of your DVD menu. Things you will want to change include

> ✔ **Title text:** Double-click the title to start editing it. Enter the title of your movie in the Change Text dialog box that appears. Most templates also have a place for a subtitle, but if you can't think of a good subtitle for the

movie, just put your name so that people know who made the movie. To change the appearance of text, select it and then use the Properties window (to the right of the DVD Layout window) to change the font, size, color, and style.

✔ **Background image:** Some (but not all) programs allow you to customize the background image in your DVD menu. In Premiere Elements, you can even use a video clip in the background. To use a still picture or video clip, simply click and drag it from the Media window and drop it Menu Background box as shown in Figure 16-6. In that figure, you can see that I've customized the background image of one of my scene selection menus. Background video clips loop indefinitely, and you can smooth the transition as the clip loops by checking the Apply Default Transition Before Loop option.

✔ **Button position:** Usually, you can click and drag buttons to new locations. Try to keep the buttons away from the very edges of the screen, however. As I describe in Chapter 9, overscan can cut the edges off video images on some TVs.

✔ **Button labels:** Most programs let you change button labels. In Figure 16-6, you can see that I've given my scene buttons names like "Old Faithful" and "Swimming." These names are much more descriptive than the default names "Scene One," "Scene Two," and so on. To change a label, double-click the button to open the DVD Marker dialog box as shown in Figure 16-7. Type a new name for the button in the Name field. Try to keep the name short and succinct.

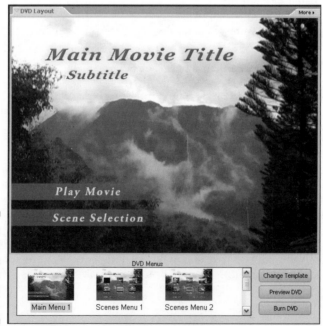

Figure 16-5:
Use this window to customize your DVD menu.

Drop picture or video clip here to change the menu background.

Figure 16-6:
Spend some
time
personal-
izing your
scene
menus.

Creates a transition as the background clip loops.

✔ **Button image:** Scene buttons usually show a thumbnail of the scene, and it's almost always the first video frame of the scene. Sometimes you want to use a different frame, however. In Premiere Elements, click and drag left or right on the timecode listed next to the Thumbnail Offset window, as shown in Figure 16-7. Try to find a frame that visually describes the contents of the scene. When you're done customizing the button, click OK to close the DVD Marker dialog box.

✔ **Audio:** Some programs such as Adobe Premiere Elements allow you to have audio in your DVD menus as well. Just as with still images and video clips, you can click and drag audio clips from the Media window and drop them on the Audio box in the Properties window. Try to choose audio that isn't overly distracting. If you added a custom video clip to the menu background, the background audio is probably that clip's accompanying audio. If you want to get rid of the background audio altogether, click Reset next to the Audio box.

Make sure you check all of the menu screens for your DVD menu. In Premiere Elements, you can check the different screens by clicking them at the bottom of the DVD Layout window.

Button name

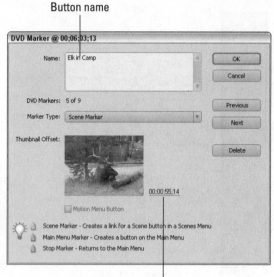

Figure 16-7:
Customize
button
names and
thumbnails.

Click and drag to change thumbnail.

The first version of Adobe Premiere Elements included a DVD menu creation feature, but it was severely stunted. It did not allow you to customize the text or graphic appearance of your menus, making it very hard to create a nice menu that looked like your movie. If you have the first version of Premiere Elements, I strongly recommend an upgrade to Premiere Elements version 2 or later, which includes the more powerful menu-editing features shown here.

Previewing your menu

You can preview the function of your DVD menus right in Premiere Elements. To do so, click the Preview DVD button in the DVD Layout window. A Preview DVD window appears as shown in Figure 16-8. This window includes standard controls like those found on a DVD player, and the menus — as well as your whole movie — are fully functional. Controls in the Preview DVD window include

✔ **Main menu:** Opens the first menu page for the movie.

✔ **Previous/Next Scene:** Jumps back and forth through the *chapters* (another name for clips) in your movie.

Previous scene   Playback controls   Main menu

Next scene   Cursor controls

✔ **Playback controls:** Allows you to play, pause, cue forward, or rewind the video.

✔ **Cursor controls:** These move the onscreen cursor from one onscreen button to the next, working much like the arrow buttons on a DVD player's remote. Click the center cursor-control button to click the currently selected onscreen button.

Preview your DVD carefully, listening to the audio in the menus and paying close attention to how easy the buttons are to see and use. When you're done previewing, click the red Close (X) button in the upper-right corner of the Preview DVD window to close it.

Burning DVDs

Don't worry; you won't need to keep a fire extinguisher handy for this section. *Burning* CDs or DVDs actually means recording the discs (presumably because a laser is involved in the recording process). Although "burn" is slang, it's a term commonly used by computer hardware gurus, ad-copy editors, and writers of *For Dummies* books. Affordable CD and DVD burners are now widely available.

If you have a CD burner but not a DVD burner, that's okay. You can still follow the steps shown here to create a VCD or SVCD instead. So go ahead, fire up whatever kind of burner you happen to have and get ready to roast some movies!

Many different DVD authoring programs are available. As I mentioned previously in the "Making Effective Menus" section, the exact steps vary depending on the program you're using, but you should see basic settings and options similar to those shown here for Adobe Premiere Elements. When you're done editing your movie and have created a menu, you're ready to burn a DVD. In Premiere Elements, place a blank recordable DVD of the proper type in your DVD burner and follow these steps:

1. **Click the DVD button on the Premiere Elements toolbar to open the DVD workspace, if it isn't already open.**

2. **At the bottom of the DVD Layout window, click Burn DVD.**

   The Burn DVD dialog box appears as shown in Figure 16-9.

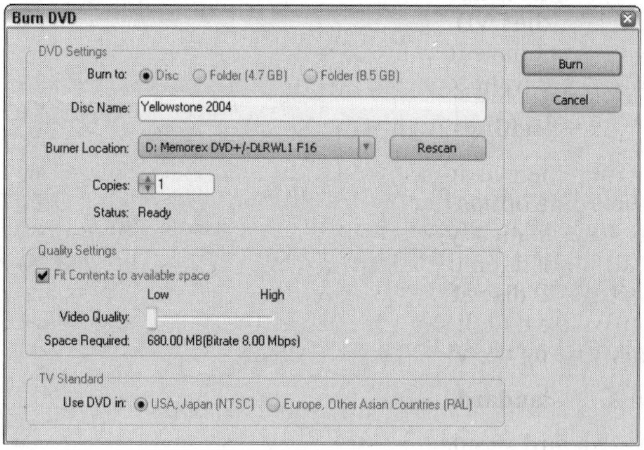

Figure 16-9:
Adjust settings for your DVD here.

3. **Choose whether you want to burn the DVD to a disc, or to a folder.**

   Premiere can record a copy or *disc image* of the DVD to a folder on your hard drive if you wish. You can then use a different program later to actually burn the DVD. If you record to a folder, make sure you choose the size — 4.7GB or 8.5GB — that matches the size of the blank disc on which you plan to record the disc.

If you want to record 8.5GB DVDs, you must have a dual-layer DVD burner, as well as 8.5GB dual-layer blank discs.

4. **Provide a name for the disc.**

In Figure 16-9, I've given the DVD the name of my movie.

5. **Choose which drive you want to use to burn the disc.**

If your computer has more than one recordable disc drive — for example, a CD-R drive and a DVD-R drive — choose the correct one here.

6. **Choose how many copies you want.**

If you're like me, you usually only print one copy of a document or burn one copy of a CD when you perform other tasks. However, when it comes time to record your movies onto DVD, it makes a lot of sense to burn multiple copies at once. If you plan to share your movie with others, burn enough discs for everyone to whom you want to give a copy, and don't forget to burn at least one for yourself. When you choose to burn two or more copies, Premiere Elements automatically asks you to insert a new disc when it's time to burn each new copy.

Recording DVDs can take hours, depending on the length of your movie. Most of that time is not actually spent burning the disc, but encoding your movie in the DVD format. If you choose to burn multiple copies at once, you won't have to wait through the lengthy encoding process again when you want to burn another copy later.

7. **Adjust quality settings.**

Most of the time you are going to want leave the Fit Contents to Available Space option checked. When this option is enabled, Premiere Elements automatically encodes your movie in the highest possible quality that will fit on the disc. If the whole movie won't fit on a single recordable DVD disc at maximum quality, Premiere Elements reduces quality to make it fit. If you uncheck this option, you can manually control quality using the Video Quality slider.

8. **Choose a TV standard.**

The TV standard should match the local TV standard for your audience. See Chapter 3 for more on TV standards.

9. **Click Burn.**

Premiere Elements starts encoding your movie and burning the disc. A progress window similar to Figure 16-10 appears.

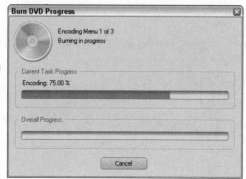

Figure 16-10:
The DVD
encoding
process can
take a long
time.

I like to start the DVD burning process in the evening when I am done using the computer for the day. DVD encoding takes a long time and uses most or all of your computer's memory and processor resources. Even short five- or ten-minute movies can take an hour or more to encode and burn, depending on your computer, and longer movies can take many hours to complete.

Part V
The Part of Tens

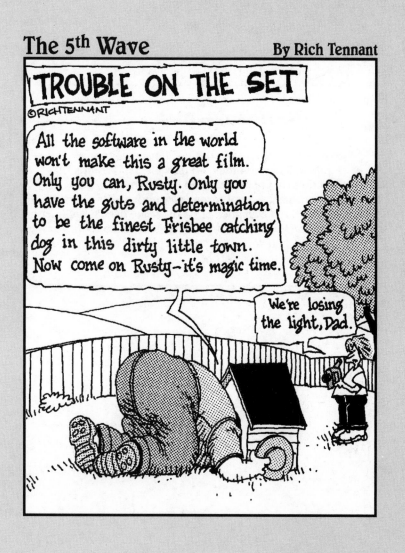

In this part . . .

1 don't know about you, but my life seems to progress from one list to another — I have lists of errands that I need to run, lists of groceries to buy at the store, and lists of video scenes to shoot for my next movie. This part of *Digital Video For Dummies* provides some lists as well: ten advanced movie making techniques, ten video tools you won't want to do without, and ten video-editing programs, compared feature for feature.

Chapter 17

Ten Advanced Video Techniques

*I*f you're new to digital video, you probably find even the most basic editing features in programs like iMovie and Windows Movie Maker exciting. And it *is* exciting to pick and choose scenes, add transitions, and give your movie a soundtrack. But at some point you'll want to take your moviemaking to the next level. You'll want to shoot better quality video with your camera, and use more advanced editing techniques on the computer.

This chapter introduces you to that next level of the moviemaking art. I show you how to do special effects using camera tricks, advanced editing techniques, fine-tune the quality of the audio and video that you record, and more.

Beam Me Up, Scotty!

Think of all the special effects you've ever seen in movies and TV shows. I'll bet that one of the most common effects you've seen is where a person or thing seems to magically appear or disappear from a scene. Sometimes a magician snaps his finger and blinks out of the picture. Other times people gradually fade in or out, as when crews on *Star Trek* use the transporter.

Making people appear and disappear from a scene is surprisingly easy. All you need is a camcorder, a tripod, and some simple editing software. Even a basic program like Apple iMovie or Windows Movie Maker will suffice. Basically you just position the camcorder on the tripod and shoot *before* and *after* scenes. The disappearing subject should only appear in one of the scenes.

After you've recorded and captured your "before" and "after" clips, edit them into the timeline of your video-editing program (as I have done in Figure 17-1). If you don't use a transition between the clips, the subject appears to "pop" into or out of the scene. If you want the subject to fade into the scene, apply a Dissolve transition between the two clips (see Chapter 9 for more on using transitions).

To make a subject magically appear or disappear effectively, follow these basic rules:

- ✔ **Use a tripod.** A tripod is absolutely mandatory to make this effect work. You won't be able to hold the camera steady enough by hand.

- ✔ **Don't move the camera between shots.** The camera must remain absolutely still between the before and after shots. If you have to reposition the camera, or if someone bumps it, reshoot both scenes. If your camcorder has a remote control, use it to start and stop recording so that your finger doesn't move the camera at all.

- ✔ **Shoot the "before" and "after" scenes quickly.** If you're shooting outdoors and you let several minutes pass between shooting the "before" and "after" scenes, shadows and lighting might change. Even subtle light changes will be apparent when you edit the two scenes together later.

- ✔ **Don't disturb the rest of the scene.** If your subject moves a chair or picks up an object between the "before" and "after" shots, the scenes will appear inconsistent when edited together.

Figure 17-1:
Make your subject magically appear (or disappear)!

Seeing Double

Have you ever wondered if you have an evil twin somewhere in the world? With some simple videography tricks and an advanced video-editing program like Adobe Premiere Elements, you can easily make your evil twin a visual reality, as shown in Figure 17-2. Don't worry, no human cloning is necessary for this effect.

Like the effect described in the previous section, this effect requires the use of a tripod. You should shoot both scenes quickly to ensure they each have the same lighting.

To make this effect work, you first shoot one-half of the image, and then shoot the other half. This creates two clips that will be combined to make a single scene. As you can see in Figure 17-3, one clip is placed in track Video 1, and the other clip — we'll call it the *overlay clip* — is placed in track Video 2. You then apply the Crop effect to the overlay clip so it only covers half the screen. (See Chapter 11 for more on working with video effects.) Notice in Figure 17-4 that I have cropped 50 percent off the right side of my overlay clip. To apply the Crop effect, follow these steps:

1. **If the Effects and Transitions window isn't visible, choose Window⇨ Effects to open the Effects window.**

   The Effects and Transitions window is located on the left side of the screen under the Media window.

2. **Open the Video Effects folder, and then open the Transform subfolder.**

3. **Click and drag the Crop effect from the Effects window to an overlay clip in the Timeline.**

   An overlay clip should be in track Video 2 or higher.

4. **Click the overlay clip in the Timeline to select it.**

5. **Open the Properties window for the clip.**

   The Properties window is located on the right side of the screen under the How To window. If you don't see the Properties window at all, choose Window⇨Properties.

6. **Click the arrow next to the Crop effect to expand it as shown in Figure 17-4.**

7. **Click and drag left or right on the Left, Top, Right, and Bottom numbers to crop the overlay image.**

In Figure 17-4, I have basically cut the overlay image in half by cropping 50 percent from the right.

Figure 17-2:
Are you really seeing double?

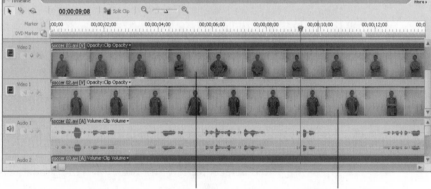

Figure 17-3:
You can use overlays in the Timeline to provide creative illusion.

Overlay clip   Background clip

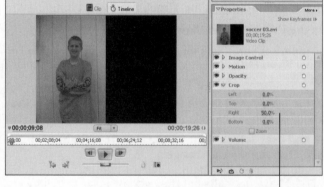

Figure 17-4:
I used the Crop effect to remove half of the overlay clip.

Adjust crop numbers here.

Forcing a Perspective

We humans perceive the world as a three-dimensional space. When you look out upon the world, you see color and light, and you can tell which things are close to you and which things are farther away. This is called *depth perception*. Bats use a sort of natural radar for depth perception, which is fine for winged creatures that flap in the night, but we humans perceive depth using two eyes. Our eyes focus on objects, and our brains interpret the difference between what each eye sees to provide depth perception. Without two eyes, the world would look like a flat, two-dimensional place, and activities that require depth perception (say, a game of catch) would be very difficult, if not impossible.

A video camera only has one eye, which means it has no depth perception. This is why video images appear as two-dimensional pictures. You can use this to your advantage, because you can make objects look like they're right next to each other when they're actually very far apart. Video professionals use this trick often, and call it *forced perspective*.

Consider the video image in Figure 17-5. It looks like a locomotive and train cars parked in a train yard, but looks are deceiving in this case. As you can see in Figure 17-6, the locomotive in the foreground is a scale model, and the train cars are real and about 50 yards away.

Figure 17-5: A typical industrial scene?

Figure 17-6:
Nope! The
camera's
eye is easily
deceived.

To make forced perspective work, you must

✔ **Compose the shot carefully.** The illusion of forced perspective works
only if the scale looks realistic for the various items in the shot. You'll
probably have to fine-tune the position of your subjects and the camera
to get just the right visual effect.

✔ **Focus.** If objects are very far apart, getting both of them in focus may be
difficult. To control focus, follow these steps:

1. **Set the zoom lens at the widest setting by pressing the zoom
control toward "W" on the camcorder so the lens zooms all
the way out.**

2. **Turn off auto-focus (as described in your camcorder's owner's
manual).**

3. **Set the focus to infinity.**

Some manual focus controls have an Infinity setting. If your camcorder does not, manually adjust the focus so objects that are 20
or more feet away are in focus.

4. **Position the camera 5 to 10 feet from the closer subject in your
forced-perspective shot.**

Check carefully to make sure everything is in focus before you
shoot; move the camera if necessary. With most camcorders,
everything beyond a distance of about five feet will probably be in
focus when you zoom out and set focus to infinity.

In Figures 17-5 and 17-6, I showed you how a small object in the foreground blends well with a large object in the background. But it can also work the other way around. In fact, model-railroad enthusiasts often use forced perspective to make their train layouts seem bigger than they really are. Mountains, trees, and buildings in the background are made smaller to provide the illusion that they are farther away.

Creating a Picture-in-Picture

You're watching the game, and during the action a picture appears of one of the stars as the commentators discuss that player. On the nightly news, a feature story is illustrated by a little video window off to the side of the news anchor. These are picture-in-picture effects, and if you have a video-editing program that supports multiple timeline tracks and video clip animation, you can make your own picture-in-picture effects too.

Programs that can do picture-in-picture effects include Adobe Premiere Elements, Apple Final Cut Express, Avid Express, and other advanced editing programs. These programs offer the multiple timeline tracks and animation features needed to do this effect.

Creating a picture-in-picture effect with a program like Premiere Elements is surprisingly easy. It's so easy, in fact, that you'll wonder why you didn't try it earlier. Follow these steps:

1. **Place the video clip or still image that will serve as the main background in the Video 1 track.**

2. **Place the clip or image that will be the smaller picture-in-picture in track Video 2 or higher.**

   This clip is called the overlay clip. Make sure that the timeline's play head is somewhere on the overlay clip you just inserted in track Video 2.

3. **Click the overlay clip once to select it.**

   The video image of the clip appears in the Monitor window.

4. **Click once on the video image in the timeline.**

   Notice that when you click a video image in the Monitor, resizing handles appear around the edges of the image.

5. **Click and drag a corner of the video image in the Monitor to make the image smaller.**

6. Click and drag the center of the overlay image to move it to a new location.

The center of the image in the Monitor window looks like crosshairs. When you reposition the overlay clip, don't just look at one frame of video. Play the background video to make sure your overlay clip doesn't obscure important elements in the video. Also, remember not to put picture-in-picture effects too close to the edge of the screen, or else they may get cut off by TV overscan (I describe overscan in Chapter 9).

Figure 17-7 shows how a picture-in-picture effect looks in Premiere Elements. Now that you know the basics of creating this effect, follow these tips to make your picture-in-picture effects better:

- Try to use clips that contrast each other to ensure that the smaller picture-in-picture doesn't get lost in the larger background. In Figure 17-7, the background has a lighter background, and the smaller picture has a darker background.

- Use drop shadows to help visually offset the picture-in-picture. This is especially helpful when there is little or no contrast between the two clips. The Drop Shadow effect is found in the Perspective subfolder of the Premiere Elements Video Effects folder.

- Listen carefully to the audio. If you want the audio from the picture-in-picture to be more prominent, you may need to temporarily turn down the volume for the background clip's audio. See Chapter 10 for more on working with audio.

- Consider adding transitions to the beginning and end of the picture-in-picture clip. Without transitions, the picture-in-picture seems to pop in and out of the video image abruptly. A transition helps soften the appearance of the picture-in-picture, while at the same time helping the user shift focus to the desired clip. The Zoom transition (see Chapter 9 for more on working with transitions) is a good choice.

In this section, I showed you how to create a picture-in-picture effect the hard way because these basic techniques will work in most advanced video-editing programs. If you have Premiere Elements, you can also use some handy effects presets to quickly create picture-in-picture effects. In the Effects and Transitions window, click the Video FX button, and then click the arrow next to Presets. In the PiP categories, you will find presets that quickly apply picture-in-picture effects to clips. Simply drag and drop a PiP preset to an overlay clip in the timeline to apply it. After you have applied the preset, you can use the techniques described in this section to customize the effect.

Click-and-drag handles

Figure 17-7:
Picture-in-picture effects have many uses.

Background clip · · · · · · Picture-in-picture clip

Making Your Own Sound Effects

Believe it or not, some professional videographers will tell you that sound is actually more important than video. The reasoning goes like this: A typical viewing audience is surprisingly forgiving of minor flaws and glitches in the video picture. The viewer is able to easily "tune out" imperfections, which partially explains why cartoons are so effective. However, poor sound has an immediate and significant effect on the viewer. Poor sound gives the impression of an unprofessional, poorly produced movie.

Chapter 7 shows you how to record better-quality sound. But another key aspect of your movie's audio is the sound *effects*. I don't just mean laser blasts or crude bathroom noises, but subtle, everyday sounds — not always picked up by your camcorder — that make your movie sound much more realistic. These effects are often called Foley sounds, named for sound-effects pioneer Jack Foley. Here are some easy sound effects you can make:

- **Breaking bones:** Snap carrots or celery in half. Fruit and vegetables can be used to produce many disgusting sounds.

- **Buzzing insect:** Wrap wax paper tightly around a comb, place your lips so that they are just barely touching the paper, and hum so that the wax paper makes a buzzing sound.

- **Fire:** Crumple cellophane or wax paper to simulate the sound of a crackling fire.

- **Footsteps:** Hold two shoes and tap the heels together, followed by the toes. Experiment with different shoe types for different sounds. This may take some practice to get the timing of each footstep just right.

- **Gravel or snow:** Use cat litter to simulate the sound of walking through snow or gravel.

- **Horse hooves:** This is one of *the* classic sound effects. The clop-clop-clopping of horse hooves is often made by clapping two halves of a coconut shell together.

- **Kiss:** Pucker up and give your forearm a nice big smooch to make the sound of a kiss.

- **Punch:** Punch a raw piece of steak or a raw chicken. Of course, make sure you practice safe food-handling hygiene rules when handling raw foods: Wash your hands and all other surfaces after you're done.

- **Thunder:** Shake a large piece of sheet metal to simulate a thunderstorm.

- **Town bell:** To replicate the sound of a large bell ringing, hold the handle of a metal stew pot lid, and tap the edge with a spoon or other metal object. Experiment with various strikers, lids, or other pots and pans for just the right effect.

If you use Apple iMovie, you already have a great library of sound effects to choose from and use in your movies. iMovie comes with a selection of pre-recorded sound effects. To access them, click the Audio button on the iMovie toolbar, and then choose iMovie Sound Effects from the menu at the top of the audio pane.

Improving Audio Quality

In Chapter 7, I gave some tips on how to record better audio. Of course, we always *try* to record perfect audio, but sometimes a few flaws are inevitable. Your audio recordings may have all kinds of problems, including wind noise, electronic hums, pops, poor volume, and other unwanted sounds.

When your video has substandard audio, your first thought may be something like, "That's okay, I'll just cover it up with a head-bangin' heavy metal soundtrack." Music is certainly one way to disguise bad audio, but if you have an advanced video-editing program like Adobe Premiere Elements, you may have other options as well. Premiere offers an assortment of audio effects that can help you modify and improve the quality of your audio.

To view a list of audio effects in Premiere Elements, click the arrow next to Audio Effects in the Effects and Transitions window (see Chapter 11 for more on working with effects in Premiere). The audio effects in Premiere that you can use to improve audio quality include

- **Balance:** Use this effect to control the balance between the left and right channels in a stereo clip.

- **Bass:** Not to be confused with the large-mouthed fish whose name is spelled the same, bass sounds are the deep, low frequency sounds in an audio clip. Adding a little bass can help audio sound fuller and richer.

- **Channel Volume:** Allows you to control the volume of stereo channels independently. Unlike the Balance effect, the Channel Volume effect does not shift audio between channels. Use this if one channel seems to have a lot of unwanted noise.

- **DeNoiser:** Removes unwanted background noise during quiet parts of the clip. This effect works kind of like the Dolby noise reduction found on audio cassette tape players by removing pops and hisses from the audio.

- **Dynamics:** This is a great effect for quickly eliminating background noise while at the same time improving overall quality. The Dynamics effect also reduces *clipping,* which is the distortion that sometimes occurs when audio is too loud.

- **Highpass:** Removes lower frequencies from the audio clip. Use this effect if your clip has an unwanted low-frequency hum, or low-frequency ambient noise. A good example of this is the road noise heard in a car traveling down the highway.

- **Invert:** Inverts the audio phase (or delay) between the left and right audio channels in a stereo clip. For example, if the audio in the left channel is slightly delayed behind the right channel, a slight echo may occur in the audio clip. The Invert effect inverts the phase so that the right channel is delayed instead of the left, thus (hopefully) reducing or eliminating the echo.

- **Lowpass:** This effect is similar to the Highpass effect, but it removes higher frequencies from the audio. Use this effect to remove high-frequency buzzes or whines (such as camcorder tape drive noise) from a clip.

✔ **Notch:** Removes sound at a frequency you specify. Use this effect if the audio clip has a constant hum caused by a nearby power line or a flaw in the recording device.

✔ **PitchShifter:** Adjusts pitch in an audio clip. For example, if you sped up a clip and the voices now have an unnaturally high pitch, you can use this effect to make the voices sounds more normal.

✔ **Reverb:** Makes the audio clip sound as if it's being played in a large hall or room.

✔ **Swap Channels:** Swaps the left and right stereo channels, if for some reason you decide that the sound in the right channel should be on the left, and vice versa.

✔ **Treble:** Provides control over treble (the higher frequency sounds) in the clip. Reducing treble slightly can take the edge off audio clips that seem too harsh and have too much treble.

✔ **Volume:** Allows you to adjust volume with an effect rather than the clip's volume rubber bands.

Filtering Your Video

Say you're making a movie showing the fun people can have when they're stuck indoors on a rainy day. Such a movie wouldn't be complete without an establishing shot to show one of the subjects looking out a window at the dismal weather. Alas, when you try to shoot this scene, all you see is a big, nasty, glaring reflection on the window.

Reflections are among the many video problems you can resolve with a lens filter on your camcorder. Filters usually attach to the front of your camera lens, and change the nature of the light passing through it. Different kinds of filters have different effects. Common filter types include

✔ **Polarizing filter:** This type of filter often features an adjustable ring, and can be used to reduce or control reflections on windows, water, and other surfaces.

✔ **UV filter:** This filter reduces UV light, and is often used to protect the lens from scratches, dust, or other damage. I never use my camcorder without at least a UV filter in place.

✔ **Neutral density (ND) filter:** This filter works kind of like sunglasses for your camcorder. It prevents overexposure in very bright light conditions, reducing the amount of light that passes through the lens without changing the color. If you experience washed-out color when you shoot on a sunny day, try using a ND filter.

✔ **Color-correction filters:** Many different kinds of color-correction filters exist. These help correct for various kinds of color imbalances in your video. Some filters can enhance colors when you're shooting outdoors on an overcast day; others reduce the color cast by certain kinds of light (such as a greenish cast that comes from many fluorescent lights).

✔ **Soft filter:** These filters soften details slightly in your image. This filter is often used to hide skin blemishes or wrinkles on actors who are more advanced in age.

✔ **Star filter:** Creates starlike patterns on extreme light sources to add a sense of magic to the video.

Many more kinds of filters are available. Check with the manufacturer of your camcorder to see whether it offers filters specially designed for your camera, and also check the documentation to see what kind of filters can work with your camcorder. Many camcorders accept standard 37mm or 58mm threaded filters. Tiffen is an excellent source for filters, and its Web site (www.tiffen.com) has photographic samples that show the effects of various filters on your images. To see these samples, visit www.tiffen.com and click the link for information on Tiffen Filters. Then locate a link for the Tiffen Filter Brochure. This online brochure provides detailed information on the filters offered by Tiffen.

Dealing with the Elements

You may at times deal with extremes of temperature or other weather conditions while shooting video. No, this section isn't about making sure the people in your movies wear jackets when it's cold (although it's always wise to bundle up). I'm more concerned about the health of your camcorder right now — and several environmental factors can affect it:

✔ **Condensation:** If you quickly move your camera from a very cold environment to a very warm environment (or vice versa), condensation can form on the lens. It can even form inside the camera on the inner surface of the lens, which is disastrous because you cannot easily clean it. Avoid subjecting your camcorder to rapid, extreme temperature changes.

✔ **Heat:** Digital tapes are still subject to the same environmental hazards as old analog tapes. Don't leave your camcorder or tapes in a roasting car when it's 105 degrees outside. Professional videographers often use a cooler for storing tapes. You shouldn't use ice packs in the cooler, but simply placing the tapes in an empty cooler helps insulate them from temperature extremes.

✔ **Water:** A few drops of rain can quickly destroy the sensitive electronic circuits inside your camcorder. If you believe that water may be a problem, cover your camcorder with a plastic bag, or shoot your video at another time if possible. If you actually want to show falling raindrops in your shot, you may be able to add virtual rain later while editing. Some editing programs (such as iMovie) have effects that simulate rain — sometimes more realistically than the real thing.

✔ **Wind:** Even a gentle breeze blowing across the screen on your camcorder's microphone can cause a loud roaring on the audio recording. Try to shield your microphone from wind unless you know you'll be replacing the audio later during the editing process.

Another environmental hazard in many video shoots is the sun — that big, bright ball of nuclear fusion that crosses the sky every day. The sun helps plants grow, provides solar energy, and helps humans generate Vitamin D. But like all good things, the sun is best enjoyed in moderation. Too much sunlight causes skin cancer, fades the paint on your car, and overexposes the subjects in your video. Natural skin tones turn into washed-out blobs, and sunlight reflecting directly on your camcorder's lens causes light flares or hazing in your video image.

You'll probably shoot video outdoors on a regular basis, so follow these tips when the sun is at its brightest:

✔ **Use filters.** Earlier in this chapter, I describe how lens filters can improve the quality of the video you shoot. Neutral-density and color-correction filters can reduce the overexposure caused by the sun while improving your color quality.

✔ **Shade your lens.** If sunlight reflects directly on your lens, it can cause streaks or bright spots called *lens flares*. Higher-end camcorders usually have black hoods that extend out in front of the lens to prevent this. If your camcorder doesn't have a hood, you can make one, using black paper or photographic tape from a photographic-supply store. (Check the video image to make sure your homemade hood doesn't show up in the picture!)

✔ **If possible, position your subject in a shaded area.** This allows you to take advantage of the abundant natural light without your subject being overexposed.

✔ **Avoid backlit situations.** If your subject is in shade and you shoot video at such an angle that the background is very bright, you'll wind up with a video picture that looks something like Figure 17-8. Your camera may have a Backlight setting to compensate for this condition, but it's best to shoot subjects against a more neutral or dark background whenever possible.

✔ **Wear sunscreen.** Your video image isn't the only thing you should protect from the sun!

Figure 17-8:
Avoid
backlit
situations
such as this.

The Ken Burns Effect

Ken Burns is one of the most renowned documentarians to ever make, er, documentaries. He has the uncanny ability to make fascinating movies about historical subjects for which there is little or no original film or video footage. For example, Burns's documentary film series on the American Civil War and the Oregon Trail were put together mainly using spoken interviews and still photographs from the period.

The tricky part about what Ken Burns does is to make his work come across as interesting movies instead of just slide shows with music and narration. Burns and other documentary filmmakers do this by panning or zooming on still images as they appear on the screen. This technique adds a sense of motion and action to the movie that would otherwise be lacking in a simple slide show.

Apple iMovie includes an effect called the Ken Burns Effect, and basically this effect slowly pans or zooms on a still image. You can do the same thing with Adobe Premiere Elements, although Adobe doesn't use Ken Burns's name.

Even if you're not doing a documentary film without much video footage, the Ken Burns technique can still come in handy. Say, for example, you're making a movie about a road trip. You can periodically pan and zoom across a still image of a map that details the progress.

Panning or zooming on a still image is easy in Premiere Elements. In the Effects and Transitions window, click the Video FX button, and then click the triangle next to Presets to open the Presets folder. The Presets folder contains four subfolders that you can use on your still images:

- ✔ **Horizontal Image Pans:** These presets pan horizontally left-to-right or right-to-left across the image.

- ✔ **Horizontal Image Zooms:** These zoom in or out on the image along a horizontal plane.

- ✔ **Vertical Image Pans:** These presets pan vertically up or down the image.

- ✔ **Vertical Image Zooms:** These zoom in or out on the image along a vertical plane.

Simply drag and drop an image pan or zoom preset to a still image in the Timeline, just like any other effect. These presets modify the Motion settings for the clip. As with most effects, you'll probably have to experiment a bit to get just the desired effect. And of course, preview your edits carefully. Pans and zooms on still images are most effective if they move slowly and in only one direction. Panning back and forth might make some audience members seasick!

Freeze Frame!

It's a sunny Wednesday afternoon at soccer practice. The players are scrimmaging each other in a practice game, when suddenly the coach notices that some players are out of position. "Freeze!" he yells, and the players obediently stop in their tracks.

Just as a coach evaluating the position of players on a field, freezing the action can sometimes be useful in your movies. You can do freeze frames pretty easily, even in basic editing programs like iMovie and Windows Movie Maker. To momentarily freeze a frame of video in the middle of a clip, and then make it play again, follow these steps:

1. **In the timeline, move the play head to the exact frame that you want to freeze.**

   You can use the left and right arrow keys (Alt+Arrow in Windows Movie Maker) to move back and forth a single frame at a time.

2. **Click the clip in the timeline that you want to freeze to select it.**

3. **Split the clip at the play head.**

   In Adobe Premiere Elements, choose Timeline➪Split Clip. In Apple iMovie, choose Edit➪Split Video Clip at Playhead. In Windows Movie Maker, choose Clip➪Split.

4. Export the current frame as a still image.

In Adobe Premiere Elements, choose File⇨Export⇨Frame. In Apple iMovie, choose Edit⇨Create Still Frame. In Windows Movie Maker, choose Tools⇨Take Picture from Preview. In Premiere Elements and Windows Movie Maker, you are prompted to name and save the image file. In all three programs, the exported still image frame is automatically added to your media collection window.

5. Click and drag the still image from the media collection window and drop it on the timeline at the location of the play head.

The still image is inserted between the two clips you created when you split the original clip in step 3.

Ta-da! You've just added a freeze-frame effect to your movie, similar to the one shown in Figure 17-9. When you play the timeline, the frame appears to freeze momentarily. You may need to adjust the duration of the still frame to make it appear for a longer or shorter period of time. See Chapter 12 for more on adjusting the duration of still images.

Figure 17-9:
Frames of video can be momentarily frozen.

Frozen frame

Chapter 18

Ten Tools for Digital Video

*Y*ou just bought a new digital camcorder, and you find that it's a pretty cool device. But if you are a gadget-person and you find yourself asking, "Is that all there is?" don't worry! There are still plenty of amazing widgets left to buy.

This chapter shows you some things that make digital video and moviemaking fun and easy. Nothing in this chapter is truly mandatory, but some things (tripods, microphones) are pretty important, some are really nice to have (LightScribe drives and helmet cams), and some (music generators, multimedia controllers) will have you wondering how you ever got by without them. So sit back, fire up the credit card, and take a tour of some of the top moviemaking programs and equipment.

Tripods and Other Stabilization Devices

After a digital camcorder, a good tripod is probably the first thing you should buy. The first time you watch some of your video on a large TV screen, you'll see them: Little wiggles that seemed minute while looking through the viewfinder become major distractions as the hand-held camcorder pitches, rolls, and yaws all over the scene, seemingly recording everything *but* the intended subject.

Before you blame yourself for a lack of videography skill, keep in mind that even the most experienced video professionals use tripods whenever they can. Video tripods are widely available, starting as low as $20 at your local department store. Alas, as with so many other things in life, when you buy a tripod, you get what you pay for. High-quality video tripods incorporate several important features:

- ✔ **Dual-stanchion legs and bracing:** Dual-stanchion legs generally have two poles per leg, which gives the tripod greater stability, especially during panning shots. Braces at the base or middle of the tripod's legs also aid stability.

- ✔ **High-tech, lightweight materials:** You'll soon get tired of lugging a 15-20–pound tripod around with your camera gear. Higher-quality tripods frequently use high-tech materials (including titanium, aircraft-quality aluminum, and carbon-fiber) that are strong and lightweight, making the gear less cumbersome to transport and use.

- ✔ **Bubble levels:** These built-in tools help you ensure that your camera is level, even if the ground underneath the tripod isn't.

- ✔ **Fluid heads:** These ensure that pans are smooth and jerk-free.

- ✔ **Counterweights:** The best tripods have adjustable counterweights so the head can be balanced for your camera and lens (telephoto lenses, for example, can make the camera a bit front-heavy). Counterweights allow smooth use of the fluid head while still giving you the option of letting go of the camera without having it tilt out of position.

For a tripod with all these features, you can expect to spend at least $300, if not much, much more. If that kind of money isn't in your tripod budget right now, try to get a tripod that incorporates as many of these features as possible.

Monopods

Tripods aren't the only stabilization devices available. You may also want to keep a monopod handy for certain occasions. As the name suggests, a monopod has only one leg (just as tripods have three legs, octopods have eight, and . . . well, you get the idea). Although this means some camera movement is inevitable — you have to keep the camera balanced on the monopod — resting the monopod on the ground can give you more stability than you'd have if you simply hand-held the camera. Monopods come in handy when you have to move frequently, or when you're shooting in an area with a lot of people who might bump or trip over the legs of a tripod. In a pinch, a monopod can also be used as a makeshift boom for getting those tricky overhead shots.

Mobile stabilizers

If you've watched a sporting event on TV lately, you may have seen footage of a player running along where the camera appears to stay with the player as he or she runs. And although the camera operator was obviously moving to get the shot, the image appears to be as stable as any tripod shot. How can this be? There are two possibilities:

- ✔ The camera operator is a superhero with the special ability to hold heavy objects absolutely still, even while riding a Radio Flyer wagon down a rocky, rutted slope.
- ✔ The camera operator was using a Steadicam-style device.

Steadicam (www.steadicam.com) is a brand of camera stabilizer that allows both super-stable images and handheld mobility. A Steadicam device attaches to the camera operator with an elaborate harness, and it is powered by a complex system of counterweights, pulleys, levers, gimbals, gyroscopes, hamster wheels, and magic crystals.

Steadicams are incredibly effective, but they are also incredibly expensive. The "affordable" Steadicam JR, which is aimed at semiprofessionals and prosumers, sells for over $400! (You don't even want to know what the professional-grade units cost.)

Other, more affordable devices are available. Check your local camera shop to see what is available for mobile stabilization. If you're handy with a needle and thread, you can even make a sling to help stabilize your arm while shooting. Fashion a sling that enables you to support your forearm with your neck and shoulders. This will reduce fatigue and thus result in smoother images.

Lighting

Many video shoots can benefit from more light. Light brings out more detail and color in your video, which is why professional videographers always carefully set up lighting before shooting a scene. (Chapter 4 describes some techniques for lighting a video scene.) Lighting equipment that you'll want for your video shoots includes

- ✔ **Lights:** Most people would consider *lights* the most important pieces of lighting equipment. Incandescents, fluorescents, halogens, and most other bright light sources are useful.

- ✔ **Reflectors:** Reflectors bounce light onto a subject for a softer, more diffuse effect. You can buy professional-style reflectors, or you can make your own, as I described in Chapter 4.

- ✔ **Gels:** Gels are translucent or semi-transparent materials that cover a light to diffuse or colorize it somewhat.

- ✔ **Extension cords:** Unfortunately, power outlets aren't always conveniently located right next to every scene you want to shoot. Extension cords to the rescue!

- ✔ **Duct tape:** Use cheap, widely-available duct tape from your local hardware store, or be like the pros and pick up some theatrical gaffing tape from a musician-supply store. Duct tape is the miracle tool with a thousand-and-one uses. Use tape to hold up reflectors and gels. Secure cords to the floor so that they don't become trip hazards. Mark your coffee cup with a small strip of tape so you know which one is yours. Use it to remove embarrassing body hair.

Professional-style video lighting can be purchased at most photographic supply stores, or you can mail order it from specialty retailers like B&H Photo (www.bhphotovideo.com). Be prepared, however, to spend hundreds (if not thousands) of dollars for professional equipment.

If you're more of a budget-minded moviemaker, do what I do and head down to the local hardware store. There you can find work lights that are bright, durable, and (most importantly) cheap. Work lights often come with stands or clips that help you position your lights without spending hours on setup. While you're at the hardware store, pick up some cheap fluorescent shop lights. These fixtures can be suspended over a scene or backdrop in your makeshift home studio and put out a lot of useful light for the price. Translucent fluorescent light covers make excellent, heat-resistant diffusers for light.

Music Generators

The quickest and easiest way to add a musical soundtrack to your movie is to pop your favorite music disc in the computer's CD-ROM drive and rip some audio files onto your hard drive. I show how to do this in Chapter 7. Unfortunately, songs copied from audio CDs present a couple of significant problems:

- ✔ The songs are never *exactly* the right length. You'll often find yourself just using portions of songs, or even adding or removing video content from your project just to make the movie fit the song.

✔ The tempo and style may not be right. I'm sure your taste in music is impeccable, but most personal music libraries are missing a style or two.

✔ The copyright holder may not like your use of the song. Songs on audio CDs are copyrighted. If you put the song *We are the Champions* at the end of home movie about a soccer game, and only your family and close friends will be watching it, legal representatives of the band "Queen" probably aren't going to come beat down your door. However, if your movie becomes very popular on the Internet, or if you want to sell the movie, the copyright owners of your background music will not be pleased.

Instead of pre-recorded music, consider music generation software. As the name implies, music generators *generate* music. You pick the music style, you choose how long it should play, and set a few more options, and the generator automatically creates some soundtrack music that fits your project perfectly. A couple of music generators that I have used and enjoyed include

✔ **SmartSound Quicktracks** (www.smartsound.com). SmartSound has been making great music generation software for years. They offer a version that is specifically designed to work with Adobe Premiere Pro and Premiere Elements. It retails for $99.95, which may sound like a lot, but is actually very affordable compared to the cost of song licensing.

✔ **Super Duper Music Looper** (www.musiclooper.com). I was first introduced to this program by my son, who started using it in the computer lab of the local Boys and Girls Club. This program — published by Sony — is designed to let kids create music on the computer, but it's a surprisingly effective tool for making music, and, at $19.95, it's also very affordable. It's not as powerful as the SmartSound software, and you may find the kid-oriented user interface a bit, well, childish. But Super Duper Music Looper can output usable soundtrack music, and if nothing else, this may be a great way to get the whole family involved in your movie projects.

LightScribe DVD Drives

You've burned your movie onto DVD, and now you plan to share your DVD discs with others. Before you drop that disc in the mail, it might be a good idea to label it somehow. You could just scribble the movie's name on the disc using a Sharpie, but that looks pretty amateurish. Another option is to print up some DVD labels, but then you have to buy special label paper for your printer, and you have to use one of those special label centering tool thingies to make sure the label gets applied to the disc *just right*. This is such a pain that most of us don't bother with labels, opting for the Sharpie instead.

But wait: There is a better option! Now you can label your DVD discs neatly and professionally, without having to mess around with label paper and centering tool thingies. Many new DVD burners now incorporate a technology called LightScribe. With a LightScribe drive, you burn the DVD disc, and then flip it over. The LightScribe drive etches a label design directly onto the disc, as shown in Figure 18-1. LightScribe printing requires special LightScribe-compatible blank CD-Rs and DVD-Rs, but LightScribe media is available at many popular retail outlets.

If you're in the market for a new DVD burner, a LightScribe drive is something to consider. If you've always eschewed labels because of the hassle, a LightScribe drive may be your ticket to finally retiring that Sharpie.

Figure 18-1:
LightScribe
drives make
disc labeling
easy!

Photograph provided courtesy of Hewlett-Packard Company. Copyright Hewlett-Packard Development Company, L.P.

Microphones

Virtually all camcorders have built-in microphones. Most digital camcorders boast 48-bit stereo sound-recording capabilities, but you'll soon find that the quality of the audio you record is still limited primarily by the quality of the microphone you use. Therefore, if you care even a little about making great movies, you *need* better microphones than the one built into your camcorder.

Your camcorder should have connectors for external microphones, and your camcorder's manufacturer may offer accessory microphones for your specific camera.

One type of special microphone you may want to use is a *lavalier* microphone — a tiny unit that usually clips to a subject's clothing to pick up his or her voice. You often see lavalier mics clipped to the lapels of TV newscasters. Some lavalier units are designed to fit inside clothing or costumes, although some practice and special shielding may be required to eliminate rubbing noises.

A good place to look for high-quality microphones is a musician's supply store. Just make sure that the connectors and frequency range are compatible with your camcorder or other recording device (check the documentation). You may also want to check with your camcorder's manufacturer; it might offer accessory microphones specially designed to work with your camcorder. Finally, the Internet is always a good resource as well. One good resource is www.shure.com, the Web site of Shure Incorporated. Shure sells microphones and other audio products, and the Web site is an excellent resource for general information about choosing and using microphones.

MP3 Recorders

Recording good sound used to mean spending hundreds of dollars for a DAT (digital audio tape) recorder. However, these days, the best compromise of quality versus sound for an amateur moviemaker may be to use an MP3 player with recording ability. If you have even a cursory knowledge of today's consumer electronics market, you're probably aware of MP3 players. Some of them can also record audio, making them a handy recording tool for your movies.

I know, I know, your camcorder records audio along with video, and it's already perfectly synchronized. So what is the point of recording audio separately? Well, you may need the capabilities of an audio recorder in many situations. Take, for example, these three:

- ✔ **You may want to record a subject who is across the room.** In this case, have the subject hold a recorder (or conceal it so it's off camera), and attach an inconspicuous lavalier microphone to the subject.

- ✔ **You may want to record only a special sound, on location, and add it to the soundtrack later.** For example, you might show crashing waves in the distant background, but use the close-up sound of those waves for dramatic effect.

- ✔ **You can record narration for a video project.** After you've recorded your narration, tweak it till it suits your needs and then add it to the soundtrack of your movie.

Don't forget a slate!

If you use a secondary audio recorder, one of the biggest challenges you may face is synchronizing the audio it records with video. Professionals ensure synchronization of audio and video using a *slate* — that black-and-white board that you often see production people snapping shut on camera just before the director yells, "Action!"

The slate is not just a kitschy movie thing. The snapping of the slate makes a noise that can be picked up by all audio recorders on scene. When you are editing audio tracks later (see Chapter 10), this noise shows up as a visible spike on the audio waveform. Because the slate is snapped in front of the camera, you can later match the waveform spike on the audio track with the visual picture of the slate snapping closed on the video track. If you're recording audio with external recorders, consider making your own slate. This makes audio-video synchronization a lot easier during the post-production process.

Countless other uses for audio recorders exist. You may simply find that an external, dedicated recorder records better-quality audio than the built-in mic in your camcorder.

Before you buy an MP3 player, check the specifications to make sure that it can record audio. Also, make sure that it can record using an external microphone. Many MP3 players can record audio, but some of them only allow you to record from a low-quality built-in microphone.

Multimedia Controllers

I don't know about you, but I find that manipulating some of the playback and editing controls in my video-editing software using just the mouse isn't always easy. Sure, there are keyboard shortcuts for most actions — and you may find yourself using those keyboard shortcuts quite a bit — but there's an even better way. You can also control most Windows or Macintosh programs with an external *multimedia controller,* such as the SpaceShuttle A/V from Contour A/V Solutions. The SpaceShuttle A/V, shown in Figure 18-2, features five buttons and a two-part, dial control in an ergonomically designed housing. The overall design of the SpaceShuttle A/V is based on professional video-editing controllers. The unit plugs into a USB port (which can be found on virtually any modern computer). You can find out more about the SpaceShuttle A/V online at

```
www.contouravs.com
```

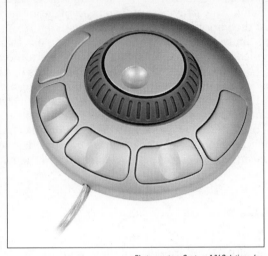

Photo courtesy Contour A/V Solutions, Inc.

The SpaceShuttle A/V sells for about $50, and it works quite well with Apple iMovie, Adobe Premiere Elements, and Windows Movie Maker. If you are using a more advanced editing program such as Adobe Premiere Elements or Apple Final Cut Express, you may want to consider the higher-end model, the ShuttlePro (shown in Figure 18-3). The ShuttlePro is similar to the SpaceShuttle A/V but with some additional buttons. The ShuttlePro can also be used with iMovie and Movie Maker, but many of the extra buttons are unused in these simpler programs.

Photo courtesy Contour A/V Solutions, Inc.

Contour provides control presets that allow their controllers to be used with many different programs. The array of buttons may look intimidating at first, but I have found that the various functions are simple to figure out, and the ergonomic design certainly makes the controllers easier to use than keyboard shortcuts. In most video-editing programs, SpaceShuttle buttons can be used to play forward, play backward, pause, or move to edit points in a movie project. But most useful are the dials. The spring-loaded outer ring acts as a shuttle control, and the inner dial rolls video forward or back a frame at a time (like the jog control in many editing programs, only the dial is a *lot* easier to use). The controllers even work with device-control capabilities to control external camcorders and tape decks during capture. The buttons are customizable, too, meaning you can apply new functions to them if you want.

Video Converters

You have a computer with a FireWire port, and you want to capture some analog video. What are you going to do? You have many, many solutions, of course. You could install a video-capture card, but a good one is expensive, and installing it means tearing apart your computer. If you're lucky, you might be able to connect an analog video source to the analog inputs on your digital camcorder, and *then* connect the camcorder to the FireWire port. This method is clumsy, however, and it simply won't work with some camcorders.

A simpler solution may be to use an external *video converter* — usually a box that connects to your computer's FireWire port. The box includes analog inputs, so you can connect an analog VCR or camcorder to the box. The unit itself converts signals from analog media into DV-format video, which is then captured into your computer — where you can easily edit it using your video-editing software.

 If you have worked with analog video a lot, you're probably aware that some quality is lost every time you make a copy of the video (especially if it's a copy-of-a-copy). This is called *generational loss.* Not to worry: A video converter like those described here doesn't present any more generational loss than a standard video-capture card does; after the signal is converted to digital, generational loss is no longer a problem until you output the video to an analog tape.

Most converter boxes can also be useful for exporting video to an analog source. You simply export the DV-format video from your editing program, and the converter box converts it into an analog signal that you can record on your analog tape deck. Among other advantages, this method of export saves a lot of wear and tear on the tape-drive mechanisms in your expensive digital camcorder. Features to look for in a video converter include

✔ Analog output

✔ PC or Mac support (as appropriate)

✔ Color-bar output

✔ Multiple FireWire and analog inputs/outputs

Video converters typically range in price from $200 to $300 for consumer-level converters. Table 18-1 lists a few popular units.

Table 18-1		Video Converters	
Manufacturer	*Model*	*Street Price*	*Web Site*
Canopus	ADVC-50	$200	www.canopuscorp.com/
Plextor	ConvertX Digital Video Converter	$75–100	www.plextor.com/
Pinnacle Systems	Dazzle Digital Video Creator 90	$75–100	www.pinnaclesys.com/

Helmet Cams

If you participate in any high-action activities such as bicycling, motorcycling, skiing, or something similar, you probably can't wait to shoot some exciting video of your pastime. And why not? High-action activities are excellent video subjects, and one of the most interesting video shots you can get is one that shows the player's-eye-view.

Alas, it's really not prudent (or safe) to hold a camcorder as you ride your mountain bike down a narrow, rocky trail. A solution is to stow your camcorder in a backpack or other safe location and use a small external camera to shoot the video action. These small cameras are often called *helmet cams* because many people attach them to the side or top of a helmet. They connect to your camcorder with a cord and are small enough that you can safely mount them in a variety of locations. Several companies offer small accessory cameras:

✔ **bulletcam.com** at www.bulletcam.com

✔ **CatchIt Cam** at www.catchitcam.com

✔ **HelmetCamera.com** at www.helmetcamera.com

✔ **SportZshot.com** at www.sportzshot.com

✔ **Viosport.com** at www.viosport.com

Usually the image quality captured by a small helmet cam is inferior to that recorded by your camcorder, but it's a small price to pay for great action shots. Before you choose any helmet cam, check the manufacturer's Web site to ensure that it is compatible with your camcorder.

Although these small cams are often called "helmet" cams, I recommend you avoid attaching them to a helmet or any other place that may cause injury. And of course, protect your camcorder. The vibration and shaking (not to mention the danger of crashing) involved with riding a bicycle or skiing down a slope can damage your camcorder (among other things).

Video Decks

Because it's so easy to simply connect a FireWire cable to your camcorder and capture video right into your computer, you may be tempted to use your digital camcorder as your sole MiniDV tape deck. If you're on a really tight budget, you may not have much of a choice, but otherwise I strongly recommend a high-quality video deck. A video deck not only saves wear and tear on the tape drive mechanisms in your expensive camcorder, but it can also give you greater control over video capture and export back to tape.

Professional video decks are expensive, but if you do a lot of video editing, they quickly pay for themselves — both in terms of the greater satisfaction and quality you're likely to get from your finished movie, and in less money spent on camcorder maintenance. Table 18-2 lists some MiniDV decks to consider.

Table 18-2	DV Video Decks		
Manufacturer	*Model*	*Formats*	*Retail Price*
JVC	SR-VS30U	MiniDV, S-VHS	$700–1,000
Sony	GVD-200 VCR Walkman	Digital 8	$600–700
Sony	GVD-1000 VCR Walkman with 4" LCD screen	MiniDV	$1,100–1,300

If you're shopping for a professional-grade MiniDV deck and money is no object, you can also look for decks that support the DVCAM or DVCPRO tape formats. These are more robust, professional-grade DV tape formats — and decks that support these formats generally also support MiniDV.

Even if you don't think a MiniDV deck is worth the expense, you may still want to consider a S-VHS deck. S-VHS (short for *Super*-VHS) is a higher-quality version of the venerable VHS videotape format. Many S-VHS decks are available for as little as $120 if you shop around. If you plan to export your movies back to tape, you'll get better recording quality if you export to an S-VHS deck instead of a conventional VHS deck. You can export from your computer directly to an S-VHS deck by using one of two methods:

✔ If you have an analog-video capture card such as the Pinnacle Studio Deluxe, or an analog-video converter like the Dazzle Hollywood DV Bridge, connect the S-VHS deck directly to the outputs for your analog device.

✔ Connect your digital camcorder to the FireWire port on your computer, and then connect the S-VHS deck to the analog outputs on the camcorder.

Your camcorder acts as a converter, changing digital video from the computer into analog video for the S-VHS deck. Most modern digital camcorders allow you to do this, but a few older MiniDV and Digital8 camcorders may cause problems, so test your equipment to see what works. If your camcorder won't output analog audio at the same time as you export digital video from the computer, you'll have to record the video onto the camcorder tape before exporting it to an analog video deck.

Chapter 19

Comparing Ten Video-Editing Programs

A few years ago, it looked like Microsoft was set to take over the world. Whenever Microsoft created a program — be it an operating system, a word processor, or a Web browser — it quickly became the most popular choice in its segment. So when Microsoft released Windows Movie Maker a few years ago, many feared that video editing would become another Microsoft enterprise.

I feature Windows Movie Maker throughout this book because it is a pretty good entry-level moviemaking program. But the video-editing market is possibly the most diverse in the software industry, with countless companies already offering editing programs and new companies entering the fray on a regular basis. When it's time to choose a video-editing program, you have a lot of choices. This chapter helps make your choice a little easier by providing a quick cross-reference of features, prices, and specifications for ten of today's most popular moviemaking programs. Here I compare the following ten programs:

- ✔ Adobe Premiere Elements
- ✔ Adobe Premiere Pro
- ✔ Apple iMovie
- ✔ Apple Final Cut Express
- ✔ Apple Final Cut Pro

✔ Avid Xpress DV

✔ Microsoft Windows Movie Maker

✔ NTI CD & DVD Maker

✔ Pinnacle Studio

✔ Pinnacle Liquid Edition

Reviewing the Basics

In your review of video-editing programs, you need to start somewhere, and it might as well be with the basics. Table 19-1 helps you identify which programs will work on your computer, how much they cost, and where to find more information. Keep in mind that I have listed suggested retail prices in U.S. dollars, current as of this writing. Software vendors may change their prices in the future, or you might be able to take advantage of upgrade specials or discounted sale prices. Also, I only list prices for the basic software. Sometimes you can get software packaged with hardware — for example, Pinnacle sells capture cards that include the Studio or Liquid Edition software — but I don't list those packages here because there are too many possible combinations.

Before you purchase or install any software, make sure you check the specific system requirements for that program. Table 19-1 tells you whether each program works on a Mac, a Windows PC, or both, but beyond that, there are many other system requirements you should review. (See Chapter 2 for information on getting your computer ready for editing video, regardless of which program you decide to use.)

Table 19-1	Basic Video Editors		
Program	*Retail Price*	*Platform*	*Web Address*
Adobe Premiere Elements	$99	Windows	www.adobe.com
Adobe Premiere Pro	$699	Windows	www.adobe.com
Apple iMovie	Free (see Appendix B)	Macintosh	www.apple.com/ imovie/
Apple Final Cut Express	$299	Macintosh	www.apple.com/ finalcutexpress/
Apple Final Cut Pro	$999	Macintosh	www.apple.com/ finalcutpro/
Avid Xpress DV	$495	Macintosh/ Windows	www.avid.com

Program	Retail Price	Platform	Web Address
Microsoft Windows Movie Maker	Free (see Appendix C)	Windows	www.microsoft.com/ windowsxp/moviemaker/
NTI CD & DVD Maker	$79	Windows	www.ntius.com
Pinnacle Studio	$99	Windows	www.pinnaclesys.com
Pinnacle Liquid Edition	$499	Windows	www.pinnaclesys.com

Importing Media

Moviemaking isn't much fun if you don't have some audio and video to work with. Virtually all editing programs can import directly from a DV (digital video) camcorder, and some can also import media in a variety of formats. Table 19-2 lists the formats in which these ten editing programs can capture. Some programs support additional formats not listed here, but the formats in Table 19-2 are the ones you're most likely to encounter. In Table 19-3, I have also noted which programs have a batch-capture feature (which, as mentioned in Chapter 11, can be a big timesaver when you capture video).

Table 19-2		Supported Formats for Importing Media				
Program	AVI	CD Audio	MPEG	MP3	QuickTime	Windows Media
Adobe Premiere Elements	X		X	X	X	X
Adobe Premiere Pro	X		X	X	X	X
Apple iMovie		X (using iTunes)		X	X	
Apple Final CutExpress		X	X		X	
Apple Final Cut Pro		X	X		X	
Avid Xpress DV	X		X	X		

(continued)

Table 19-2 *(continued)*

Program	AVI	CD Audio	MPEG	MP3	QuickTime	Windows Media
Microsoft Windows Movie Maker	X	X (using Windows Media Player)	X	X		X
NTI CD & DVD Maker	X	X	X	X		X
Pinnacle Studio	X	X	X	X		X
Pinnacle Liquid Edition	X	X	X	X	X	

Table 19-3 — Support for Video Capture

Program	DV	Analog	Batch Capture
Adobe Premiere Elements	X		
Adobe Premiere Pro	X	X	X
Apple iMovie	X		
Apple Final Cut Express	X		
Apple Final Cut Pro	X	X	X
Avid Xpress DV	X		X
Microsoft Windows Movie Maker	X		
NTI CD & DVD Maker	X		
Pinnacle Studio	X	X	
Pinnacle Liquid Edition	X	X	X

Editing Your Movies

The primary differences between editing programs are the actual editing features offered by each one. Table 19-4 lists the number of video tracks, audio tracks, and transitions available in each program. Generally speaking, the more tracks you have to work with, the better. Figure 19-1 shows a timeline in Adobe Premiere Elements that currently has two separate video tracks and two audio tracks — and more can be easily added if necessary. This arrangement provides a great deal of flexibility when you're editing. Table 19-4 also lists which programs offer tools to perform basic "cleanup" tasks on your video, such as improving color or lighting.

Figure 19-1:
Multiple
video and
audio tracks
give you
more editing
flexibility.

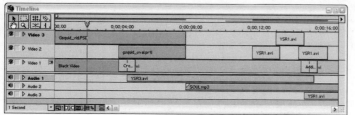

Table 19-4	**Basic Editing Capabilities**			
Program	*Video Tracks*	*Audio Tracks*	*Transitions*	*Video Cleanup Tools*
Adobe Premiere Elements	99	99	79	X
Adobe Premiere Pro	99	99	73	X
Apple iMovie	1	3	13	X
Apple Final Cut Express	99	99	100+	X
Apple Final Cut Pro	99	99	100+	X
Avid Xpress DV	99	99	100+	X
Microsoft Windows Movie Maker	1	2	60	
NTI CD & DVD Maker	1	2	338	X
Pinnacle Studio			266	X
Pinnacle Liquid Edition	Unlimited	Unlimited	200+	X

Table 19-5 identifies more advanced editing features. Here you can see which programs allow you to animate objects onscreen, control transparency of video clips, or key out certain parts of a video image using chroma keys or other similar tools. Keying is important if (for example) you want to do bluescreen effects. I show how to do bluescreen and other compositing effects in Chapter 11.

Table 19-5	Advanced Editing Capabilities		
Program	*Animation*	*Transparency*	*Keying*
Adobe Premiere Elements	X	X	X
Adobe Premiere Pro	X	X	X
Apple iMovie			
Apple Final Cut Express	X	X	X
Apple Final Cut Pro	X	X	X
Avid Xpress DV	X	X	X
Microsoft Windows Movie Maker			
NTI CD & DVD Maker			
Pinnacle Studio			
Pinnacle Liquid Edition	X	X	X

Most video-editing programs offer some built-in special effects. Table 19-6 shows you how many video effects and audio effects are offered in each program. You can also see which programs allow you to control effects using keyframes (which generally indicates far more advanced effects capabilities). Keyframes allow you to control an effect dynamically throughout a clip, as opposed to just applying it uniformly to an entire clip. Finally, some programs come with prerecorded sound effects that you can use in your movies. Interestingly, prerecorded sound effects are more common in the cheaper, low-end editing programs.

Table 19-6	Special-Effects Capabilities			
Program	*Video Effects*	*Audio Effects*	*Keyframe Control*	*Sound Effects*
Adobe Premiere Elements	79	24	X	
Adobe Premiere Pro	94	22	X	

Program	Video Effects	Audio Effects	Keyframe Control	Sound Effects
Apple iMovie	20+	0		X
Apple Final Cut Express	100+	25+	X	
Apple Final Cut Pro	100+	25+	X	X
Avid Xpress DV	100+	7+ audio tools	X	
Microsoft Windows Movie Maker	28	0		
NTI CD & DVD Maker	124	0		
Pinnacle Studio	30	10	X	X
Pinnacle Liquid Edition	Hundreds	Yes	X	

Table 19-7 lists some generators included with the various editing programs. Sorry, none of these generators will power your refrigerator during a brownout — what they do is produce elements that are useful in video production. A *bar-and-tone generator* produces color bars (see Figure 19-2) and a steady audio tone that, when recorded on tape, can be used to calibrate the colors and audio levels on broadcast and display equipment. Some programs also have a *counting leader* generator, which produces a visible, ten-second countdown for the beginning of the movie. Counting leaders also help professional video engineers calibrate their equipment, although a counting leader is basically just a novelty unless you actually produce video for broadcast.

Figure 19-2: Color bars are calibrating broadcast and display equipment to work with your tape.

A *soundtrack generator,* on the other hand, is something we can all appreciate and use. Some video-editing programs (like Pinnacle Studio and Apple Final Cut Express) come with programs like SmartSound QuickTracks or Apple Soundtrack, which automatically generates high-quality soundtrack music in a variety of styles to match your project.

Table 19-7	Generators		
Program	*Bars and Tone*	*Counting Leader*	*Soundtrack*
Adobe Premiere Elements	X	X	
Adobe Premiere Pro	X	X	
Apple iMovie			
Apple Final Cut Express	X	X	X
Apple Final Cut Pro	X	X	(with Final Cut Studio)
Avid Xpress DV	X	X	
Microsoft Windows Movie Maker			
NTI CD & DVD Maker			
Pinnacle Studio			X
Pinnacle Liquid Edition	X		

Exporting Your Movies

All video-editing programs provide tools to help you export your movie to the rest of the world. Table 19-8 shows you which popular export formats are available in each program. Most programs now come with tools to help you author DVDs as well — and that's noted in Table 19-8 as appropriate.

Table 19-8	Export Options					
Program	*AVI*	*DVD*	*MPEG*	*QuickTime*	*Real Media*	*Windows Media*
Adobe Premiere Elements	X	X	X	X		X
Adobe Premiere Pro	X	X	X	X	X	X

Program	AVI	DVD	MPEG	QuickTime	Real Media	Windows Media
Apple iMovie		iDVD		X		
Apple Final Cut Express		iDVD	X	X		
Apple Final Cut Pro		iDVD	X	X		
Avid Xpress DV		X	X	X	X (Windows only)	X (Windows only)
Microsoft Windows Movie Maker	X					X
NTI CD & DVD Maker		X	X			
Pinnacle Studio	X	X	X		X	X
Pinnacle Liquid Edition	X	X	X	X	X	X

Part VI
Appendixes

The 5th Wave   By Rich Tennant

"It's a site devoted to the 'Limp Korn Chilies' rock group. It has videos of all their performances in concert halls, hotel rooms, and airport terminals."

In this part . . .

Sometimes, when you're making movies, you just need a quick reference to provide some essential bit of knowledge. I've provided several Appendixes to *Digital Video For Dummies* that serve as quick references on several subjects. Appendix A is a glossary of the various technical terms and acronyms that seem to pop up everywhere when you work with video. The remaining appendixes help you get the most out of the three video-editing programs shown throughout this book: Apple iMovie, Windows Movie Maker, and Adobe Premiere Elements.

Appendix A

Glossary

alpha channel: Some digital images have transparent areas; the transparency is defined using an alpha channel.

analog: Data recorded as a wave with infinitely varying values is analog data. Analog recordings are usually electromechanical, so they often suffer from generational loss. *See also digital, generational loss.*

aspect ratio: The shape of a video image (its width compared to height) is the *aspect ratio*. Traditional television screens have an aspect ratio of 4:3, meaning the screen is four units wide and three units high. Some newer HDTVs use a "widescreen" aspect ratio of 16:9. Image pixels can also have various aspect ratios. *See also HDTV, pixel.*

audio clipping: The audible distortion that occurs when recorded audio is too loud; for example, when someone yells straight at the microphone. If your audio recording device has volume level (VU) meters, clipping occurs when the meters show red bars at the top. *See also VU meter.*

bars and tone: A video image that serves the function of the "test pattern" used in TV broadcasting: Standardized color bars and a 1-kHz tone are usually placed at the beginning of video programs. This helps broadcast engineers calibrate video equipment to the color and audio levels of a video program. The format for color bars is standardized by the SMPTE. *See also SMPTE.*

bit depth: The amount of data that a single piece of information can hold depends upon how many bits are available. Bit depth usually measures color or sound quality. A larger bit depth means a greater range of color or sound.

black and code: The process of recording black video and timecode onto a new camcorder tape. This helps prevent timecode breaks. *See also timecode, timecode break.*

Bluetooth: A wireless networking technology that allows devices to connect to the Internet (or to computers) using radio waves. Some newer digital camcorders incorporate Bluetooth technology, although its practical applications for digital video have not yet been realized.

capture: The process of recording digital video or other media from a camcorder or VCR tape onto a computer's hard drive.

CCD (charged coupled device): This is the unit in camcorders that interprets light photons and converts the information into an electronic video signal. This signal can then be recorded on tape. Digital still cameras also use CCDs.

chrominance: A fancy word for color. *See also luminance.*

clip: One of various segments making up the scenes of a video program. Individual clips are edited into your video-editing program's timeline to form complete scenes and a complete story line. *See also storyboard, timeline.*

clipping: *See audio clipping.*

coaxial: Most wires that carry a cable TV signal use coaxial connectors. Coaxial connectors are round in cross-section, and have a single thin pin running through the middle of the connector. Coaxial cables carry both sound and video. Most TVs and VCRs have coaxial connectors; digital camcorders usually do not. Coaxial cables usually provide inferior video quality to component, composite, and S-Video cables. *See also component video, composite video, S-Video.*

codec: A scheme used to compress, and later decompress, video and audio information so it can pass more efficiently over computer cables and Internet connections to hard drives and other components.

color gamut: The total range of colors a given system can create (by combining several basic colors) to display a video image. The total number of individual colors that are available is finite. If a color cannot be displayed correctly, it is considered *out of gamut.*

color space: The method used to generate color in a video display. *See also color gamut, RGB, YUV.*

component video: A high-quality connection type for analog video. Component video splits the video signal and sends it over three separate cables, usually color-coded red, green, and blue. Component video connections are unusual in consumer-grade video equipment, but they provide superior video quality to coaxial, composite and S-Video connections. *See also analog, coaxial, composite video, S-Video.*

composite video: A connection type for analog video, typically using a single video-connector cable (color-coded yellow). The connector type is also sometimes called an *RCA connector,* usually paired with red and white audio connectors. Composite video signals are inferior to S-Video or component video because they tend to allow more signal noise and artifacts in the video signal. *See also analog, coaxial, component video, S-Video.*

DAT (digital audio tape): A digital tape format often used in audio recorders by professional video producers.

data rate: The amount of data that can pass over a connection in a second while contained in a signal. The data rate of DV-format video is 3.6MB (megabytes) per second.

device control: A technology that allows a computer to control the playback functions on a digital camcorder (such as play, stop, and rewind). Clicking Rewind in the program window on the computer causes the camcorder tape to actually rewind.

digital: A method of recording sound and light by converting them into data made up of discrete, binary values (expressed as ones and zeros). *See also analog.*

DIMM (Dual Inline Memory Module): A memory module for a Mac or PC. Most computer RAM today comes on easily replaced DIMM cards. *See also RAM.*

Digital 8: A digital camcorder format that uses Hi8 tapes. *See also digital, DV, MicroMV, MiniDV.*

driver: Pre-1980, the person in control of a car or horse-drawn carriage. Post-1980, a piece of software that allows a computer to utilize a piece of hardware, such as a video card or a printer.

drop-frame timecode: A type of timecode specified by the NTSC video standard, usually with a frame rate of 29.97fps. To maintain continuity, two frames are dropped at the beginning of each minute, except for every tenth minute. *See also timecode.*

DV (Digital Video): A standard format and codec for digital video. Digital camcorders that include a FireWire interface usually record DV-format video. *See also codec, FireWire.*

DVCAM: A professional-grade version of the MiniDV digital-tape format developed by Sony. DVCAM camcorders are usually pretty expensive. *See also digital, DVCPro, MiniDV.*

DVCPro: A professional-grade version of the MiniDV digital-tape format developed by Panasonic. Like DVCAM camcorders, DVCPro camcorders are usually very expensive. *See also digital, DVCAM, MiniDV.*

DVD (Digital Versatile Disc): A category of disc formats that allows capacities from 4.7GB up to 17GB. DVDs are quickly becoming the most popular format for distributing movies. Recordable DVDs (DVD-Rs) can hold 4.7GB (single-layer discs) or 8.5GB (dual-layer discs).

dual-layer DVD: A type of recordable DVD that can hold up to 8.5GB of data. *See also DVD.*

EDL (Edit Decision List): A file or list that contains information about all edits performed in a program. This list can then be used to reproduce the same edits on another system, such as at a professional video-editing facility. Most advanced editing programs can generate EDLs automatically.

EIDE (Enhanced Integrated Drive Electronics): Most modern PCs and Macs have hard drives that connect to the computer using an EIDE interface. For digital video, you should try to use EIDE disks with a speed of 7200 rpm.

exposure: The amount of light allowed through a camcorder's lens. Exposure is controlled with a part of the camcorder called the iris.

field: One of two separate sets of scan lines in an interlaced video frame. Each field contains every other horizontal resolution line. Immediately after one field is drawn on the screen, the other is drawn in a separate pass while the previous frame is still glowing, resulting in a complete image. *See also frame.*

FireWire: Also known by its official designation IEEE-1394, or by other names such as i.Link, FireWire is a high-speed computer peripheral interface standard developed by Apple Computer. FireWire is often used to connect digital camcorders, external hard drives, and some other devices to a computer. The speed of FireWire has contributed greatly to the affordability of modern video editing. *See also USB.*

frame: Still image, one in a sequence of many that make up a moving picture. *See also frame rate.*

frame rate: The speed at which the frames in a moving picture change. Video images usually display 25 to 30 frames per second, providing the illusion of movement to the human eye. Slower frame rates save storage space, but can produce jerky motion; faster frame rates produce smoother motion but have to use more of the recording medium to store and present the images.

gamut: *See color gamut.*

gel: A translucent or colored sheet of plastic that is placed in front of a light to diffuse the light or change its appearance.

generational loss: A worsening of the signal-to-noise ratio (less signal, more noise) that occurs every time an analog recording is copied; some values are lost in the copying process. Each copy (especially a copy of a copy) represents a later, lower-quality *generation* of the original. *See also analog.*

HD (High-Definition) video: Some newer camcorders can record HD video, which offers a much higher-quality picture than standard NTSC, PAL, or SECAM video. HD video requires a special HDTV to watch. *See also HDTV, NTSC, PAL, SECAM.*

HDTV (High-Definition Television): A new set of broadcast-video standards that incorporate resolutions and frame rates higher than those used for traditional analog video. *See also HD video, NTSC, PAL, SECAM.*

IEEE-1394: *See FireWire.*

i.Link: *See FireWire.*

interlacing: Producing an image by alternating sets of scan lines onscreen. Most video images are actually composed of two separate fields, drawn on consecutive passes of the electron gun in the video tube. Each field contains every other horizontal resolution line of a video image. Each field is drawn so quickly that the human eye perceives a complete image. *See also progressive scan, field.*

iris: *See exposure.*

jog: *See scrub.*

key light: A light used to directly illuminate a subject in a video shot.

lavalier: A tiny microphone designed to clip to a subject's clothing. Lavalier mics are often clipped to the lapels of TV newscasters.

lens flare: A light point or artifact that appears in a video image when the sun or other bright light source reflects on the lens.

luminance: A fancy word for brightness in video images. *See also chrominance.*

MicroMV: A small digital-camcorder tape format developed by Sony for ultra-compact camcorders. *See also digital, Digital 8, DV, MiniDV.*

MiniDV: The most common tape format used by digital camcorders. *See also digital, Digital 8, DV, MicroMV.*

moiré pattern: A wavy or shimmering artifact that appears in video images when tight parallel lines appear in the image. This problem often occurs when a subject wears a pinstriped suit or coarse corduroy.

NLE (nonlinear editor): A computer program that can edit video, audio, or other multimedia information without confining the user to an unchangeable sequence of frames from first to last. Using an NLE, you can edit the work in any order you choose. Popular video NLEs include Apple iMovie, Adobe Premiere Elements, and Windows Movie Maker.

NTSC (National Television Standards Committee): The broadcast-video standard used in North America, Japan, the Philippines, and elsewhere. *See also PAL, SECAM.*

online/offline editing: When you edit using full-quality footage, you are performing *online* editing. If you perform edits using lower-quality captures, and intend to apply those edits to the full-quality footage later, you are performing *offline* editing.

overscan: What happens when a TV cuts off portions of the video image at the edges of the screen. Most standard TVs overscan to some extent.

PAL (Phase Alternating Line): The broadcast-video standard used in Western Europe, Australia, Southeast Asia, South America, and elsewhere. *See also NTSC, SECAM.*

PCI: Peripheral Component Interconnect, a standard type of connection for computer expansion cards (such as FireWire cards). Any new card must be placed in an empty PCI slot on the computer's motherboard.

pixel: The smallest element of a video image, also called a *picture element.* Bitmapped still images are made up of grids containing thousands, even millions of pixels. A screen or image size that has a resolution of 640 x 480 is 640 pixels wide by 480 pixels high.

Plug and Play: A hardware technology that allows you to easily connected devices such as digital camcorders to your computer. The computer automatically detects the device when it is connected and turned on.

progressive scan: A scan display that draws all the horizontal resolution lines in a single pass. Most computer monitors use progressive scan. *See also interlacing.*

RAM (Random Access Memory): The electronic working space for your computer's processor and software. To use digital video on your computer, you need lots of RAM. *See also VRAM.*

render: To produce a playable version of an altered video image. If an effect, speed change, or transition is applied to a video image, your video-editing program must figure out how each frame of the image should look after the change. Rendering is the process of applying these changes. Usually, the rendering process generates a preview file that is stored on the hard drive. *See also transition.*

resolution: The number of pixels in an image. An image with a resolution of 720 x 480 is 720 pixels wide and 480 pixels high. *See pixel.*

RGB (Red-Green-Blue): The color space (method of creating onscreen colors) used in computer monitors; all the available colors result from combining red, green, and blue pixels. *See also color space, YUV.*

sampling rate: The number of samples obtained per second during a digital audio recording. When audio is recorded digitally, the sound is sampled thousands of times per second. 48kHz audio has 48,000 samples per second.

scrub: To move back and forth through a video program, one frame at a time. Some video-editing programs have a scrub bar located underneath the video preview window (also called the *jog control*). *See also shuttle.*

SECAM (Sequential Couleur Avec Memoire): Broadcast video standard used in France, Russia, Eastern Europe, Central Asia, and elsewhere. *See also NTSC, PAL.*

shuttle: To roll a video image slowly forward or back, often to check a detail of motion. Professional video decks and cameras often have shuttle controls. Some video-editing programs also have shuttle controls in their capture windows. *See also scrub.*

slate: The black-and-white hinged board that moviemakers snap closed in front of the camera just before action commences. The noise made by the snapping slate is used later to synchronize video with sound recorded by other audio recorders during the shoot.

SMPTE (Society for Motion Picture and Television Engineers): This organization develops standards for professional broadcasting equipment and formats. Among other things, the SMPTE defines standards for bars and tone, counting leaders, and timecode.

storyboard: A visual layout of the basic scenes in a movie. The storyboard can be used to arrange clips in a basic order before you do finer edits using the timeline. *See also clip, timeline.*

S-VHS: A higher-quality version of the VHS videotape format. S-VHS VCRs usually have S-Video connectors. *See also S-Video.*

S-Video: A high-quality connection technology for analog video. S-Video connectors separate the color and brightness signals, resulting in less signal noise and fewer artifacts. Most digital camcorders include S-Video connectors for analog output. Analog capture cards and S-VHS VCRs usually have S-Video connectors as well. *See also analog, capture, coaxial, composite video, component video, S-VHS.*

timecode: The standard system for identifying individual frames in a movie or video program. Timecode is expressed as *hours:minutes:seconds:frames* (as in 01:20:31:02). This format has been standardized by the SMPTE. Non–drop-frame timecode uses colons between the numbers; drop-frame timecode uses semicolons. *See also SMPTE, timecode break.*

timecode break: An inconsistency in the timecode on a camcorder tape. *See also timecode.*

timeline: The working space in most video-editing programs. Clips are arranged along a timeline, which may include different video tracks, audio tracks, or other features. The timeline usually shows more detail and allows finer editing control than the storyboard. *See also clip, storyboard.*

title: Text that appears onscreen to display the name of the movie, or to give credit to the people who made the movie. *Subtitles* are a special type of title, often used during a video program to show translations of dialogue spoken in foreign languages.

transition: The method by which one clip ends and another begins in a video program. A common type of transition is when one clip gradually fades out as the next clip fades in. *See also clip, render.*

USB (Universal Serial Bus): This is a computer port technology that makes it easy to connect a mouse, printer, or other device to a computer. Although USB usually isn't fast enough for digital-video capture, some digital camcorders have USB ports. Connected to a computer's USB port, these cameras can often be used as Webcams. Most computers built after spring 2002 use a newer, faster version of USB called USB 2.0.

video card: This term can refer to either of two different kinds of devices inside a computer: the device that generates a video signal for the computer's monitor, or the card that captures video from VCRs and camcorders onto the computer's hard drive. Some hardware manufacturers refer to their FireWire cards as video cards because FireWire cards are most often used to capture video from digital camcorders. *See also capture, FireWire.*

VRAM (Video Random Access Memory): Computer video cards have built-in memory, often called VRAM. When you are working with digital video, you want a video card with lots of VRAM. Ideally, VRAM should not share your computer's system RAM. *See also RAM.*

VU meter: Short for *volume unit meter,* this is the meter found on audio recording devices. VU meters measure the volume of audio being recorded. Some VU meters use a needle and scale, but most use LEDs. When the scale gets up into the red zone, audio clipping occurs, causing distortion in the audio. *See also audio clipping.*

waveform: A visual representation of an audio signal. Viewing a waveform on a computer screen allows precise synchronization of sound and video.

YUV: The acronym for the color space used by most TVs. For some reason YUV stands for *luminance-chrominance. See also chrominance, color space, luminance, RGB.*

zebra pattern: An overexposure-warning feature that some high-end camcorders have. A striped pattern appears in the viewfinder over areas of the image that will be overexposed unless the camcorder is adjusted to compensate.

Appendix B

Using Apple iMovie

*O*ne of the programs I feature in this book is Apple iMovie. If you're using a Mac, this is an excellent free video-editing program that's probably already installed on your computer. iMovie pioneered free, simple home video editing when it was first introduced in 1999, and it continues to be a good choice today. It's also very nearly your only choice. As I write this book, Avid is the only other company offering a free or low-cost video editing program for Mac OS X. Avid's program is called Avid Free DV (www.avid.com/freeDV/), and Avid offers versions of this program both for Windows and Mac computers.

This appendix shows you briefly how to obtain and install the latest version of iMovie on your computer. I also show you how to find and install plug-ins to expand iMovie's capabilities.

Installing and Upgrading iMovie

The video-editing instructions in this book assume you have iMovie 3 or later. If you've recently purchased a new Mac, you probably already have such a version. Version 3 of iMovie incorporated some important improvements, among them the capability to import QuickTime media clips into the program. iMovie also comes with iLife, a suite of software that includes current versions of iTunes, iPhoto, and iDVD.

To check your version of iMovie, launch the program from your applications folder and choose iMovie⇨About iMovie. A splash screen appears (as shown in Figure B-1), showing you the current version number.

Figure B-1:
Make sure you have the latest version of iMovie.

To update iMovie, or just to check and see whether an update is available, do one of the following:

- Visit www.apple.com/imovie and click one of the download links on that page.

- If Software Update runs automatically on your system, check for iMovie updates when it runs.

- To run Software Update manually, open the System Preferences window (Apple⇨System Preferences) and open the Software Update icon. Click the Update Now button in the Software Update settings dialog box that appears.

When you download an update, you'll see a desktop icon for an iMovie installer disk image. Double-click that icon to temporarily mount a disk image for the installer, and then double-click the icon for the mounted disk image. A window opens displaying an installer package icon. Yep, now you have to double-click that too. I know, it's a whole lotta icons to double-click, but it's actually a pretty simple process.

When you double-click the installer package, the first window you probably see is an Authorization dialog box. If you see a message stating that you must enter an administrator password, click the little lock icon at the bottom of the dialog box and enter an administrator password. When that's done, just follow the instructions onscreen to install your update.

When you're done installing the software, you can get rid of the mounted-disk image by dragging it to the Trash bin. You can also delete the disk image file if you like, although I recommend backing up your update files in a safe place (for example, on a recordable CD).

Sometimes when you install a newer version of iMovie, you may also be required to install a new version of QuickTime or other software as well. Usually the Apple Web site offers recommendations on other software to download. Also, when you launch your updated version of iMovie, you may see warnings about required software that isn't installed.

I strongly recommend that you use Software Update in the OS X Applications folder to download required software updates, especially QuickTime. I have found that not all parts of the Apple Web site talk to each other — meaning that links on Web sites don't always lead to the latest and greatest version. Fortunately, Apple does a pretty good job of keeping the available downloads in Software Update, er, *updated,* so I recommend using it first.

Enhancing iMovie with Plug-Ins

The Apple Web site is a pretty useful resource for all things iMovie. If you aren't already there, go ahead and pay a visit to www.apple.com/imovie. Among other things, you can usually find cool audio and video effects that you can download and install as plug-ins to iMovie. Plug-ins are developed by Apple and third-party software vendors, and they may add a variety of capabilities to iMovie, including

✔ New transitions

✔ Borders or frames for the video image

✔ Advanced overlays and video effects

The current selection of plug-ins for iMovie may vary, but scroll down the iMovie Web page and look for links to downloadable plug-ins. Figure B-2 shows an X-Ray effect that comes on an effects sampler from GeeThree (www.geethree.com).

Figure B-2: This X-Ray effect from GeeThree gives my video image an eerie look.

Appendix C

Using Windows Movie Maker

*I*f you've been around personal computers for more than a few minutes, you probably know that a rivalry exists between Apple and Microsoft. Early in the digital video boom, Apple released iMovie, introducing many Macintosh users to the world of moviemaking. Microsoft quickly followed suit with its own video-editing program, Windows Movie Maker. Windows Movie Maker was first released as part of the Windows ME (Millennium Edition) operating system, and was later included with Windows XP as well. Like Apple iMovie for Mac users, Windows Movie Maker is free for any Microsoft Windows user.

Microsoft buried Windows Movie Maker deep in the Windows Start menu, so it's not exactly the easiest thing to find. To launch Windows Movie Maker in XP, choose Start➪All Programs➪Accessories➪Windows Movie Maker.

Upgrading Windows Movie Maker

The first version of Windows Movie Maker was released in 2000 and came with both Windows Me and Windows XP. Version 1 was an extremely limited program, and if you still have Version 1 listed, I strongly recommend an upgrade. Newer versions of Windows Movie Maker offer some welcome and important improvements, including

- **Real transitions:** Yes, it's true. In the first version of Movie Maker, your only available transition was a dissolve. But now Windows Movie Maker has 60 — yes, *sixty* — great transitions to choose from.

- **Video effects:** Windows Movie Maker offers 28 video effects that can be applied to your movies. That's 28 more effects than were available in Movie Maker version 1.

- **A title designer:** If you wanted to make titles for the first version of Windows Movie Maker, you had to do it using Windows Paint. Later versions of Windows Movie Maker include a real title editor.

To upgrade your version of Windows Movie Maker, open the program and choose Help➪Windows Movie Maker on the Web. This takes you to the Windows Movie Maker Web site, where you should see an Update link that takes you to a place where you can download the latest version. Alternatively, you can visit `www.microsoft.com/windowsxp/moviemaker/`.

Getting Acquainted with Windows Movie Maker

One thing that Windows Movie Maker definitely has going for it is a user interface that is really easy to understand and use. As does virtually every other video-editing program ever made, Movie Maker has a storyboard/timeline viewer at the bottom of the screen. The middle of the Movie Maker screen is filled with three items:

- ✔ **Movie Tasks:** This panel is actually a collection of clickable menus covering all of the things you can do in Windows Movie Maker, including capturing video, using transitions and effects, and exporting the movie.

- ✔ **Browser:** The very middle of the screen serves as a clip browser if you're viewing a collection of clips, or it shows available transitions and effects if you've chosen to view those items by clicking them in the Movie Tasks panel.

- ✔ **Preview window:** No surprises here. The preview window contains playback controls that allow you to preview clips and your project.

As you can see in Figure C-1, Windows Movie Maker's timeline is quite similar to the timeline in most other video-editing programs. The timeline includes tracks for video, audio, background music or narration, and titles. Movie Maker's timeline also provides a separate track for transitions. If you don't see the transition and audio track in your timeline, click the plus sign next to the video track.

Making movies with Windows Movie Maker is pretty straightforward. The Movie tasks panel provides a step-by-step process that you can follow to capture video, edit the movie, and finally export your finished project to a CD, the Internet, or a camcorder tape. When you're done editing a movie, click one of the export formats listed under Finish Movie and follow the simple onscreen instructions to export your project. For more information on using Windows Movie Maker, click the links under Movie Making Tips.

Movie Tasks

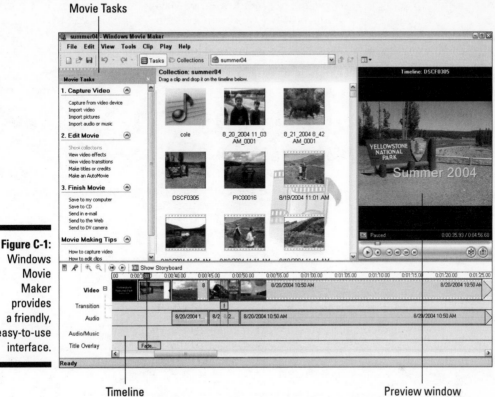

Figure C-1:
Windows
Movie
Maker
provides
a friendly,
easy-to-use
interface.

Timeline

Preview window

Appendix D

Installing and Configuring Adobe Premiere Elements

In This Appendix

▶ Installing Premiere Elements

▶ Customizing Premiere Elements for your needs

Most of the tasks in this book focus on things that can be done in basic video-editing programs like Apple iMovie and Windows Movie Maker. Those simple programs are reasonably capable, and considering the price of each (free), they are each a tremendous bargain.

But as you make movies, at some point, you'll want to do something that just can't be done in iMovie or Movie Maker. Eventually, you'll probably want to step up to a slightly more advanced editing program like Adobe Premiere Elements. Adobe pioneered desktop video editing with Premiere more than a decade ago, when it was originally intended as an advanced desktop video editor for professionals. In 2004, Adobe spun off Premiere into two versions: Adobe Premiere Pro ($699) for professionals and Adobe Premiere Elements ($99) for consumers. But don't let the huge price difference fool you into thinking that Premiere Elements is a stunted, lightly featured program. Premiere Elements offers an incredible level of editing power for the price, and unless you actually are a video pro, you probably won't need anything else.

Unfortunately, since the release of Premiere Pro and Elements, Adobe no longer offers a Macintosh-compatible version. If you have a Mac, your next step up from iMovie is Final Cut Express, which retails for $299. In terms of features, Final Cut Express is roughly equivalent to Premiere Elements, and most of the Premiere Elements tasks in this book can also be performed in Final Cut Express.

In this appendix, I show how to install Premiere Elements, even if you're just installing the free trial-version for now. I also show how to adjust the program settings in Premiere Elements to ensure that it works best for you.

Installing Adobe Premiere Elements

Adobe Premiere Elements is widely available at many computer and electronics retailers, and is often packaged along with Adobe Photoshop Elements. This package is a tremendous value because it retails for just $149 (the stand-alone Premiere Elements retails for $99), and you get not only a great video-editing program but also a first-class photo-editing program. Photoshop Elements comes in handy when you want to improve images taken with a digital still camera, as well as when you want to clean up still frames extracted from video projects (I show how to work with still frames in Chapter 12).

If you're not ready to purchase Premiere Elements, you can download a free trial from www.adobe.com/products/premiereel/.

Click the Tryout link under downloads to download a free trial version of Premiere Elements. This trial version lacks the ability to burn DVDs, and it expires 30 days after installation. Keep in mind that the download is huge; the tryout download for Premiere Elements version 1 was about 500MB, and you should assume that the tryout for Premiere Elements 2 will be even bigger. (The trial download wasn't yet ready as of this writing, but it should be available by the time you read this.)

Actually installing Adobe Premiere Elements is pretty easy. Just put the disc in the drive and follow the onscreen instructions to install. During the setup process, you will be asked to activate your copy of Premiere Elements. If you don't activate your copy of Premiere Elements online within 30 days, it will cease to function. After the program is installed, launch it by choosing Start⇨All Programs⇨Adobe Premiere Elements. When the program launches, you see a screen that looks like Figure D-1. From here, you can create a new project, open an existing project, or quickly start capturing video. A convenient list of your most recent projects (if you have any) appears as shown in Figure D-1.

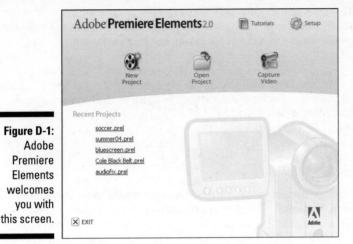

Figure D-1:
Adobe
Premiere
Elements
welcomes
you with
this screen.

Configuring Adobe Premiere Elements

Adobe Premiere Elements is a pretty advanced program, so I recommend that you take a few minutes and check its program settings to make sure that Premiere Elements is tailored to the way you like to work. When you see the welcome splash screen shown in Figure D-1, click Setup in the upper-right corner of the screen. A Setup dialog box appears as shown in Figure D-2.

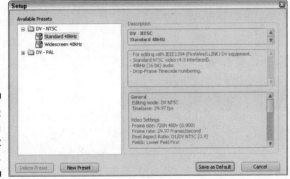

Figure D-2:
Choose a
default
preset.

The Setup dialog box is where you choose the default preset for your projects. A preset is basically just a group of default settings that are applied to new projects when you create them. These settings cover a variety of movie specifications, including

- ✔ **Broadcast video format:** As I explain in Chapter 2, different parts of the world use different broadcast video formats. The Americas and Japan use the NTSC format, whereas much of Asia and Europe use the PAL format. France, Russia, and a few other places use the SECAM format, but in Premiere Elements, it's safe to just use the PAL format for SECAM video. Your default preset should match the type of video (NTSC or PAL) that you work with most.

- ✔ **The video image aspect ratio:** Most video is considered either full-screen (with a 4:3 aspect ratio) or widescreen (with a 16:9 aspect ratio). As explained in Chapter 2, aspect ratios are the basic shape of the video image. If most of your video is full-screen, choose a Standard preset. If you have a camcorder that can shoot widescreen video and you use that format a lot, choose a widescreen preset.

- ✔ **Audio quality:** If you're capturing video from a digital camcorder, keep the default audio sample rate of 48,000 samples per second. This is the rate used by DV format video, and there's really no good reason to change it.

- ✔ **Capture format:** If you are capturing video from a DV camcorder, keep the DV Capture preset. However, if your video camera records in a different format (for example, 640 x 480 MPEG-2 video), change the capture format.

- ✔ **Default timeline setup:** By default, Premiere Elements creates a timeline with three video tracks and three audio tracks. You can easily add more tracks later if you need them, but if you want to change the default number of tracks, you can.

To create a custom preset, first select one of the default presets that most closely matches the settings you plan to use in your custom preset. Then click the New Preset button, and use the New Preset dialog box to adjust settings. Click OK to close all dialog boxes when you are done.

After you have created a new movie project, you can further customize the way Premiere Elements works. With a project open, choose Edit➪Preferences and then choose any Preferences group. A Preferences dialog box appears as shown in Figure D-3. You can access any Preference group by clicking it in the left side of the dialog box. A lot of the settings here are things I show how to customize elsewhere in the book, but there are some settings that you may want to review that aren't covered under other subjects. These settings include

- ✔ **Auto Save:** By default, Premiere Elements automatically saves a backup copy of your work every 20 minutes. You can change this interval, or disable Auto Save completely. Auto Save doesn't overwrite your existing project file, so if you're away from your desk and the cat steps on the keyboard, deleting hours of work, you won't lose everything.

✔ **Label Colors and Defaults:** If you like to color-code all your stuff to help keep it organized, these Preference groups let you choose colors.

✔ **Media:** This group specifies the default folder on your hard drive where you store media. When you click Import to import media into Premiere Elements, this is the first folder you see. Change the default folder if you prefer a different location.

✔ **Scratch Disks:** Don't worry, Premiere Elements isn't going to automatically scratch all of your CD and DVD discs! A scratch disk is the default location where items like captured video files, DVD encoding files, or rendered video previews are stored. If you have a second hard drive where you prefer to store your video files, choose it here. As you can see in Figure D-3, you can choose scratch disk locations for several different kinds of files.

If you have a second hard drive that is used mainly for video, I still recommend that you use My Computer or Windows Explorer to create a folder on the drive specifically for Adobe Premiere Elements work. You can name the folder "Premiere Elements Scratch" or something similarly descriptive.

✔ **User Interface:** Do you have to wear sunglasses while you work in Premiere Elements? If so, there are two possible explanations. Either you are too cool, or the interface window is too bright. If the sunglasses cannot be explained by your coolness, use the User Interface Preferences group to adjust the interface brightness.

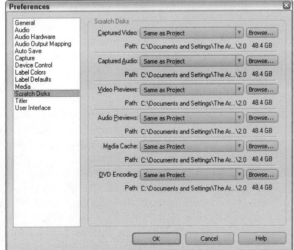

Figure D-3:
Adjust
program
preferences
in Premiere
Elements.

Index

• *B* •

● *E* ●

● *F* ●

USINESS, CAREERS & PERSONAL FINANCE

0-7645-5307-0

0-7645-5331-3 *†

Also available:
- Accounting For Dummies †
  0-7645-5314-3
- Business Plans Kit For Dummies †
  0-7645-5365-8
- Cover Letters For Dummies
  0-7645-5224-4
- Frugal Living For Dummies
  0-7645-5403-4
- Leadership For Dummies
  0-7645-5176-0
- Managing For Dummies
  0-7645-1771-6

- Marketing For Dummies
  0-7645-5600-2
- Personal Finance For Dummies *
  0-7645-2590-5
- Project Management For Dummies
  0-7645-5283-X
- Resumes For Dummies †
  0-7645-5471-9
- Selling For Dummies
  0-7645-5363-1
- Small Business Kit For Dummies *†
  0-7645-5093-4

OME & BUSINESS COMPUTER BASICS

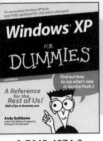

0-7645-4074-2

0-7645-3758-X

Also available:
- ACT! 6 For Dummies
  0-7645-2645-6
- iLife '04 All-in-One Desk Reference
  For Dummies
  0-7645-7347-0
- iPAQ For Dummies
  0-7645-6769-1
- Mac OS X Panther Timesaving
  Techniques For Dummies
  0-7645-5812-9
- Macs For Dummies
  0-7645-5656-8

- Microsoft Money 2004 For Dummies
  0-7645-4195-1
- Office 2003 All-in-One Desk Reference
  For Dummies
  0-7645-3883-7
- Outlook 2003 For Dummies
  0-7645-3759-8
- PCs For Dummies
  0-7645-4074-2
- TiVo For Dummies
  0-7645-6923-6
- Upgrading and Fixing PCs For Dummies
  0-7645-1665-5
- Windows XP Timesaving Techniques
  For Dummies
  0-7645-3748-2

OOD, HOME, GARDEN, HOBBIES, MUSIC & PETS

0-7645-5295-3

0-7645-5232-5

Also available:
- Bass Guitar For Dummies
  0-7645-2487-9
- Diabetes Cookbook For Dummies
  0-7645-5230-9
- Gardening For Dummies *
  0-7645-5130-2
- Guitar For Dummies
  0-7645-5106-X
- Holiday Decorating For Dummies
  0-7645-2570-0
- Home Improvement All-in-One
  For Dummies
  0-7645-5680-0

- Knitting For Dummies
  0-7645-5395-X
- Piano For Dummies
  0-7645-5105-1
- Puppies For Dummies
  0-7645-5255-4
- Scrapbooking For Dummies
  0-7645-7208-3
- Senior Dogs For Dummies
  0-7645-5818-8
- Singing For Dummies
  0-7645-2475-5
- 30-Minute Meals For Dummies
  0-7645-2589-1

NTERNET & DIGITAL MEDIA

0-7645-1664-7

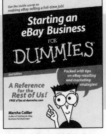

0-7645-6924-4

Also available:
- 2005 Online Shopping Directory
  For Dummies
  0-7645-7495-7
- CD & DVD Recording For Dummies
  0-7645-5956-7
- eBay For Dummies
  0-7645-5654-1
- Fighting Spam For Dummies
  0-7645-5965-6
- Genealogy Online For Dummies
  0-7645-5964-8
- Google For Dummies
  0-7645-4420-9

- Home Recording For Musicians
  For Dummies
  0-7645-1634-5
- The Internet For Dummies
  0-7645-4173-0
- iPod & iTunes For Dummies
  0-7645-7772-7
- Preventing Identity Theft For Dummies
  0-7645-7336-5
- Pro Tools All-in-One Desk Reference
  For Dummies
  0-7645-5714-9
- Roxio Easy Media Creator For Dummies
  0-7645-7131-1

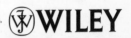

SPORTS, FITNESS, PARENTING, RELIGION & SPIRITUALITY

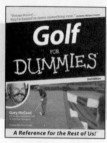

0-7645-5146-9

0-7645-5418-2

Also available:

- Adoption For Dummies
0-7645-5488-3
- Basketball For Dummies
0-7645-5248-1
- The Bible For Dummies
0-7645-5296-1
- Buddhism For Dummies
0-7645-5359-3
- Catholicism For Dummies
0-7645-5391-7
- Hockey For Dummies
0-7645-5228-7

- Judaism For Dummies
0-7645-5299-6
- Martial Arts For Dummies
0-7645-5358-5
- Pilates For Dummies
0-7645-5397-6
- Religion For Dummies
0-7645-5264-3
- Teaching Kids to Read For Dummies
0-7645-4043-2
- Weight Training For Dummies
0-7645-5168-X
- Yoga For Dummies
0-7645-5117-5

TRAVEL

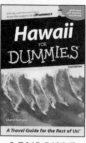

0-7645-5438-7

0-7645-5453-0

Also available:

- Alaska For Dummies
0-7645-1761-9
- Arizona For Dummies
0-7645-6938-4
- Cancún and the Yucatán For Dummies
0-7645-2437-2
- Cruise Vacations For Dummies
0-7645-6941-4
- Europe For Dummies
0-7645-5456-5
- Ireland For Dummies
0-7645-5455-7

- Las Vegas For Dummies
0-7645-5448-4
- London For Dummies
0-7645-4277-X
- New York City For Dummies
0-7645-6945-7
- Paris For Dummies
0-7645-5494-8
- RV Vacations For Dummies
0-7645-5443-3
- Walt Disney World & Orlando For Dummies
0-7645-6943-0

GRAPHICS, DESIGN & WEB DEVELOPMENT

0-7645-4345-8

0-7645-5589-8

Also available:

- Adobe Acrobat 6 PDF For Dummies
0-7645-3760-1
- Building a Web Site For Dummies
0-7645-7144-3
- Dreamweaver MX 2004 For Dummies
0-7645-4342-3
- FrontPage 2003 For Dummies
0-7645-3882-9
- HTML 4 For Dummies
0-7645-1995-6
- Illustrator CS For Dummies
0-7645-4084-X

- Macromedia Flash MX 2004 For Dummies
0-7645-4358-X
- Photoshop 7 All-in-One Desk Reference For Dummies
0-7645-1667-1
- Photoshop CS Timesaving Techniques For Dummies
0-7645-6782-9
- PHP 5 For Dummies
0-7645-4166-8
- PowerPoint 2003 For Dummies
0-7645-3908-6
- QuarkXPress 6 For Dummies
0-7645-2593-X

NETWORKING, SECURITY, PROGRAMMING & DATABASES

0-7645-6852-3

0-7645-5784-X

Also available:

- A+ Certification For Dummies
0-7645-4187-0
- Access 2003 All-in-One Desk Reference For Dummies
0-7645-3988-4
- Beginning Programming For Dummies
0-7645-4997-9
- C For Dummies
0-7645-7068-4
- Firewalls For Dummies
0-7645-4048-3
- Home Networking For Dummies
0-7645-42796

- Network Security For Dummies
0-7645-1679-5
- Networking For Dummies
0-7645-1677-9
- TCP/IP For Dummies
0-7645-1760-0
- VBA For Dummies
0-7645-3989-2
- Wireless All In-One Desk Reference For Dummies
0-7645-7496-5
- Wireless Home Networking For Dummies
0-7645-3910-8

ALTH & SELF-HELP

Diabetes FOR **DUMMIES**

A Reference for the Rest of Us!

0-7645-6820-5 *†

Low-Carb Dieting FOR **DUMMIES**

A Reference for the Rest of Us!

0-7645-2566-2

Also available:

- Alzheimer's For Dummies
  0-7645-3899-3
- Asthma For Dummies
  0-7645-4233-8
- Controlling Cholesterol For Dummies
  0-7645-5440-9
- Depression For Dummies
  0-7645-3900-0
- Dieting For Dummies
  0-7645-4149-8
- Fertility For Dummies
  0-7645-2549-2

- Fibromyalgia For Dummies
  0-7645-5441-7
- Improving Your Memory For Dummies
  0-7645-5435-2
- Pregnancy For Dummies †
  0-7645-4483-7
- Quitting Smoking For Dummies
  0-7645-2629-4
- Relationships For Dummies
  0-7645-5384-4
- Thyroid For Dummies
  0-7645-5385-2

UCATION, HISTORY, REFERENCE & TEST PREPARATION

Speak Spanish — the fun and easy way!

Spanish FOR **DUMMIES**

A Reference for the Rest of Us!

0-7645-5194-9

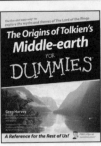

The fun and easy way to explore the myths and themes of The Lord of the Rings

The Origins of Tolkien's Middle-earth FOR **DUMMIES**

A Reference for the Rest of Us!

0-7645-4186-2

Also available:

- Algebra For Dummies
  0-7645-5325-9
- British History For Dummies
  0-7645-7021-8
- Calculus For Dummies
  0-7645-2498-4
- English Grammar For Dummies
  0-7645-5322-4
- Forensics For Dummies
  0-7645-5580-4
- The GMAT For Dummies
  0-7645-5251-1
- Inglés Para Dummies
  0-7645-5427-1

- Italian For Dummies
  0-7645-5196-5
- Latin For Dummies
  0-7645-5431-X
- Lewis & Clark For Dummies
  0-7645-2545-X
- Research Papers For Dummies
  0-7645-5426-3
- The SAT I For Dummies
  0-7645-7193-1
- Science Fair Projects For Dummies
  0-7645-5460-3
- U.S. History For Dummies
  0-7645-5249-X

Get smart @ dummies.com®

- Find a full list of Dummies titles
- Look into loads of FREE on-site articles
- Sign up for FREE eTips e-mailed to you weekly
- See what other products carry the Dummies name
- Shop directly from the Dummies bookstore
- Enter to win new prizes every month!

- Separate Canadian edition also available
- Separate U.K. edition also available

Available wherever books are sold. For more information or to order direct: U.S. customers visit www.dummies.com or call 1-877-762-2974.
U.K. customers visit www.wileyeurope.com or call 0800 243407. Canadian customers visit www.wiley.ca or call 1-800-567-4797.